A Golden Age of Jazz Revisited 1939-1942

What other people are saying about *A Golden Age of Jazz Revisited 1939 – 1942 ...*

The commentary is lively, trenchant, and deeply interesting to one who is fond of this era in music but has only a slight knowledge of it. Right off the bat I was delighted to be reunited with Jelly Roll Morton's beautiful "Mamie's Blues," which I heard once twenty years ago and have been wanting to hear again ever since. I'd never heard (or even heard of) James P. Johnson's "Snowy Morning Blues," but it's gorgeous.

- Richard Snow, former editor-in-chief, *American Heritage* magazine

Schumacher writes in a clear, lighthearted style but hardly wastes a word, and the result is that the book contains a tremendous amount of information that serves both those who know the period well and those who do not. Indeed, for anyone who has never really been attracted to this music before, this is the perfect introduction, but aficionados will enjoy it just as well, and find much that is new. The transfers of the recordings are extremely well done, in clear, undistorted sound, but without any hiss or clicks.

- Piotr Michalowski, Jazz Musician, university professor, *Southeastern Michigan Jazz Association Update*, January 2009

This book is must for any of us who remember the remarkable program "Jazz Revisited" that came our way weekly through National Public Radio. ... The book is laid out so that each year is given a review of the history of the times plus some really interesting facts about the recording industry as well as little known facts of the time. ... Mr. Schumacher writes exactly like he spoke on those programs of so long ago, that is in a very intelligent and concise manner. The book is a real easy read. I found it enjoyable throughout.

- Herb Young, book reviewer for *The International Association of Jazz Record Collectors Journal*, Spring 2009

[Hazen Schumacher's] background on the period and each recording is thoughtful, concise, and well done. I can almost hear [his] radio voice reading the text. The musical choices are all fun and interesting ...

- Geoffrey Wheeler, author of *Jazz by Mail*

A Golden Age of Jazz Revisited 1939-1942

Three years of musical excitement when jazz was the world's popular music

Hazen Schumacher and John Stevens

NPP Books

www.nppbooks.com

NPP Books, P.O. Box 1491 Ann Arbor, Michigan 48106, USA

Printed in the United States of America

International Standard Book Number (ISBN): 978-0-916182-15-1 (Soft cover, 7.44" by 9.69", CDs sold separately)
Library of Congress Control Number: 2008926747

Publisher's Credits

Word Processing
Rebecca Earwood

Composition
Christopher R. Buchanan
Kimberly Hopper

Copy Editing
Jaime E. Lieber
Anna Taylor

Cover Design
Mary Christianson

Dedication

To the History of Jazz

A special thanks to Antoinette F. Domino, owner and publisher of NPP Books, who loved jazz and lost her courageous struggle with cancer over six years ago.

Typeset in Adobe Garamond Pro 12/14

The paper used meets the requirements of the American National Standard for Information Sciences — Permanence of Paper for Printed Library Materials, ANSI Z39.48-1984

The CDs that accompany this book are sold separately. Visit **www.nppbooks.com** to purchases the two CD set.

Acknowledgements

Between the time of the writing of this book and its publication, co-author John Stevens died. He was an admired colleague, a stylish writer and a wonderful human being. He was responsible for much of this book and I miss him as this project comes to its conclusion.

This book could not have been published without the support, commitment, and efforts of Dr. Edward Domino of NPP Books in Ann Arbor and of the Hamburg (Germany) Jazz Museum, Wilke-Jan "Bix" Eiben, Director, and his associates, Wolfgang Westermann and Boris Plantiko. Becky Earwood took a difficult manuscript and converted it into Word; Christopher Buchanan and Kimberly Hopper took a messy Word document and converted it into a pdf file after many hard months of editing, corrections, changes, etc.

Most of the label pictures are from the Michigan Radio Collection in the Hamburg Jazz Museum. Others came from collectors Gary Herzenstiel, Bob Hodge, Duncan Schiedt, and Julian Vein. Also, thanks to Gary, Ron Pikielek and Mike Montgomery of the International Association of Jazz Record Collectors for guidance on how to contact collectors.

Some of the important women in my life were most helpful in editing, rewriting, and rearranging portions of the book. They are daughters Mare Schumacher and Nancy Walter, and my adoring, but long-suffering wife, Rusty. The three have carried over their helpful critiques of my public speaking into my writing attempts, and I thank them for their skills and their careful handling of a crotchety patriarch.

The CDs[1] which accompany this book contain 49 of the 55 noteworthy records, all that will fit on two CDs. The records came from my own library and that of radio station WEMU in Ypsilanti, Michigan, which also assisted in the pre-production transfer of the records. Special thanks to WEMU's Music Director, Linda Yohn, to Station Manager Art Timko, Chief Engineer Ray Cryderman, and our long-time friend, Michael Jewett. Dr. Wolfgang Westermann then handled the legal and technical production details of the CDs in France and Germany. Mary Christianson of Christianson Design created the book and CD covers. Professor Luis Fernandez of Northern Arizona University was particularly helpful in critiquing the language used regarding racial matters.

♪ H.S. 2008♪

[1] For this edition of the book, the CDs are sold separately. To purchase the CDs, visit nppbooks.com.

Table of Contents

What Am I Here For?

Introduction

Almost everyone has a connection to a favorite type of music, and many can trace that connection to their years as a teen or a young adult. Music critic Whitney Balliett put it this way in *The New Yorker*: "The music that teenagers like penetrates their bones." It's as if we stop discovering new music at some point in our lives and continue to explore the music we already love.

For me the music that captured my soul was the jazz of the late 1930s and early 1940s. As a teenager in Detroit I grabbed at every chance to hear the popular music of the time at concerts, in movie theaters, and especially on the radio. My chances increased when I went into service and was stationed first near New York City and later near Los Angeles. The little money found in my pockets paid for prowling the jazz haunts of those two great cities.

Years later, after service and college, I discovered that my tastes had changed. Now, instead of the mostly ensemble recordings of the big band era, I was more interested in the small group records of the same period. Though the big band sounds were deep in my 'bones,' the recordings of Teddy Wilson & Billie Holiday and the small groups of Count Basie, Duke Ellington, Benny Goodman, and Lionel Hampton soared into my heart and head as well. I marvelled at the exquisite solos and the virtuosity of interplay in the small group sessions. So I looked at the whole period with different eyes (and ears!), reaching the conclusion that something extraordinary had gone on. I certainly enjoyed and appreciated the jazz of the '50s and on, but the earlier period stayed with me.

A special period for jazz that this book will examine began in the summer of 1939. The Great Depression was pretty well over. Records were selling briskly and jukeboxes hummed. The airwaves throbbed to jazz. The general public knew the names of more jazz musicians than they ever had before or would since. Hundreds of bands criss-crossed the land. Jazz had moved out of the back alleys and into Carnegie Hall. War was approaching – but in the USA it was to a boogie beat. The period ended abruptly three years later when America's entry into World War II and a musicians' recording strike coincided.

Popular music in this three-year period was exceptional in quantity, quality, and diversity. William Gottlieb wrote in his book, "The Golden Age of Jazz," that the late '30s through the '40s was "the only time when the most widely-acclaimed music was the best music."

Sounding a similar note was S. Frederick Starr. In his review of Gunther Schuller's "The Swing Era," Starr suggested: "For sheer excitement and creative ferment the years 1930-45 have no equal in the long history of jazz. In that period jazz attained the highest level of enduring art and at the same time gained mass popularity." Record producer John Hammond praised the musicians who played on the superb

Teddy Wilson & Billie Holiday sessions: "It simply was a Golden Age; America was overflowing with a dozen truly superlative performers on every instrument."

Many of the great jazz performers were active during the three years 1939-42, from the New Orleans veterans to the young musicians who would take jazz into its next phase. In "Since Yesterday," author Frederick Lewis Allen said that the period "...accompanied the sharpest gain in musical knowledge and musical taste that the American people had ever achieved."

People all over the world had become enthralled with this vital and distinctively American art form. While the dance bands were drawing crowds, jazz was noticed by scholars both here and in Europe.

The music was in flux. In 1939 many jazz writers insisted that only the New Orleans style, improvised by small groups, was worthy of the name "Jazz." They decried swing bands as imposters. Three years later, others insisted that bebop was the only jazz, and that big bands were as old-fashioned as Dixieland. Leaving a precise definition of jazz to each reader's choice, this book will be broadly inclusive in its approach.

Was there truly a "Golden Age" of jazz? Some insist that there was and that it ended in the late '20s with the Louis Armstrong Hot Five and the Bix Beiderbecke-Frankie Trumbauer records. Others might argue that it didn't begin until the 1940s with Charlie Parker or the 1950s with Miles Davis.

We think that the period covered in this book was "a" golden age and we have organized it around 55 recordings to illustrate the point. These are not offered as the 55 best records, but rather to show the styles and repertoires of key jazz groups and artists. Most are available in modern formats. A full listing of the artists, compositions, and dates may be found in the text and in Appendix F.

The number of recordings made during this time was in the thousands. For those readers who wish to delve further, Appendix A lists 1,200 recordings from the period. Both the list of 55 and Appendix A include only those recordings available to the general public for sale during the period. We have not included the radio transcriptions nor the recordings from radio broadcasts, concerts, private sessions, etc. These only became available later, and are still being discovered and distributed today.

With an introductory overview for each year, the chapters are chronological with comments about the chosen records set amid cultural, political, and news events. Sub-headings are titled with the names of popular compositions.

Each of the 55 noteworthy records is named and described, along with a photograph of the original label, and its WIN (Why It's Noteworthy) details.

Often a record's description will be followed by an appropriate feature essay about related topics, e.g. "Jazz in Europe," "Alternate Masters," "Glenn Miller's Year," etc..

Short items of jazz-related news, such as recording sessions, radio programs, concerts, etc. are sprinkled throughout the text.

H.S.

Chapter One

It All Comes Back to Me Now...

Prelude

The summer of 1939 could be called the last summer of American innocence. The United States was not yet involved in the conflicts that would become World War II.

After a long Depression, Americans once again had some money in their pockets, and popular culture was experiencing a boom in movies, radio, and music. The economy had recovered to the point where Americans could afford entertainment and other luxuries. Slightly more than four million Americans declared annual incomes of over $2,000, a respectable middle-class wage, and more personal disposable income was available.

Opinion surveys showed that nearly every American sympathized with Britain and France against the Axis Powers (Germany and Italy) and with China against Japan— but they hoped that the United States could stay out of a war. The United States had only 200,000 soldiers, fewer even than the small Dutch army. Most U.S. naval vessels built during the 1930s had been assigned to the Pacific and it wasn't until two years later— when the Japanese attacked Pearl Harbor— that they would seem to be in any danger.

The world hungered for the promises held out by the New York World's Fair, opened by President Franklin D. Roosevelt in 1939. NBC relayed the opening ceremony to about 200 experimental receivers, television's first live TV news report. "Sooner than you realize it, television will play a vital role in the life of the average American," promised one newspaper ad.

The centerpieces of the Fair were the Trylon and Perisphere, a tall, thin pyramid and a gleaming white globe. Rainbow colors festooned the wide streets. Orange-and-blue electric tractors pulled rubber-wheeled cars filled with gawking tourists past streamlined buildings. A must-see stop was the General Motors Building, where one was transported over the Futurama diorama showing the highways of tomorrow. Almost every visitor took home a plastic pickle pin from the Heinz exhibit. Pavilions from sixty nations surrounded the Court of Peace and, of course, there were rides and amusements galore. "On the cusp of the Fair had gathered the hopes of the decade as well as its ashes," wrote historian Alice G. Marquis. Little did anyone know that it wouldn't be long before the Fair finances sank in a sea of red ink.

In deference to "nice" people, movie screens and airwaves were scrubbed to eliminate coarseness or suggestiveness. In Hollywood the Hays Office had established a decency code for film producers in 1930. Customs and postal inspectors barred novels by D.H. Lawrence and Henry Miller, while Erskine Caldwell was read only on the sly. *National Geographic*, with its occasional photos of bare-breasted women, was considered risqué. Yet, many critically-applauded and popularly-beloved films were introduced in 1939, including *Gone with the Wind, The Wizard of Oz, Mr. Smith Goes to Washington, The Little Princess, Stagecoach*, and *Beau Geste*. In his book, "Hollywood's Golden Year, 1939," Ted Sennett argued that 1939 was "Hollywood's golden era at its peak."

In sports, 1939 was a big year for baseball. On July 4, New York Yankees first baseman Lou Gehrig gave his tearful farewell in Yankee Stadium. He declared himself the "luckiest man on the face of the earth" despite the fact that he had been diagnosed with a deadly malady that would later be known as Lou Gehrig's disease. The first night baseball game in the American League was played that summer at Comiskey Park in Chicago. Working as a groundskeeper in the park was Jimmy Yancey, soon to be "discovered" as a top boogie-woogie pianist.

Another sport was gaining in popularity— professional football. In the National Football League championship game, the Green Bay Packers beat the New York Giants, 27-0.

♪ DOCTOR JAZZ ♪

Into this well-scrubbed and innocent era burst a golden age of jazz – a music reaching its own maturity after years of evolution. Jazz had been spawned around the turn of the century when Jelly Roll Morton, King Oliver, and Louis Armstrong played their first gigs in Storyville, the red light district of New Orleans. It started out as a provocative music; even the word "jazz" (spelled "jass" in its earliest form) was often a euphemism for sex.

The music kept its seedy ties as it spread to Chicago, Kansas City, New York, and the rest of the country. Then, with the coming of Prohibition, it stayed alive in illegal speakeasies and nightclubs, many under the management of gangsters. It was no accident that jazz flourished in Harlem, wide-open Chicago, and Kansas City. The Mob used the clubs as headquarters and, for the most part, gave the bands plenty of musical leeway.

Starting in the early 1930s arrangers and instrumentalists broadened the music's appeal by smoothing some of the rough and sometimes raunchy edges. The music's audience expanded and many, especially affluent young white collegians, sought out the music. Not only did these early fans frequent the clubs where jazzmen played, they also sought out the shops in black neighborhoods that sold jazz records.

People all over the world became enthralled with this vital and distinctively American art form. Jazz now was the darling of intellectuals, evidenced by the prolific output of European books and periodicals discussing its uniqueness. As Bruno Bettleheim observed, "Whenever art is vital, it is always equally popular with the ordinary man and the most refined person."

♪ RADIO RHYTHM ♪

Before the popularity of jazz and the advent of radio, families entertained themselves by playing the piano at home. But the piano gathered dust when the phonograph, then the radio, took its place in the parlor. By 1939, many families had bulky radio-phonograph combinations as large as washing machines of today.

Now, Americans found that their radios offered amusing and affordable entertainment. Emerson sold a $10 table-model radio. There were receivers in nine of ten American homes, not to mention in 7.5 million automobiles. Sets played in many stores and businesses. The average person listened almost five hours a day. Of the almost 800 radio stations, two-thirds were affiliated with one of four major networks: CBS, NBC Red, NBC Blue (later ABC), and Mutual.

The Blue Network began Walter Damrosch's "Music Appreciation Hour" in 1928. There had been live network symphony concerts since 1926, and five years later NBC began its broadcasts of the Metropolitan Opera. By 1939, 12 million listeners tuned in for the Met broadcasts; many others tuned in to jazz and popular music.

According to Federal Communications Commission data, some sort of music filled one-half the total broadcast hours. Most of the music was live, either created in the studios or through "remotes" from nearby hotels or ballrooms. Newark's WJZ did the first remote in the fall of 1921, when it used Western Union lines to pick up Vincent Lopez's orchestra from the Pennsylvania Grill in midtown Manhattan. The announcer invited listeners to drop in the next Friday to see the broadcast, and hundreds did just that. In 1922, the station broadcast the Paul Whiteman band from several locations. Fred Waring and his Pennsylvanians had been on the air since the early 1920s.

Gradually band shows invaded the regular prime-time schedules, too. One of the earliest, "The Fitch Bandwagon," began on NBC in 1933. The sponsor was a manufacturer of shampoo ("Don't despair, use your head, save your hair"). For years it was headlined by Phil Harris and his band, but later featured a different band each week. NBC hit it big in 1938 with "The Kollege of Musical Knowledge," in which bandleader Kay Kyser served as quizmaster. (The affable Kyser could neither play nor read music, but he signed a three-year contract for $1 million.)

Although the British Broadcasting Corporation

(BBC) carried no advertisements, British listeners eavesdropped frequently on commercial stations from the Continent. Radio Paris had aired a Sunday evening series of light music since 1929. Terry Randall and His Sensational London Band went across the Channel to broadcast from Radio Luxembourg. Recorded dance music, including jazz, was a staple on many of these stations; in fact, the English company, Vocalion Records, was a frequent sponsor.

Back in the United States, the record labels of the day contained a warning against radio use, but no one seemed to pay any attention. At first, record companies were fearful that playing records on the air would hurt sales. Later, realizing that radio play would increase their sales, they complained when an announcer failed to credit the title and artist. Just to be safe, however, the companies hedged their bets and records continued to have the warning...albeit in very small print!

By the late '30s serial dramas dominated American radio networks during the late morning and early afternoon hours. These "soap operas" (so named because many of the sponsors were makers of laundry soap) mostly ran only fifteen minutes, several times a week. Housewives cooked, ironed, and sewed amid the amnesia, terminal illnesses, and marital difficulties of "When a Girl Marries," "Ma Perkins," "Just Plain Bill," etc. Late afternoons belonged to adventure serials for kids. Many a youngster gulped his supper in front of the Magnavox so he would not miss an announcement of a new premium offered on "Jack Armstrong," "Captain Midnight," or "Tom Mix." After supper, the whole family listened to comedy and variety programs.

Also, by the late '30s, most stations had a live organist, and the big ones hired their own live studio orchestras. A few were hiring "disc jockeys" (that title was not in general use yet) who played at least some jazz. A program of gramophone recordings had been a regular Thursday night feature on the BBC since 1927. In New York in the '30s, recognizing the influence of radio host Martin Block on WNEW, bandleaders welcomed chances to plug their records on his "Make-Believe Ballroom."

As war spread in Asia and threatened in Europe, news on the radio was becoming more important in those pre-TV days. H.V. Kaltenborn and other commentators attempted to put world events in perspective for listeners. A survey by *Fortune* magazine found Americans trusted radio more than print news. Sports programs were very popular, too. In 1939 the New York Yankees finally succumbed, and now all of the sixteen white major league baseball teams permitted sponsored broadcasts.

♪ DANCING IN THE DARK ♪

Along with increasingly widespread acceptance of jazz came acceptance of dancing to jazz music. In the decade following World War I, dancing masters branded as crude and suggestive the motions of the Black Bottom and the Charleston. Popular magazines called for their ban. There were crackdowns on dance pavilions where, to the beat of the "primitive" music, unescorted couples danced, drank and...who knew what?

But as the "flappers" and the "sheiks" grew up, the dances became less shocking. As early as 1922 in Europe the BBC offered Saturday night radio dance programs, featuring, at various times, the Savoy Havana Band, the Gleneagles Hotel Dance Band, and Jack Hylton and his Dance Band. Listeners were urged to "roll back your carpets and dance," and apparently many did.

By the late '30s ballroom dancing was not only acceptable, it was a national passion in the United States. Girls adored dancing, and even boys with two left feet liked holding a girl close. Dances and proms were highlights of the school year, and society debutantes "came out" at fancy-dress balls. They also rolled back the rugs at home and danced the Lindy Hop or "jitterbugged" to records or the radio.

The young people didn't have the floors to themselves. Adults crowded dancing schools so they could show off the latest step at their clubs and parties. Each year nearly a million Americans paid studios like Arthur Murray's to teach them the latest steps. (Songwriter Johnny Mercer chronicled the craze in his song, "Arthur Murray Taught Me Dancing in a Hurry.")

♪ LET'S DANCE ♪

Dancing to jazz and mainstream acceptance of jazz did not truly come about until 1935 when the music went from "sweet" to "swing." In the mid-1930s, the so-called "sweet" bands were popular. Guy Lombardo's Royal Canadians, the prototypical sweet band, stuck to a rigid "businessman's bounce" tempo, as well as waltzes, rhumbas, and tangos. With music which can only be described as schmaltzy, Lombardo's thin muted brass, syrupy reeds, and weak-sounding strings concentrated on pop and novelty tunes. ("Boo Hoo," "It's Love, Love, Love," and "Managua, Nicaragua" were a few of his hits.) His feature acts were tinkling twin pianos and quivering vocals by tenors. Again, songwriter Johnny Mercer was on top of the trend. He called Hal Kemp's Orchestra, another sweet group, the "typewriter band," a perfect description of its staccato trumpets.

Many sweet bands bought and modified stock arrangements of popular songs from publishers. They played ballads and show tunes with lots of vocals and novelty effects such as bubbling champagne, trumpets making kissing noises, singing song titles, etc. Sweet bands packed them in at college dances and were fixtures in the hotel ballrooms. The sweet bands of Jan Garber, Freddy Martin, Sammy Kaye, and Wayne King were all popular.

In the meantime, jazz musicians were starting to "swing," and a new term was born. Duke Ellington named it in his song "It Don't Mean A Thing (If It Ain't Got That Swing)." Singer Billie Holiday noted the new word in an otherwise-forgettable tune, "Now They Call It Swing." In a word, the sweet bands did not "swing" and had to make way for the growing popularity of swing bands.

The swing bands played more up-tempo instrumentals and there were more improvised solos. Most leaders of swing bands insisted on precision in pitch and in ensemble playing. (A Benny Goodman pianist complained that during rehearsal breaks the leader asked him to sound an "A" note over and over again for the horns to tune on.) Swing bands drew on the blues, spirituals, and the works of black composers, such as Duke Ellington, Jelly Roll Morton, and Fats Waller, instead of the more "white bread" sounds of the sweet bands.

On the radio, sponsors cashed in on swing, signing bands for prime-time slots. Many bands floated to popularity on smoke rings. Raleigh sponsored Tommy Dorsey; Chesterfield, Glenn Miller; Sensation, Larry Clinton; and Old Gold, Woody Herman. A succession of top swing bands were featured on "The Camel Caravan," which advertised Camel cigarettes. Had there been a ban on tobacco ads in those days, one wonders how much big band jazz would have been broadcast.

The arrangers for the swing bands adapted original instrumentals to each band's style and soloists. At first most of the innovative arrangers were black. Fletcher Henderson, Don Redman, Benny Carter, and Sy Oliver brought in the call-and-response patterns of the black churches, along with what was termed "collective improvisation," in which whole sections of a band played melodic variations together. These arrangers also allowed soloists room in which to improvise. White bands and arrangers quickly adopted all of these techniques.

A milestone in jazz history occurred in 1935 when a series of events shifted mainstream popularity from sweet to swing. It started when the National Biscuit Company (now known as Nabisco, makers of Ritz Crackers, Shredded Wheat, Uneeda Biscuits, etc.) sponsored "Let's Dance," a three-hour Saturday night radio dance party from New York. It offered a style for everyone – Kel Murray's sweet band, Xavier Cugat's Latin group, and Benny Goodman's swing band alternated segments, with Goodman featuring "hot" arrangements by Fletcher Henderson, a black artist and bandleader. The little-known Goodman band was heard around midnight in the East – too late for most listeners to stay awake. The program was cancelled after a few months when a strike idled National Biscuit's production.

Later in that same year, Goodman suffered through a lukewarm response to his spring-summer cross-country concert tour. His band was greeted by small audiences on the East Coast, in the Midwest, and the Rockies. But Goodman was stunned when, at the conclusion of the tour, enthusiastic crowds jammed into a ballroom in Oakland, California and then the next night, into the sparkling new Palomar Ballroom in Los Angeles. Much to his surprise, these young fans shouted requests for the hottest numbers in the band's repertoire. Why the sudden and enthusiastic response? It turns out that the California teens had been listening to "Let's Dance" at 9:00 P.M. California time (midnight in the Eastern time zone). Because of the time zone differential, Goodman had been drawing far more listeners in the West than in the East. Where Goodman led, other bands followed; that is why August 21, 1935 – the night Goodman played the Palomar – is recognized as the night "hot" jazz became the popular music of this country.

♪ JUMPIN' AT THE WOODSIDE ♪

As Goodman's experience demonstrated, although radio carried jazz to every corner of the country, a band's reputation was enhanced by personal appearances. In 1939, *Metronome*, the music magazine, listed the live performance venues of nearly 300 bands. Count Basie was at the Famous Door, Cab Calloway at the Cotton Club in Harlem, Tommy Dorsey at the Hotel Pennsylvania, Guy Lombardo and Xavier Cugat at the Waldorf-Astoria, and Woody Herman ended the month at the Paramount Theater, all in New York City. Glenn Miller was at the Glen Island Casino on Long Island and Jimmy Dorsey at the Meadowbrook in New Jersey. Glen Gray & The Casa Loma Orchestra was playing the Palmer House in Chicago. Duke Ellington opened July 24 at Boston's Ritz Carlton Hotel.

Jazz sparkled through New York City and beyond. In midtown Manhattan, swing bands held forth in hotel ballrooms and first-run theaters, while clubs on 52nd Street echoed to small groups and singers. Jazz was even performed from time to time on concert stages. A four-hour jazz bash at the Hippodrome drew 3,000 attendees. Uptown, Harlem's theaters, ballrooms, rib joints and clubs resonated to the very latest jazz sounds. Downtown in Greenwich Village, Nick's became the haven for fans of Dixieland jazz. Café Society Downtown featured boogie-woogie pianists and top jazz vocalists. Just a few minutes away were Brooklyn's theaters and the ballrooms of New Jersey, Long Island, and Westchester County.

Because there were so many remote broadcasts from hotels, night clubs, and ballrooms where jazz bands performed, a radio listener, perhaps incapable of directing a stranger to his or her own Main Street, knew that the Meadowbrook was "...on the Newark-Pompton Turnpike in Cedar Grove, New Jersey," that the Southland wasn't in the South, but in Boston, that Elitch Gardens was in Denver and Eastwood Gardens in Detroit, that the Aragon and the Trianon were in Chicago, and that the Lincoln Hotel was just off Times Square.

Success depended on making these nationwide appearances, so many bands took to the road. Artie Shaw traveled widely after setting attendance marks at the Palomar. Louis Armstrong, Paul Whiteman, Benny Goodman, and Harry James were among the majority simply "on tour." The term "journeyman musician" meant many things because, in addition to playing nightly dances and proms, the bands found work in radio broadcasts, studio recording sessions, benefits, and private parties. With a musical book that might include 250 arrangements, there were always new numbers to be learned and rehearsed.

Most bandsmen caught what sleep they could while bumping along in buses. Often they did not know what town they were in, let alone where they were to play the next week. No wonder it was a young person's game; by age thirty most had seen enough of the road.

Many cruise ships featured jazz bands, but at least one passenger on a British liner in May 1939 decided enough was enough. After the band went to bed, he pitched over the side a banjo, saxophone, drums, bass, and two violins. The other passengers were irate, and the villain grudgingly agreed to make restitution.

Because few hotels or big-city theaters that offered extended stays were open to them, black bands were even more itinerant. Many cities had no hotels that would house them nor restaurants that would serve them. Duke Ellington minimized these problems by leasing two railroad Pullman cars for his band, while even a living legend like Louis Armstrong shared an unheated bus with his players. But this was just one of many challenges facing black musicians of the time.

♪ WHAT DID I DO TO BE SO ♪ BLACK AND BLUE?

Goodman's band and the other hot swing jazz bands owed much of their musical punch to the African-American jazz artists who influenced them, wrote arrangements for them, and sometimes played with them. But recognition of black artists was infrequent and, at times, non-existent. Hence, the story of a golden age of jazz cannot be told without touching upon the status of race in America at the time.

In the South, Jim Crow laws doomed all but a few African-Americans to hardscrabble lives. In the North, Jim's sophisticated cousin "James Crow," confined blacks to a cramped and stunted existence. Discrimination – legal or customary – applied to virtually all aspects of life: medical care, housing, employment, travel, recreation, and entertainment – even burial. Music offered one of the few escapes. Because they had fewer opportunities than did whites, blacks suffered disproportionately in the Depression. Sharecroppers in the South were hurt most, but in urban areas, many domestics were laid off and factory workers took wage cuts. An estimated 40 percent of blacks in cities were unemployed, far higher than the rate for whites.

By 1939, however, there were also signs that at least some Americans were not satisfied with accepting the status quo. For example, President Franklin D. Roosevelt's wife Eleanor resigned from the Daughters of the American Revolution over its refusal to rent Constitution Hall for a recital by Marian Anderson, an African-American concert singer. Interior Secretary Harold Ickes and Roosevelt helped the contralto to reschedule for an Easter Sunday concert at the Lincoln Memorial; it attracted 85,000 people.

In that same year, Billie Holiday recorded "Strange Fruit," with its graphic lyrics about lynching of African-Americans. Holiday's company wouldn't record the song, but one of the jazz labels did. Radio stations wouldn't play the record for years, but "Lady Day" sang it at every live performance and the song became her classic.

Prior to the '30s, the world of jazz was almost as segregated as the rest of American society. African-Americans played in their own bands, appearing before largely black audiences. For the most part, they were unknown to whites. Although in the 1920s many whites became aware of black art, music, and literature, the net effect was to see the black as "exotic." Author Langston Hughes said of the Harlem Renaissance, "It was the period when the Negro was in vogue." Ironically, black patrons were not welcome at the poshest clubs in Harlem. Black and white musicians sometimes "jammed" together in informal sessions, but the few mixed recordings groups seldom played together in public.

By the late '30s there were many places to work for musicians – white and black. Many bands were on the road for at least part of the year; of these, about fifty had national reputations. Hundreds more played close to home, their reputations seldom extending a hundred miles.

In both Germany and Japan, authoritarian regimes attempted to ban jazz, fearing the music's inherently individualistic stance. (Among German youth, listening to jazz became a sign of resistance to the Nazi regime.) Besides, it was created and played by what Nazis termed "inferior" blacks and Jews. Yet, at the same time as the German derision, Benny Goodman and His Orchestra topped all the popularity polls in the United States, Goodman was a Jewish man leading a racially-mixed band.

By the end of the 1930s, while most of the public was familiar with only the white swing bands of Goodman, Glenn Miller, Tommy Dorsey, and their peers, musicians in those very bands were listening to, and being inspired by, the best of the black bands – Duke Ellington, Count Basie, Chick Webb, and

Jimmie Lunceford. The white public knew black jazz musicians Fats Waller and Louis Armstrong primarily as singers and entertainers, and many never did recognize their instrumental virtuosity. (Armstrong, incidentally, insisted that Lombardo's was his favorite band and, irony of ironies, Lombardo's "sweet" band, The Royal Canadians, for many years held the all-time attendance record at Harlem's Savoy Ballroom, considered the "hottest" venue of them all. Another white band, Glenn Miller's, would break the record.)

Metronome magazine in August, 1939 proclaimed Charlie Barnet's the "blackest white band." The story noted the band's "distinctly negroid" style and accused Barnet of imitating Ellington, which was exactly what Barnet admitted he was trying to do. At about the same time, Jimmie Lunceford's was billed as "the whitest of the black bands." But the fine Lunceford group never attracted a big following among whites, in part because it got little radio exposure. A columnist in the black *Chicago Defender* called it "radio's color line." Actually, a few black groups, including Earl Hines and Fats Waller, were heard regularly on network radio.

Even on college campuses, the black bands were not always treated fairly. Two orchestras were hired for the 1939 J-Hop at the University of Michigan in Ann Arbor, but Henry Busse's run-of-the-mill white sweet group was paid more than Count Basie's black swing band, and Basie's group had to travel 40 miles to Detroit for a place to sleep.

Whether music sounded "black" or "white" is certainly open to question. Critics and musicians were given "blindfold" tests in which they listened to records by black or white artists. More often than not they were unable to correctly identify bands or individual musicians as black or white. Yet the stereotypes persisted as critics, artists, and listeners held to their black and white classifications.

♪ THE MUSIC GOES 'ROUND AND 'ROUND ♪

Amidst the live performances and radio programs, record sales were lively. And the recording industry had matured along with jazz music. Phonograph records – all breakable, two-sided 78 rpms until the late '40s – spread jazz throughout the world. (The regular 10 inch 78s allowed around three minutes of music, and the less-frequently recorded 12 inch discs, up to five minutes.)

The first jazz recordings were made in 1917 by a white group called the Original Dixieland Jass Band. Actually, some black jazz musicians had declined the opportunity to record earlier, fearing, first of all, that other musicians would copy their tricks and, secondly, that record sales would limit their bookings. They were right about the imitators, but wrong about the profits. Jazz pioneer Joe "King" Oliver was told in New York that he sounded "just like Johnny Dunn." Dunn had copied Oliver's style from records and used the sound to make his group popular. This trick didn't always work though. Horn men across the land imitated Louis Armstrong's solos they heard in recordings, but by the time they had them mastered, Satchmo was playing even higher or faster or better.

Although during the '20s records by Armstrong and blues singers, such as Bessie Smith, sold well, more customers bought the "symphonic jazz" of Paul Whiteman. (Many critics thought it was neither "symphonic" nor "jazz.") Although his "Three O'Clock In The Morning" was recorded at a time when there were only 3 million phonographs in the United States, Victor eventually sold nearly 4 million discs. This was a boon for the record company – at the time, companies figured they could make a profit if a record sold 5,000 copies.

In 1929 record sales plummeted after the stock market crash. For the next few years American firms recorded little jazz. To meet continued interest in Europe, John Hammond, the promoter and entrepreneur, contracted with English companies to record American jazzmen, such as Benny Carter, Fletcher

Henderson, and Benny Goodman. These recordings, later released in the United States, are among the few small group jazz sides made until Americans began buying records again. U.S. record sales had plummeted from 120 million in 1928 to 5 million in 1933, but rebounded to 140 million in 1939. Swing accounted for 85 percent of that total.

The conditions were right for Americans to spend their dollars on music. Although 5 million Americans were still unemployed, automobile plants were paying unskilled workers as much as $40 a week, an acceptable wage for the time. More than 1 million teen-agers had after-school jobs, which allowed them to purchase records or at least to feed the jukeboxes. Although no one was sure how many coin machines there were, their spread alarmed the American Federation of Musicians (AFM), which was convinced the boxes were replacing live musicians.

The same corporations that controlled radio also dominated the recording industries. In the late '20s, successful Columbia Records backed off from its involvement with the struggling CBS radio network. Ten years later the revived and profitable CBS network bought the American Record Company, which included the dying Columbia Records, plus Brunswick and other labels. This new combine challenged the top conglomerate, Radio Corporation of America-Victor Records-National Broadcasting Company. Decca was the third of the major record companies.

Victor was still king of the hill with its 35c Bluebird and its black label Victor, 75 cents in 1939, but reduced to a more competitive 50c in 1940. Columbia, had its 35c (Vocalion & Okeh) and 50c (red label Columbia) discs, as did Decca (35c blue & 50c black). Independents, with limited distribution, scrambled for the leftovers and many had to charge $1.00 or more a record. A short time later, in 1942, Capitol Records broke the lock of the three majors by signing available artists and settling early with the musicians' union during the strike (or ban) that idled the other companies.

♪ ECHOES OF HARLEM ♪

Whether considering records, radio, or live performances, it's hard to ignore that jazz artists were forerunners in promoting racial justice – at least within their own world. Benny Goodman, a white bandleader, integrated his band in 1939 with Fletcher Henderson, a black pianist. To the bandleader's delight, the newly-integrated band filled the Hollywood Bowl on August 5, 1939. The press made much of the fact that Fletcher Henderson had become the band's regular pianist. There was a certain irony in the controversy over Henderson. On his rare recorded solos, Henderson sounded stodgy. (Apparently Goodman had hired Henderson out of gratitude for the arrangements he had written for Goodman, rather than for his pianistic skills.) His piano style belonged to the late '20s. Johnny Guarnieri (white, and a descendant of the violin-making family) quickly replaced Henderson in the band. Goodman was notorious for the fast turnover of musicians, in part because he was such a taskmaster but also because of his high musical standards.

Earlier, black artists Teddy Wilson and Lionel Hampton had been part of Goodman's small groups (trios and quartets) but, as such, were considered specialty acts. At concerts and broadcasts, these small groups performed between orchestral sets. (Hampton occasionally sat in on drums with the band, but Henderson was the first black with a regular chair.)

So it was that the promotion of Henderson remained an important symbol. *Down Beat* magazine commended Goodman for integrating his band, and NBC reported no listener protests when Henderson debuted on the radio on "Camel Caravan." Goodman deserved credit for this move, but perhaps John Hammond, Goodman's mentor-producer and brother-in-law, who was always pushing him, should have it. Hammond was a superb talent scout and crusader for racial justice. Financially secure (his mother was a Vanderbilt, one of America's wealthiest families), Hammond, who served on the board of the National Association for the Advancement of Colored People (NAACP), earlier had convinced Goodman to use

Henderson's arrangements and to employ Wilson and Hampton in his small groups. In the fall of 1939 Hammond sneaked black guitarist Charlie Christian onto the bandstand to play; Goodman recognized talent and Christian stayed. A year later black trumpeter Cootie Williams was lured away from Duke Ellington. More artist than humanitarian, Goodman was simply hiring the most talented musicians he could find, and these integrated groups produced some of Goodman's finest artistic efforts.

More acceptable than a black instrumentalist sitting among white instrumentalists were the few black singers who performed with white bands for, as James Lincoln Collier pointed out, vocalists sat by themselves on the stage. Since they did not physically mix with the band, the integration was considered more acceptable. But this was tolerated by the public only when it went in one direction— a black singer like Lena Horne might perform with a white band, but no white woman could sing with a black band, at least not in live performances. In the mid-'30s Duke Ellington's managers rejected an African-American vocalist because her skin was not black enough. In recording studios, many white women sang with black small groups: Helen Ward with Teddy Wilson, Helen Forrest with Lionel Hampton, Ginny Simms with Eddie South. Record buyers also had no problem with such racially-mixed pairs as Tommy Dorsey's Jo Stafford and Sy Oliver or Gene Krupa's Anita O'Day and Roy Eldridge, but their live performances together provoked protests. Americans were not ready for this form of racial integration. In 1930, thirty states had laws banning interracial marriages, and the prohibition was not deemed unconstitutional until well into the 1960s.

In its October 15, 1939 edition, *Down Beat* devoted considerable attention to the racial issue. Its front-page headline asked, "Should Negro Musicians Play in White Bands?" Fellow white band leader Jimmy Dorsey praised Goodman for his move to integrate his band. Woody Herman, another white band leader, feared Southerners would boycott mixed bands. Duke Ellington was concerned that white leaders might deplete the black bands, taking their best players. Few other leaders were willing to be quoted on the topic and some uncredited remarks were outright racist. Regardless of the leaders' fears, however, integration was proceeding as jazz was growing up.

Guitarist Charlie Christian with Benny Goodman.

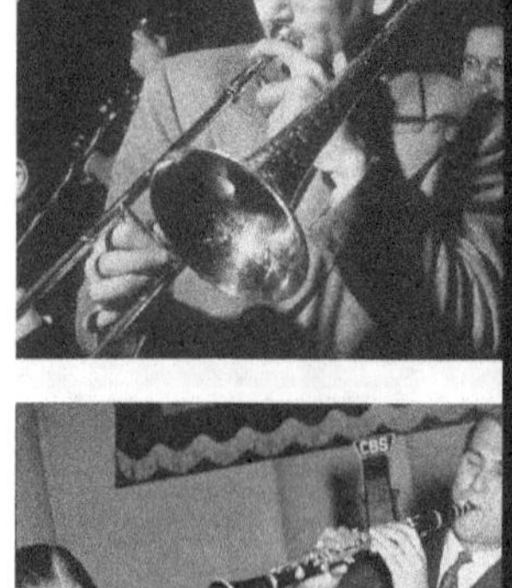

Chapter Two

Somewhere Over the Rainbow

July recording

Louis Prima & His Orchestra recorded four sides for Decca, the last Prima recordings which French Discographer Charles Delaunay could take seriously. Sniffed Delaunay, "Later Louis Prima recordings are increasingly commercial." Prima chose to concentrate on ethnic humor and novelty numbers with an occasional serious instrumental.

July recording

Harry James and His Orchestra recorded two sides for Brunswick. The first had a vocal by James' new singer, Frank Sinatra.

August 6 radio milestone

Vocalist Dinah Shore premiered her new radio show on the Mutual network. She would remain a radio and TV favorite into the 1990s.

August recording

Red Nichols & His Orchestra, "Wail of the Winds." His haunting theme song was one of Nichols' few big band recording successes. Ten years earlier, Nichols had led an internationally-famous group (Red Nichols & His Five Pennies) which included future leaders such as Tommy and Jimmy Dorsey, Benny Goodman, Gene Krupa, Glenn Miller, Jack Teagarden, and others. The Nichols band was a major competitor to Paul Whiteman's number-one group in the late '20s.

1939

The fateful headline on September 1, 1939 read "Germany Attacks Poland." Over a million Nazi troops, supported by tanks and bombers, swept across Poland from the west while Russians struck from the east, just a month after the Germans and Russians had signed a non-aggression pact. The repercussions of the alliance, Stalin cooperating with Hitler, were felt around the world. Many Communists could not tolerate this move and left the party to protest the agreement.

The world was at war again, but oblivious visitors at the New York World's Fair (in hopes of winning a contest for a week in Warsaw) were completing essays describing "What I want to see in Poland." Large crowds of tearful visitors filed through the gold-domed Polish pavilion.

In Washington, the government turned toward preparation for war. Learning that the Germans were working on nuclear fission, émigré scientists in the United States convinced Albert Einstein to write a letter alerting President Franklin Roosevelt. FDR appointed an Advisory Committee on Uranium which, by the end of the year, quickly began a program to beat the rest of the world to building an atomic bomb.

On September 17, national hero and aviator Charles A. Lindbergh made his first of many anti-intervention speeches on network radio. While living in Europe, he had met most of the military leaders and had received an award from the German government. He argued now that neither Stalin nor Hitler posed much threat to world peace and that the United States should stay out of the war. (A favorite swing-era dance step was the "Lindy Hop," named for Lindbergh's 1927 solo flight across the Atlantic. The aviator, who hated the nickname "Lindy," winced every time he heard it.)

A man associated more with love than war, Sigmund Freud, was making news in London. The father of psychoanalysis, and the man who made discussions of sex respectable, was 83 years old. Plagued by jaw and mouth cancer – caused by a cigar-smoking habit he could not quit – his life ended when a sympathetic doctor gave him the lethal morphine overdose Freud requested.

♪ SWING IS HERE ♪

By 1939 the stage was set for an exciting era in jazz. Americans had left the tired and stodgy sweet orchestras to discover jazz, and particularly the hot sounds of swing bands. Record sales were at all-time highs – twenty-five times higher than during the Depression. People were listening to live and recorded music on radios in their homes and cars, and seeking jukeboxes for recorded music outside of the home. Bands played live music in hundreds of ballrooms, hotels, resorts, nightclubs, and concert halls. Adults as well as young people danced to swing music and, now that Prohibition was over, jazz fans attending live events could enjoy cold beer with their music.

Jazz musicians came of age— the musician's repertoire had been expanded to a rich blend ranging from early New Orleans to latter-day Cole Porter. And most of the musicians could play the hundreds of tunes turned out by Hollywood, Broadway, and Tin Pan Alley, as well as songs by Jelly Roll Morton, Duke Ellington, George Gershwin, and Fats Waller. They played music in a way that would continue to sound current many decades later.

This musical sophistication of the day was accompanied by criticism and serious writing about jazz. *Down Beat*, *Metronome,* and *Variety* detailed the world of popular music for Americans; *Melody Maker* did the same for English fans as did other magazines in Europe. Jazz discographies were being compiled and books were being written, mostly by Europeans.

♪ JUKE BOX SATURDAY NIGHT ♪

Record sales were booming and those who preferred "renting" their listening pleasure could drop a nickel in a jukebox. This habit prodded the American Federation of Musicians (AFM) into taking its complaints against "canned music" to the public through ads in *Saturday Evening Post* and other popular magazines. The record companies should have taken notice since the AFM was unhappy, and not just about jukeboxes. It was also taking aim at those who made money from all uses of recordings, including home players.

Nonetheless, an unprecedented burst of recording activity came on to the jazz scene. The phonographs and jukeboxes were flooded with hundreds of excellent selections played by high-quality professional musicians. It took the combined efforts of the Imperial Japanese Navy and the American Federation of Musicians to close it off three years later.

Duke Ellington at a jam session.

MUSIC MAKERS

In contemporary accounts, written by authorities of their period, Paganini was described as the greatest of classical violinists and Franz Liszt as the premiere pianist, but we'll never know for sure since we've never actually heard them play. Fortunately, we can make our own evaluations of jazz musicians because recording technology came along at just the right time. Much of jazz history has been preserved in recordings. From among the thousands of recordings made between mid-1939 and mid-1942, chosen for this book are 55 noteworthy records. These are by no means the 55 *best* sides, but together they are representative of the major artists, styles, and compositions of the period.

The record descriptions begin on the next page. All of the label photos show early 78rpm issues; these are taken of discs actually played by collectors of the day.

Each record is identified in the following ways: number and artist, composition, date of recording, position on the CDs accompanying this book, a WIN statement (Why It's Noteworthy), and pertinent comments.

1. Charlie Barnet & His Orchestra
CHEROKEE
July 17, 1939
CD 1, Track 1

Why It's Noteworthy (WIN): A composition which became the radio theme of one of the top-level, jazz-oriented big bands, played with vigor, precision, and musical humor.

"Cherokee" was written by British bandleader Ray Noble as part of a suite intended to describe various American Indian groups. A number of bands recorded it, but the Barnet recording was a big hit and then became Barnet's radio theme. The tune played a role in later jazz when saxophonist Charlie Parker re-arranged it in his classic recording of "Ko Ko," a major contribution to early bebop. (Parker's "Ko Ko" is not to be confused with Ellington's "Ko-Ko" (Record 16), an entirely different composition.)

Charlie Barnet played his enthusiastic tenor sax throughout this record, stating the theme and then improvising in his romping style. Also, he could play alto sax and was one of the few reedmen in this period to use the soprano saxophone. Many of his arrangements stand out from other big band records, with the sound of his soprano sax leading the reed section.

"Cherokee" was arranged for Barnet by Billy May, who made substantial contributions to the library of this band. The next year May left Barnet for Glenn Miller and did much to loosen up the sound of that group. Later, May wrote for radio, TV, and films, and led a successful big band of his own.

"Cherokee" was probably such a big hit because of the wah-wah brass, combined with the reed sounds

which open the record, followed by Barnet's statement of the melody. This arrangement came in handy the next year when a music-licensing hassle denied Barnet the right to use "Cherokee" as his theme. Instead, Barnet recorded a new theme, "Redskin Rhumba," that used the same distinctive opening. When a listener heard the new theme, it was easily identifiable as Barnet's band, even if it wasn't "Cherokee."

Charlie Barnet playing tenor saxophone.

2. Erskine Hawkins & His Orchestra
TUXEDO JUNCTION
July 18, 1939
CD 1, Track 2

WIN: A train-influenced composition played with sensitivity by a band which began its life in a black college in the Deep South.

Recorded the day after "Cherokee" and for the same label (RCA's Bluebird), this track was the latest in a long series of blues and jazz recordings with themes relating to trains of the rural South. The slow tempo, the trumpet muted with a plunger, the ensemble playing, and the solos, all added to the train motif.

Hawkins himself played the opening and closing trumpet, but in the middle of the record there is a striking solo by Dud Bascomb, an influential but little-known trumpeter. An alto saxophone solo by Bill Johnson and clarinet by Heywood Henry add to the tapestry.

After hearing the Hawkins band play "Tuxedo Junction," a group of Glenn Miller's musicians requested the sheet music and Miller recorded it. His recording sold a million copies, many more than the original Hawkins version. (Incidentally, authorities Martin Williams and Gunther Schuller chose the Hawkins record over Miller's for their excellent *Smithsonian Collection of Big Band Jazz.*) Other bands also recorded it and, because it was requested so often, almost every band had an arrangement.

The Hawkins orchestra first came north together in 1936, when Hawkins and a few classmates from the Alabama State Teachers College formed a band they called "The Bama State Collegians." In 1940 they would record their biggest seller, "After Hours."

3. Fats Waller & His Rhythm
SQUEEZE ME
August 10, 1939
CD 1, Track 3

WIN: A major composer, influential pianist, playful singer, and leader of a swinging small group showed off all his talents in one recording.

Thomas "Fats" Waller here performs one of his own compositions with enthusiasm and humor. The tune has a built-in jazz feeling, and Waller and his crew cavort through it with great spirit. Relaxed solos on tenor saxophone by Gene "Honey Bear" Sedric and on trumpet by John Hamilton mesh easily with Waller's joyful piano and irreverent vocal. This was one of hundreds of Waller small-group sides recorded from 1934 until the leader's early death in 1943.

Waller's clowning often disguised the very serious talent of one of the most imaginative of composers, pianists, and vocalists. Composer Waller's "Squeeze Me" ranks in popularity just behind his "Honeysuckle Rose" and "Ain't Misbehavin'."

In May of 1941, Waller took time out from his small-group sessions to record five piano solos, including his own "Honeysuckle Rose," Ellington's "Ring Dem Bells," and his mentor James P. Johnson's "Carolina Shout." It's obvious from these sides why top pianists such as Art Tatum and Count Basie, looked at Waller as their inspiration.

Waller played "stride" piano, in which the left hand alternates single notes and chords. Free-wheeling, humorous, and as insouciant as he was, he had one musical prohibition: boogie-woogie. He considered it a low form of music and would not play it.

4. Eddie Condon & His Chicagoans
NOBODY'S SWEETHEART
Aug. 11, 1939
CD 1, Track 4

WIN: A group of top-notch musicians playing a spirited rendition of a standard— at a time when Dixieland was rarely performed.

This label is loaded with information for the collector or historian. Near the top, in parentheses, is the master recording number, 66073, which would stay with this item through all reissues (the number is also etched into the surface of the record). Below that is the album number, 121. Then, 12 sides are noted, of which this is the first. On the bottom line is the Decca issue number of the day, 18040A.

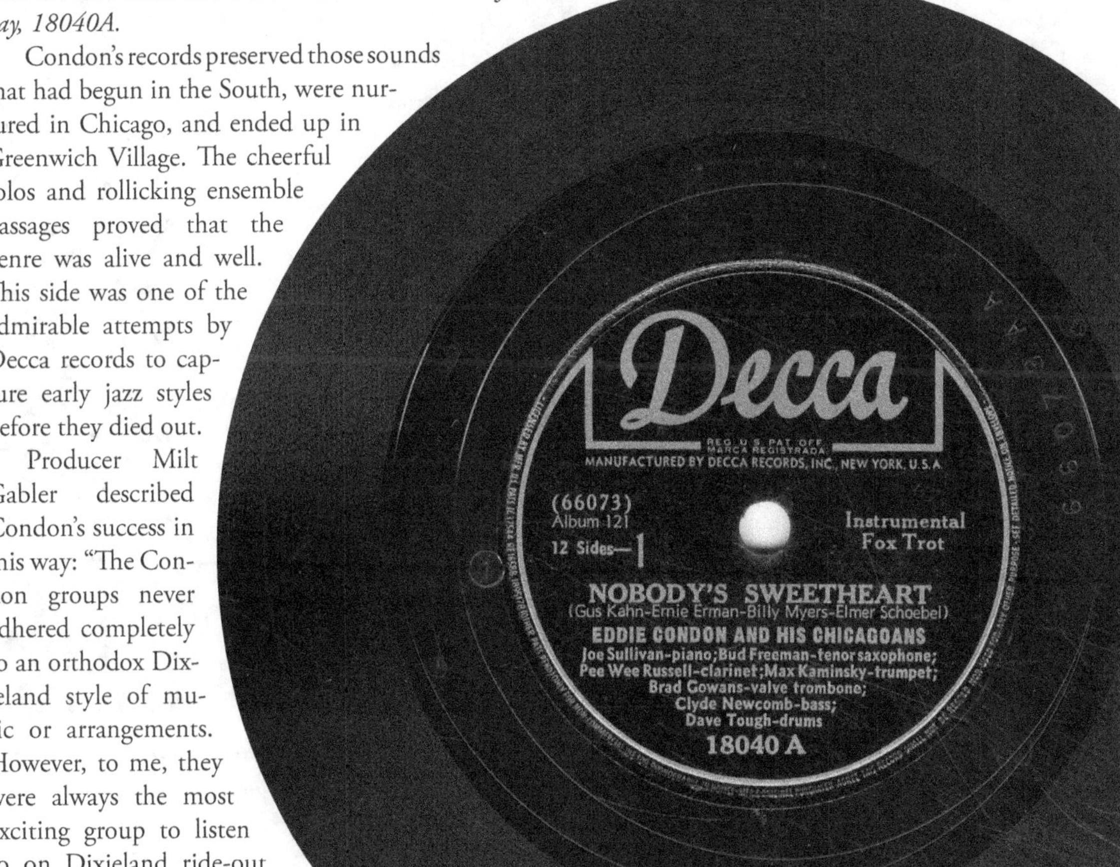

Condon's records preserved those sounds that had begun in the South, were nurtured in Chicago, and ended up in Greenwich Village. The cheerful solos and rollicking ensemble passages proved that the genre was alive and well. This side was one of the admirable attempts by Decca records to capture early jazz styles before they died out.

Producer Milt Gabler described Condon's success in this way: "The Condon groups never adhered completely to an orthodox Dixieland style of music or arrangements. However, to me, they were always the most exciting group to listen to on Dixieland ride-out last choruses." (Condon did not like his music to be labeled "Dixieland" or "Chicago-style." He brushed aside all labels when he titled his autobiography "We Called It Music.")

On this recording Condon had gathered some of the best musicians ever to play this kind of jazz. A few, such as tenor saxophonist Bud Freeman, trumpeter Max Kaminsky, and pianist Joe Sullivan, had played and would play in major big bands. Others, such as clarinetist Pee Wee Russell, spent most of their musical life in small groups. Still others, Dave Tough for example, could play any style and, later, Tough even drove the bebop-flavored Woody Herman First Herd.

Russell opens the record, and weaves in and out during the whole first chorus. Then follow solos by Brad Gowans on valve (not slide) trombone— an instrument not played by many in those days; Freeman on tenor saxophone; Kaminsky with a fine plunger-mute offering; and Sullivan on piano.

Condon was a fixture at a club called Nick's in Greenwich Village for years, then had his own clubs in the Village and, later, uptown. His contributions to jazz are legendary (including an incident in the '20s when his assignment was to get Fats Waller to a session on time...and sober!) Condon was a great drinker and storyteller. Among his best is his recipe for a hangover: "First, take the juice of one quart of whiskey..." He said of the bebop musicians, "They flat their fifths, we drink ours."

This side was recorded for a 78rpm album of the day, part of Decca's "Gems of Jazz" series, which often listed personnel of the sessions. In this period such a black label Decca sold for 50 cents.

Jazz musician Fats Waller (R) with fellow musicians Bobby Hackett (on trumpet) & Eddie Condon (2L) & photographer Charles Peterson (2R) backstage after a performance at Apollo Theater, Harlem.

5. Quintette of the Hot Club of France

H.C.Q. STRUT

August 25, 1939, London

CD 1, Track 5

WIN: This selection, from the only non-American group which influenced jazz musicians in this period, featured two outstanding soloists and jaunty, swinging ensemble sections.

This quintet, the only important European jazz group of the swing era, was an unlikely instrumental combination of violin, string bass, and three guitars. The outstanding figures were Gypsy guitarist Django Reinhardt (born in Belgium) and French violinist Stephane Grappelly (sometimes spelled 'Grappelli').

Reinhardt was much admired and imitated in this period when the guitar was becoming more prominent as a solo instrument in jazz groups. He was the first European to impress American jazz musicians. Reinhardt and the facile Grappelly both solo on this track, their own clever compositions. ("HCQ" for 'Hot Club Quintette' were the group's initials in French.) Both had recorded with visiting American jazzmen and impressed them with their improvising abilities.

Few American fans were aware of the Quintette since most of its music was on European labels not generally available in the U.S. After World War II, Reinhardt came to the U.S., but had an unsuccessful tour. He went back to Europe where he died in 1953. He became a jazz legend: the Modern Jazz Quartet featured a composition called "Django;" Woody Allen placed him as a central figure in his movie *Sweet and Lowdown*; and groups still imitate his work in the early 21st century.

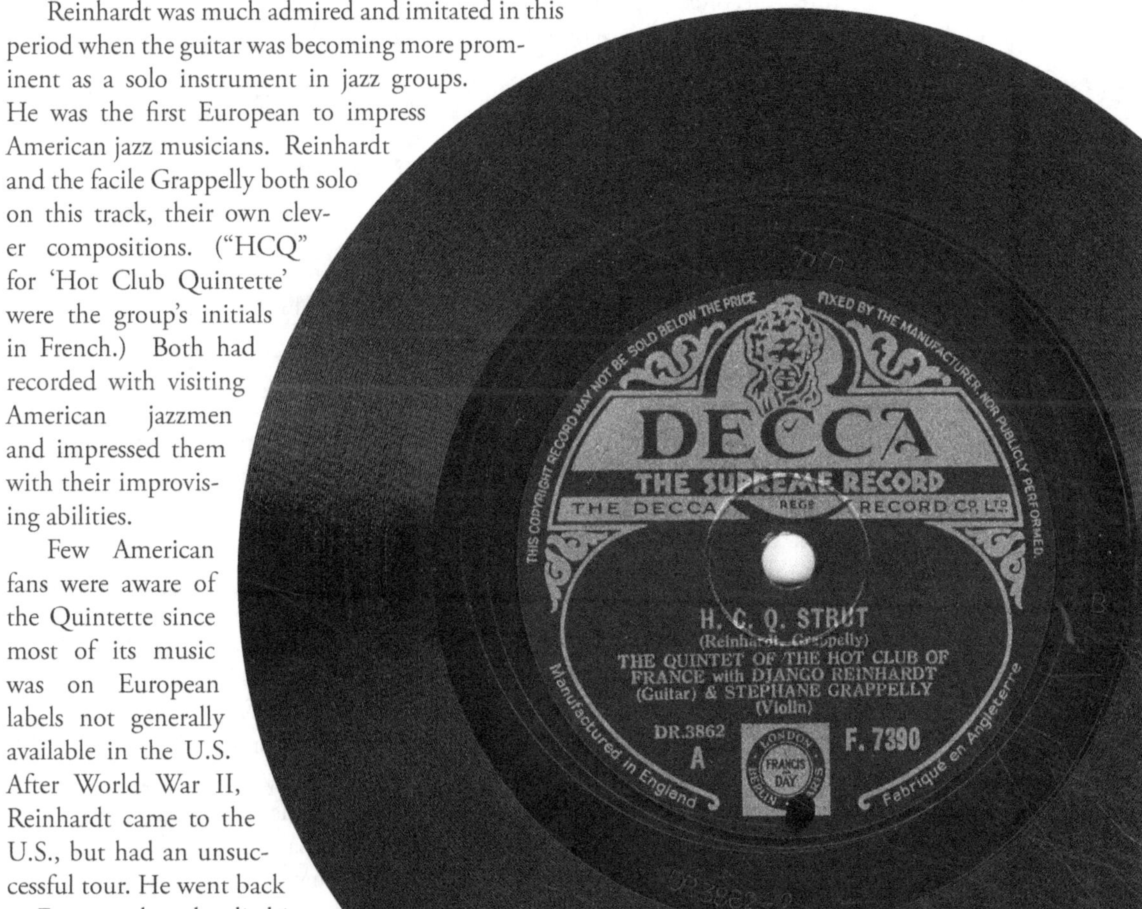

Long-lived, Grappelly went on to greater fame after the HCQ, playing all around the world, even recording jazz duets with classical violinist Yehudi Menuhin.

"H.C.Q. Strut" (even in France, jazz was "Hot" and club was "Club") was one of dozens of sides by this wonderful group. Most of their recordings were of standards, movie tunes, and Broadway tunes; in other words, they performed the same repertoire that their American counterparts played.

The original issue of this side was on the British Decca label, noted for its high technical quality. During World War II, this label's engineers were involved in war-related audio and sonar projects. American Decca was started in 1934 by the British parent company.

Notice that Reinhardt and Grappelly are the only artists named on the label, even though there were three other players in the group.

Jazz In Europe

Whether Europeans appreciated jazz more than Americans is debatable, but certainly they took great interest in the music. (Some sources indicate that at this time Europeans bought more jazz records per capita than Americans did.) The popularity of the Quintette of the Hot Club of France on the continent and in England is but one example.

Early American jazz records sold well on British, French, German, Dutch, Swiss, and Swedish record labels. Some American companies tried to overcome language barriers by issuing only instrumentals overseas. Fats Waller, Louis Armstrong, and Red Nichols were among those who recorded both vocal and instrumental versions of the same compositions.

A greater acceptance of people of color allowed black American musicians to move freely around Europe. In the '30s both Louis Armstrong and Duke Ellington played before British royalty; it's sad to note that Ellington didn't perform at the White House untl 1971. The Duke likened playing and traveling in Europe to dining on steak after a lifetime of hot dogs. Lesser-known players, such as trumpeter Bill Coleman and trombonist Dicky Wells, played, recorded, lived in, and were feted in France. Writer Leonard Feather reported that the French had developed a belief that only black musicians could play jazz well; he called this attitude their "Crow Jim" policy.

Tenor saxophonist Coleman Hawkins, saxophonist-arranger Benny Carter, and cornetist Rex Stewart recorded in Europe with Dutch, British, French, and Swiss musicians. (A noteworthy group was a Dutch band called The Ramblers.) American violinist Eddie South did some of his best recordings with Reinhardt and Grappelly. If few European groups matched the American bands, there were many first-class individual musicians. Pianist George Shearing recorded in London in 1941-42 before coming to the U.S., and England's Nat Gonella played trumpet and sang in the style of Louis Armstrong.

For decades black bands had been traveling to Europe. Now German submarines were prowling the Atlantic Ocean, effectively closing the only the road to Europe in those pre-aircraft days. (Pan American Airways would begin its Boeing Clipper service that year, but it took only a few passengers at a time.) The lucrative overseas market was closing to musicians of all colors. Fats Waller and Duke Ellington toured Europe in the spring of 1939 but, by fall, Jimmie Lunceford had to cancel his tour because the war had started. Lunceford's tour became the first jazz casualty of World War II.

Even during their darkest days in World War II the British continued issuing jazz records. Such bands as Jack Hylton, Bert Ambrose, Geraldo Bright, Sid Phillips, and Lew Stone bolstered civilian morale. The Royal Air Force Dance Band recorded inspired Dixieland music during the war, then stayed together afterwards as The Squadronaires.

Sometimes European producers came to the U.S. to record. The foray by English bandleader Spike Hughes in 1933 resulted in few good recordings, but most critics praise the sessions arranged five years later by French critic Hughes Panassie, who felt that not enough "real" jazz was being recorded. Union regulations, that protected the jobs of local musicians on both sides of the Atlantic, limited international visits and recording efforts.

Often European affiliates of American companies have done more than their American counterparts in reissuing LPs and CDs of pre-World War II American jazz. For example, French RCA and French CBS both reissued a trove of Ellington's records not available here at the time ('50s & '60s). French RCA also reissued artists ranging from Benny Moten's Kansas City band through Dizzy Gillespie. French MCA issued dozens of LPs with the artists who recorded in the '30s and '40s for American Decca. With the advent of CDs, Classics Records started to reissue the total recorded outputs of many major American jazz artists, and some not so major. Without these European efforts, not much of this American musical heritage would have been available in the post-78rpm formats.

Not only did Europeans appreciate listening to jazz, but the first serious writing about jazz was produced by Europeans as well. Englishman Brian Rust and Frenchman Charles Delaunay compiled the first two major discographies for the 1939-42 period. (Delaunay's father, painter Robert, was a member of Gertrude Stein's salon in the '20s.) Only since the 1960s have American writers caught up with the Europeans. Musician-pundit Eddie Condon was skeptical of European jazz critics; he said of Frenchman Hughes Panassie, "Do we teach them (how) to jump on grapes?"

♪ BROADWAY MELODY ♪

On August 25 what was to be the thirteenth and last edition of *George White's Scandals* opened in New York. Dancer Ann Miller and comedians Willie Howard, Ben Blue, and the Three Stooges starred. The revue which once had shocked Broadway for its naughty humor now seemed old hat – another sign that times were changing.

The demand for novelty tunes had not diminished, though. A big hit of 1939 was "Three Little Fishies." Saxie Dowell, a sideman in Hal Kemp's orchestra, simply added verses and some boop-boops to a two-bar nursery ditty. The verse could be sung either in English ("Down in a meadow in a little bitty pool") or in sort of fish-Latin ("Down in da medy in an itty biddy poo"). The only way to sing the chorus was "Boop boop dittem dottem wottem chu!" Singer Mildred Bailey recorded the song, and another version was a million-seller for Kay Kyser.

Even nonsense tunes had their troubles with the censors. Thus, for a song that was originally about a woman of the streets, the lyricist had to substitute the nonsense word "floogie" for the original "floozie" and "foot" for the original "fleet." It ended up as "The Flat Foot Floogie (With A Floy Floy)." The tune received a singular honor: the lyrics were microfilmed and stowed in the time capsule at the World's Fair site. No one could guess what those who were to dig up the capsule in 6939 A.D. would make of them.

♪ UPTOWN DOWNBEAT ♪

In September, sweet bands were featured throughout New York. The Waldorf-Astoria headlined Hal Kemp and Xavier Cugat. Larry Clinton was at the Paramount and Ozzie Nelson at the Strand Theater. The New Year's Eve broadcast by Guy Lombardo & His Royal Canadians was already a tradition. Humorist Garrison Keillor tells of fighting to stay awake as a youngster to hear Lombardo play "Auld Lang Syne" at midnight. Later, Keillor confessed that he had been certain the Royal Canadian players were like the Mounties, dressed in scarlet tunics and playing while on horseback.

Bandleader Paul Whiteman assured the *New York Times* that swing was just a fad and would pass within six months. He said that collegians already saw it as "high school stuff." (On the other hand, Whiteman was hedging his bets by releasing records by his Swing Wing, a small group of his jazz-oriented musicians.) Even if he no longer showed up in the popularity polls, Whiteman was still the highest-paid leader in the business. (Years earlier, Whiteman had hired and encouraged Bix Beiderbecke, the Dorsey Brothers, Red Norvo, Mildred Bailey, Jack Teagarden, and many other swing-era stars. Years later, he was the first bandleader to be a TV star.)

In spite of Whiteman's remarks, the swing bands were doing all right, thank you. When Artie Shaw played the Strand in October, his band received record pay of $13,500 for each of two weeks. In his autobiography, Shaw complained about playing nursemaid and teacher to temperamental musicians. Once, a disgusted Shaw walked off the bandstand in the middle of a performance and went to Mexico. But, in a few weeks, he formed a new band that made a million-selling record of "Frenesi," a tune he picked up south of the border. Shaw's stormy love-hate affair with music continued, as well as his avocational inquiries into literature and the arts. Admirers argued that Shaw was too intellectual for his own good.

While Artie Shaw saw himself as a tortured artist, other leaders held a variety of self-images. Louis Armstrong considered himself an entertainer, his job to please his audiences. Glenn Miller, leading the most popular band of all, looked at himself as a businessman, as did Tommy Dorsey. Duke Ellington, "class" personified, wooed his audiences by telling them that he "loved them madly." Benny Goodman, reputed to be a strict disciplinarian as a leader, threw himself into the joy of playing jazz.

6. Count Basie's Kansas City Seven
LESTER LEAPS IN
September 5, 1939
CD 1, Track 6

WIN: One of the outstanding small group sessions found throughout recorded jazz, utilizing a variation on "I Got Rhythm," and featuring an exciting interaction between the tenor saxophone of Lester Young and the piano of Count Basie.

Count Basie, like many big band leaders, set up small group sessions to let his best players stretch out and improvise with more freedom than the big band recordings allowed. This track showcases Lester Young, one of the giants in jazz history, who approached the tenor saxophone with unmatched delicacy and lightness. Basie's well-placed piano notes interact brilliantly with Young's horn.

The guitar-bass-drums group shows why it was called "The All-American Rhythm Section" (Guitar – Freddie Green, Bass – Walter Page, Drums – Jo Jones). The other side of the original 78 of this record was "Dickie's Dream," a salute to trombonist Dickie Wells.

Propelled by whispers rather than shouts, this track shows that "hot" jazz does not have to be loud. As in so many jazz compositions, this uses the chords of Gershwin's "I Got Rhythm." This exemplary track is included in many compilations, including the *Smithsonian Collection of Classic Jazz.* This track is a perfect example of great jazz, i.e., it swings, the improvisation is highly imaginative, and the artistic collaboration is superb.

Alternate Masters

The French artist Claude Monet did a number of "serial" paintings showing the Cathedral at Rheims at different times of the day. Imagine one day finding several more Monet paintings of the same cathedral. The equivalents in jazz are the "alternate" or unissued takes, including one of "Lester Leaps In."

At recording sessions, artists usually recorded more than one performance of a tune to insure against technical glitches and/or to provide producers or the musicians themselves a choice of which version (or "take") to release. After such a decision was made, some companies destroyed the rejected takes, some put them aside, and many just forgot about them. Since jazz musicians improvised while recording, this meant that many rejected takes might contain different, but acceptable, interpretations of the same composition. Thus many good jazz recordings were lost to posterity. Since some companies did keep acceptable but rejected takes, or an employee might have sneaked some out, many of these performances (or "alternate takes") have shown up later on LPs and/or CDs, either legitimately used or pirated (stolen).

As the technology advanced and recording tape came along (the early master recordings were all on small discs), even partial takes might be retained. Eventually, recording might start when the players entered the studio and keep going until they left, thus making it possible to later release whole sessions including bad takes, jokes, profanity, etc. rather than just the preserved takes.

Beginning with microgroove technology in the late 1940s, the record companies began releasing these "alternate takes" from the '20s, '30s, and '40s and listeners discovered a whole new body of music. There was an identification system used in the recording industry for identifying both original released takes and alternates.

The system worked in this way. During the Basie session mentioned above, Brunswick assigned "Lester Leaps In" to its 35 cent Vocalion label and gave it the master recording number of 25297. On the initial U.S. release, the number was printed under the Vocalion "issue" number 5118 and etched into the disc just outside the label. The same number, 25297, was printed on the labels of English Columbia DB5073 and English Parlophone R2915, which were issued at about the same time as the American Vocalion. That number, 25297, let the prospective buyer know they were getting the original "Lester Leaps In."

This master recording or "matrix" number (usually abbreviated "mx") identified a particular performance forever. For example, Columbia Records purchased the Brunswick and Vocalion labels in 1939, but each reissue of "Lester Leaps In" carried mx 25297. This number was used also to identify non-Columbia reissues such as the *Time-Life Giants of Jazz* collection and the *Smithsonian Collection of Classic Jazz*. In other words, no matter what label or what format, the original "Lester Leaps In" can be identified by the designation mx25297, even today.

To continue with the history of "Lester Leaps In," Brunswick's files showed that the Basie group recorded two acceptable takes that day in 1939. Following company policy, the version picked for release was called Take 1 (mx25297-1) and was the master used for the first and most subsequent reissues. It turned out that Young's solo on take 2 was equally exciting, but quite different. Take 2 was never released in the 78rpm era. It did find its way on to some independent jazz LPs in the '50s and '60s, then in the late '70s Columbia issued the two takes side-by-side on an LP. To extend our analogy, listening to the two takes is like looking at two paintings Monet made of the same cathedral. The basic subject is the same, but the shadings and emphasis are different.

A few small jazz labels sometimes released more than one take at a time. For example, when Eddie Condon's group improvised three more-than-acceptable takes of "Lonesome Tag Blues" in 1942, Commodore issued one under the original name, the second as "Tortilla B Flat," a third as "More Tortilla B Flat." (The titles are in tribute to *Tortilla Flat*, a 1935 novel by jazz buff and Condon buddy John Steinbeck.)

Sometimes a company accidentally released different takes of the same composition. Some 78rpm copies of Benny Goodman's 1937 recording of "Can't We Be Friends?" are Take 1, and others, Take 2; the performances contain very different solos, but there's no way to tell from the label. Similarly, the first pressings of Glenn Miller's "Tuxedo Junction" mixed two almost identical takes of an arrangement which has almost all ensemble playing by a well-rehearsed band, and it's just about impossible to tell one take from the other. (Librarians have a way of checking for alternate takes: they measure the grooves on the 78rpm record. Almost always, takes that might sound identical will have slightly different lengths.)

The alternate takes from the '39 - '42 era began surfacing on LPs about ten years after they were recorded. The companies found in their vaults such treasures as:

> "Jump for Joy," which Duke Ellington wrote as the title tune for a black musical on July 2, 1941 (mx 061340-1). It had fine solos by trombonist Joe "Tricky Sam" Nanton, alto saxophonist Johnny Hodges, and vocal by Herb Jeffries. Take 2 turned out to feature equally good, but different, solos, and Ivy Anderson did the vocal – a big change, indeed.
>
> "Boogie-Woogie on St. Louis Blues," in which the brilliant pianist Earl Hines climbed on the then-popular boogie-woogie bandwagon. He recorded this number on February 13, 1940 (mx 47055-1). The record sold well not only because of Hines' piano artistry, but also because of band-member George Dixon's encouraging shouts, such as "Turn out all the lights and call the law, right now!" and "Don't stop 'til 1951." Take 2, recorded the same day, but not released for twenty years, was equally good but had no shouts.

Many rejected takes and breakdowns were retained from the 1940 Liberty Music Shop recording session in New York, featuring singer Lee Wiley and trumpeter Bunny Berigan, and issued later on LP. Hearing Wiley struggle with the lyrics and Bunny Berigan rehearse his accompaniments provide a sort of voyeuristic glimpse of major artists at work. Some tracks contain rather coarse language from the frustrated singer. (Wiley had no reason to expect that the breakdowns and her comments would leave the studio.)

The countless Benny Goodman alternate and rejected takes, false starts, and breakdowns expanded the documentation of the Goodman band, showing how difficult many of his arrangements were and how they were rehearsed often many times. These items captured the artistry of Goodman guitarist Charlie Christian also. This virtuoso player did all of his recording in '39-'42 and almost all with Goodman. (Record 35). There is an entire alternate take of "Solo Flight," the concerto written for Christian, and even a warm-up rehearsal tune, later titled "Waiting For Benny." On the negative side, purists deplored the 1960s practice of record producers, and used tape-splices to intercut Christian solos from one take to another.

Some companies discovered master takes that had never been released on 78s. Billie Holiday's "Mandy Is Two," Charlie Barnet's "I Can't Get Started," and Artie Shaw's "Deserted Farm" were just some of the sides not released at the time of recording. It's not likely that many more of these will be found now since so many years have gone by and the record bins have been scoured.

In this period the record companies began to reissue a few classic jazz recordings from the 1920s. With state-of-the-art technology, Louis Armstrong, Jelly Roll Morton, and Bix Beiderbecke sounded better than ever. (Beiderbecke, a trumpeter called the first white jazz star, died in 1931 at age 28.)

Many labels from the 78rpm era reveal more information than just artist, composer, composition, and matrix and issue numbers. Some labels had a code for the city of recording, while others, with the "race" labels such as Victor's "V" prefix, Okeh's 8000 series, Decca's 7000, and Bluebird's 8000 alerted distributors to ship those records to the black neighborhoods. The racial designation was not masked on Decca's "Sepia Series" in the early '40s.

Some companies added "A" suffixes to their issue numbers to signal to dealers which side of a disk was more likely to sell – but they were not always right. Artie Shaw's "Begin The Beguine" was a "B" side that became one of the biggest sellers of the era.

"Not licensed for radio broadcast" and "For use only in homes" warnings appeared on the 78 rpm labels but, once record companies learned that radio play stimulated sales, they never backed up the threats.

7. Lionel Hampton & His Orchestra

WHEN LIGHTS ARE LOW

September 11, 1939

CD 1, Track 7

WIN: One of the outstanding pick-up sessions organized by Lionel Hampton with musicians from different bands. This one featured all-star soloists improvising on a beautiful melody.

Notice Victor's identification of this record as a "Swing Classic," and the proviso that the record could be used "only for non-commercial use on phonographs in homes."

This is one of the dozens of sides recorded by all-star groups that Hampton organized when he was with Benny Goodman. They featured members of whatever bands happened to be in the same town as Goodman – the top players from the bands of Goodman, Duke Ellington, Count Basie, Cab Calloway, Earl Hines, and Andy Kirk. (Appendix C lists musicians who played on these Hampton dates.) During these sessions Hampton himself played drums (his first instrument), or the vibraphone (Louis Armstrong started him on that instrument at a 1930 session), or the piano (with a two-fingered percussive style). Sometimes he sang (in a light-voiced rhythmic style).

For this session, Hampton assembled three masters of the tenor saxophone: Coleman Hawkins, the player who "invented" the modern sax in the '20s and who had just returned from five years in Europe; Ben Webster, who would soon join Ellington as he and the Duke both approached creative peaks; and Chu Berry, the player touted as the best young tenor sax player at the time. Also present was the superb alto

saxophonist Benny Carter, who wrote and arranged this tune.

Chu Berry, the young Dizzy Gillespie on trumpet, Milt Hinton on bass, and Cozy Cole on drums were all from the high-quality Cab Calloway band, the best he ever had. Charlie Christian on guitar came from Benny Goodman's band. (Gillespie later said that he was awed by such company.)

On his vibraphone solo, Hampton's mallets conveyed amazing sensitivity. Carter demonstrated his usual sophistication, power, and grace. Hawkins' rough up-tempo style was very different from the tender approach he would use just one month later on "Body and Soul" (Record 9). The Hampton sessions produced many good jazz sides, and this was one of the very best.

Lionel Hampton playing the vibraphone.

8. Bob Crosby & His Orchestra

HIGH SOCIETY

October 2, 1939

CD 1, Track 8

WIN: A traditional New Orleans melody played by a big band featuring the Dixieland style. Aware of the tradition in which they played, the musicians honored the early classic solos of the genre.

This popular big band played the usual swing-era repertoire, but specialized in music associated with New Orleans small groups. Usually it was called "Dixieland" or "Chicago-style" music. The lead cornet part— which in Dixieland music would be played by one person— would be scored for three trumpets, the single wailing clarinet for four reeds, etc. The band compensated for a loss of the spontaneity, which is characteristic of Dixieland, with improvised solos and tight ensemble work. (Their small group, The Bob Cats, often played in a manner closer to the parent style.)

On this track the underrated Irving Fazola (born Prestopnik) recreated the traditional clarinet solo originated by New Orleans veteran Alphonse Picou. The solo is said to be based on the piccolo obbligato background written for this tune, originally a military march. Another highlight of this track is the interplay between the reed section and the piano of Jess Stacy.

The Crosby band had its own network radio show and played at the major venues. The band made hundreds of recordings, mostly of pop tunes but also of some Dixieland classics.

The most frequent soloist in the band was tenor saxophonist Eddie Miller, who later became a favor-

ite of the Hollywood studio conductors. Bob Crosby, the brother of super-star Bing, sang the ballads and fronted what was originally a co-op band, with each member sharing in the profits.

The tune "High Society," had a long history before this recording was made, and would continue to evolve. In 1956 a musical film adaptation of the play *The Philadelphia Story* was produced. In addition to new songs by Cole Porter, "High Society" was not only given new lyrics but was also the title of the film. The cast included three outstanding singers of the period: Louis Armstrong, Bing Crosby, and Frank Sinatra.

This record was on the blue label Decca, which sold for 35 cents at the time. Some stores offered a bargain at three for a dollar.

Brothers Bing (L) and Bob Crosby.

9. Coleman Hawkins & His Orchestra
BODY AND SOUL
October 11, 1939
CD 1, Track 9

WIN: A virtuoso performance of one of the greatest American popular songs by one of the very best tenor saxophonists in jazz history.

The sounds on this record were mostly those of the deep-toned, heavy-vibrato tenor saxophone of Coleman Hawkins, improvising on one of the finest American popular songs. After establishing the tenor sax as a major instrument in the '20s and early '30s, Hawkins spent five years in Europe. Returning in 1939, he was warned that Chu Berry, Ben Webster, and Lester Young were surpassing him. (While Young mostly used the lighter upper registers, Berry and Webster played with the Hawkins-originated deep tone.) Berry had recorded a good version of "Body and Soul" just a few months earlier, which may explain why Hawkins used this song to reassert his dominance.

In *The Jazz Tradition*, critic Martin Williams called this track "the accepted Hawkins masterpiece. The record reveals not only Hawkins' knowing use of increasingly sophisticated techniques, but his brilliant use of pacing, structure, and rhythmic relief. He saves his showiest arpeggios, opening melodiously and introducing implied double time along the way." That this uncompromising jazz performance became a million-seller is yet another indication of the widespread popularity of jazz in this period.

Hawkins briefly led a big band, but most of his numerous recordings were made with small groups.

Million-Sellers

Hawkins' "Body and Soul" was one of sixteen records produced in 1939 that sold at least a million copies. Not all of these records had instant success, however; it took a few years for some to reach the million sales mark. For example, "All or Nothing at All," recorded by Harry James in 1939, was reissued by Columbia when its vocalist, Frank Sinatra, became a star in 1943. Sales hit a million when Sinatra's career in radio, recording, and films flourished.

Sixteen million-selling records in 1939 was a particularly impressive number since only 53 recordings had ever sold that many up to that time. Most of the pre-1939 million-sellers could not qualify as jazz, nor could such 1939 hits as Gene Autry's sentimental "That Silver-Haired Daddy of Mine" or Lale Anderson singing "Lili Marlene" in German. But the charmed jazz circle of million-sellers featured big bands such as Cab Calloway, "Jumpin Jive;" Woody Herman, "Woodchoppers' Ball;" Harry James, "Ciribiribin;" Artie Shaw, "Traffic Jam;" and four sides by Glenn Miller: "Little Brown Jug," "Sunrise Serenade," "Moonlight Serenade," and "In The Mood."

The main theme of "In The Mood" had been used in jazz for years. Trumpeter Wingy Manone had recorded it in 1929 as "Tar Paper Stomp" and in 1939 as "Jumpy Nerves;" Fletcher Henderson had called it "Hot and Anxious" in a 1931 record. Composer Joe Garland worked it up into a longer composition and sold it to Artie Shaw who played it, but never recorded it in the studio. (An eight-minute version by Shaw was recorded off a radio broadcast and became available on tape and LP years later.) Glenn Miller shortened it, gave it his own treatment, and it became a hit.

Jazz musicians (clockwise from top left): Artie Shapiro (bass), Hot Lips Page (trumpet), Coleman Hawkins (saxophone), and Joe Marsala (clarinet), at a jam session.

Glenn Miller's Year

Glenn Miller's orchestra was to become the most popular of all the big bands, and 1939 was the year of his rapid ascendancy to the top. He was no instant star, though. The trombonist-arranger had paid his dues. In the late '20s he played with Red Nichols and with the popular Ben Pollack Orchestra. (Miller told this story on himself: when Pollack left the band business, the sidemen were looking for a new front man; Miller warned them that Benny Goodman would never make a good leader. They believed him and eventually chose a non-musician front man – the personable Bob Crosby.)

Miller was respected enough as a trombonist to play alongside such top players as Goodman, saxophonist Jimmy Dorsey, trombonist Jack Teagarden, and drummer Gene Krupa in the pit orchestra for the 1929 musical "Strike Up The Band," under the baton of George Gershwin.

After developing a reputation as an arranger, Miller joined the Dorsey Brothers Orchestra in 1934. The next year he helped English leader Ray Noble organize an American orchestra. Because union restrictions wouldn't allow Noble to bring his players to the U.S., he hired Miller as musical director and chief arranger. Miller proceeded to sign quality musicians such as pianist Claude Thornhill, trumpeter Charlie Spivak, saxophonist Bud Freeman, and trombonist Will Bradley. However, Noble declined the adoption of the distinctive reed blending which would be Miller's trademark later.

Miller formed his own band which struggled for a while until he signed with Victor Records late in 1938. In the next year he had the four million-sellers mentioned above. In the spring and summer of 1939, the band packed them in at the Meadowbrook in New Jersey and the Glen Island Casino on Long Island Sound. Both ballrooms originated national broadcasts and attracted big crowds from New York City. In August, a reviewer for *Variety* praised the band's "resilient dansapation," but misspelled Miller's first name, leaving off one of the "n"s.

That fall the band received the honor of playing at Carnegie Hall for the silver anniversary celebration of the American Society for Composers, Authors, and Publishers (ASCAP). In December, Glenn Miller & His Orchestra began network broadcasts for Chesterfield cigarettes, which continued until the leader went into the Army Air Corps in 1942. (For a time the program aired three nights a week and developed a huge audience.) The sponsor did require a small change in the repertoire. Miller had written a novelty number called "Sold American," based on the auctioneer's chant in a Lucky Strike cigarette commercial; after the Chesterfield cigarette contract was signed, Miller never played it again.

A good trombonist, Miller rarely soloed for fear of being compared with Tommy Dorsey. Although a sensitive musician, Miller admitted that he made his musical decisions as a businessman. Jazz aficionados scoffed at his monotonous tempos and some considered his band's distinctive reed sound outdated. His vocalists did not win over the critics, but they sold records.

The band's artistic level kept improving. It sounded more relaxed after Miller added such jazzmen as Bobby Hackett and Ernie Caceres plus trumpeter-arranger Billy May (Record 1). From Jimmie Lunceford's band Miller borrowed such techniques as wah-wah brass and the use of dynamics (gradual increase or decrease in sound levels).

A big band was no better than its arrangers. Miller was a master himself and recognized talent in others. Bill Finegan came over from Tommy Dorsey and arranged the early Miller hit, "Little Brown Jug." Jerry Gray (born Generoso Graziano) left Artie Shaw for Miller. (Shaw's "Begin The Beguine" was a Gray arrangement). Among others, Gray contributed his original composition, "String of Pearls" (Record 46). There were also occasional contributions from black arrangers Eddie Durham and Benny Carter.

The Miller orchestra averaged more than 80 studio tracks a year. (The million-selling records continued with two in 1940, one in 1941, and two in 1942.) Many of Miller's recordings were pop tunes or songs taken from movies. For example, he drew on *The Wizard of Oz* for two songs, backing up "Over the Rainbow" with "Ding, Dong, the Witch is Dead."

Miller and his band played themselves in the 1941 film *Sun Valley Serenade* and in 1942's *Orchestra Wives*. (Both are good films and still play occasionally on TV.) In both, the band was portrayed in a realistic and dignified manner. There were, however, a few replacements with actors substituting for Miller musicians. The string bass player in one film was a young comedian named Jackie Gleason and the piano player was the actor Cesar Romero. (A movie made about Miller in the '60s, *The Glenn Miller Story*, with James Stewart in the title role, was Hollywood at its worst— factually inaccurate and musically boring.)

Perfectionist that he was, Miller recorded all of his broadcasts so that he could review the performances. Since network engineers made the recordings, their technical quality was excellent. Many of these broadcasts were later issued on LPs and CDs. In one recorded form or another, there are available from the period almost 4,000 separate Miller items. (An item is defined here as one playing of a single composition, thus a 15-minute broadcast might include five items.)

Miller broke up his civilian band in the summer of 1942 and went into the Army. As Captain, and later Major, Miller formed and directed marching, concert, and dance bands. (The string section of his Army dance band was larger than his entire civilian group. He could afford such a luxury now that the Army was paying the salaries!) His bands played for civilians and soldiers, broadcast and recorded on government VDiscs, then went to England to play for troops in 1944. Some observers called it the best big band of all; it certainly was the largest! In December Miller was a passenger on a small plane that was lost on its way from Paris to England. (One theory is that it was downed accidentally by an English bomber jettisoning its load over the English Channel.)

10. John Kirby & His Orchestra
SCHUBERT'S SERENADE
October 12, 1939
CD 1, Track 10

WIN: A small group with an unusual instrumentation playing a classical composition with a romping ensemble style and appropriate solos.

Kirby's six-piece group featured a distinctive ensemble sound of muted trumpet, clarinet, alto saxophone, piano, bass, and drums; it was perfectly suited for small night clubs.

This side was typical of the way this band treated classical compositions – with respect but with a lightly swinging, up-tempo arrangement. Short solos by pianist Billy Kyle, clarinetist Buster Bailey, alto saxophonist Russell Procope, drummer O'Neil Spencer, and trumpeter Charlie Shavers were all tastefully coordinated with the group's overall sound and feeling.

Writer-musician Leonard Feather described the group this way: "This combo, with its light breezy sound and unique style, brought a new element of ingeniously orchestrated finesse to small-band jazz." All of the players in the group were imaginative improvisers with successful careers before and after their years with Kirby.

Jazz musicians of this period were much more familiar with classical music than were their predecessors. The Kirby group recorded a number of "long-hair" compositions, as did some of the big bands (Appendix D). The Kirby group's influence continues even today. In 2006, jazz violinist Regina Carter recorded "Anitra's Dance" using the Kirby arrangement.

This track was included in a 4-record 78rpm album with an unusual distinction. It was one of the very first jazz albums to be produced with original artwork on its cover.

11. Earl Hines, Piano solo
ROSETTA
October 21, 1939
CD 1, Track 11

WIN: One of the major pianists in the history of jazz showing off his solo talents on one of his own compositions.

Note the recording date on the label, not a usual practice for the major companies. Also notice how the label is getting more crowded. In addition to the legal notices, copyright notices, artist, composition, date, etc., there is a advertisement for Victor Needles. Many phonographs of the day used removable needles which had to be changed occasionally.

Pianist Earl "Fatha" Hines gained attention in the 1920s as one of the few musicians who could hold his own with Louis Armstrong. He made dozens of recordings with his big band in this period, but this track is a solo piano display of his powerful right hand and daring improvisations. He said he developed this "trumpet style" so that his piano could be heard over the horns.

Another characteristic of his playing was his uncanny ability to wander off the tempo but still come back to the original beat, as if he has a metronome in his head. On this track he plays one of his own compositions with power and vigor. (See Record 53 for Hines' big band.)

Hines' piano style was a major influence on many young pianists, including Nat "King" Cole and Stan Kenton. His career as a solo pianist was reinvigorated by a concert in the '60s and then in the early '70s he recorded "Earl Hines Plays Duke Ellington." The album is now listed in Ben Ratliff's *New York Times Essential Library: Jazz: A Critic's Guide to the 100 Most Important Recordings*, an honor indeed.

More Hidden Treasures

To revisit the Monet analogy, imagine that even more "lost" Monet cathedral pieces or works were discovered, some that were unfinished, some painted with other artists, etc. Once again, there are jazz equivalents.

In addition to the alternate takes and unreleased studio material, there were other recordings made in this period that were not offered for public sale at the time. This whole new body of music, which became available later on LPs and CDs, fits into four major categories:

Live Performances: Although portable recording equipment was bulky and unreliable, a few pioneers captured such moments as the 1940 Duke Ellington concert at Fargo, North Dakota, and some 1941 sessions by guitarist Charlie Christian in Harlem. (Kudos to the Europeans for writing the first discographies, but mistakes were made. Due to his lack of knowledge of U.S. geography, discographer Brian Rust located Fargo in Illinois!) Yet even into the 21st century, private recordings of live performances from this period were coming on the market and many collectors own privately-recorded tapes or discs.

Radio Broadcasts: So-called "air checks" or "air shots" were recorded with portable equipment or in a recording room in a radio station. Many were recorded illegally, but some were recorded and released through regular channels. Benny Goodman and Glenn Miller air checks became best-selling LPs in the 1950s. Hundreds of such broadcasts are now available, and newly-discovered items surface every year.

Film Sound Tracks: In 1938, Victor had released part of the sound track to the Walt Disney film *Snow White and the Seven Dwarfs*, but this practice didn't become routine until well into the LP era. (The first original Broadway cast recording was *Oklahoma* in 1944; it also became the first original cast million-seller when it was produced as an LP in 1949.)

Jazz groups and big bands appeared in many films which today can be seen on late-night TV, YouTube, or rented as videocassettes or DVDs. However, no soundtrack recordings were released at the time; often tunes played in the films were re-played in the regular recording studios and then released as 78 rpm singles. (Since it was improvised jazz, sometimes the film version might be quite different from the recording that was released for sale.) Some original film sound track recordings from the 1939-42 period by Basie, Ellington, Miller, and others began to appear in the 1950s.

> **Electrical Transcriptions:** In addition to all of their other activities in this period, musicians were making ETs, later called "for-radio-only recordings." Recorded in professional studios, these were sold to subscribing radio stations which had special turntables for the 16" plastic disks. By purchasing an ET service a station shut off the access to that music by its competitors. Ellington first recorded "Take the 'A' Train" on an ET and pianist Art Tatum did some rare sides. It took decades to unravel the legal and financial obstacles that finally allowed the transfer of the ETs to LPs and CDs.

Jazz record collectors run into many problems in acquiring the records of this period, and many times the title they seek might be available in a variety of formats. For example, suppose a collector wants a recording of Benny Goodman's "Sing, Sing, Sing." Sounds simple enough, doesn't it? You start with the Victor recording on July, 6, 1937, mx 09571-2 and 09572-2, two sides of a 12" 78rpm record. Then you discover that when the record became popular, Victor edited it and issued it as a 2-sided 10" 78 rpm, so now there are two choices.

But it turns out you're just starting your search. Goodman's discography shows dozens of recordings of "Sing, Sing, Sing," some privately recorded, from concerts, radio broadcasts, private parties, etc. On many LPs, you'll find the tune as played at the Goodman Carnegie Hall Concert in 1938, a smashing performance with a great piano solo by Jess Stacy (you can hear Goodman say "Jess"). That version was chosen for some collections. Then you discover that many aficionados prefer the "Sing, Sing, Sing" from the soundtrack of the movie *Hollywood Hotel,* recorded between the Victor and the Carnegie Hall recordings. And on and on it goes, through radio broadcasts, concerts, and private party recordings all the way to the 40th anniversary concert at Carnegie Hall in 1978. So, once again, just the artist and the composition are not sufficient. Collectors must have all kinds of information to find the particular recording they're after.

12. Muggsy Spanier & His Ragtime Band

DIPPER MOUTH BLUES

November 10, 1939

CD 1, Track 12

WIN: One of sixteen historic recordings on which Dixieland musicians provided re-creations of early jazz gems. This one, a "King" Oliver number, included Oliver's classic solo, still played today by Dixieland trumpeters.

This recording was one in a series called, then and now, "The Great Sixteen," in which Spanier's Dixielanders breathed new life into classic numbers. On "Dipper Mouth Blues," Spanier recreated Joe "King" Oliver's 1923 trumpet solo. At the close, trombonist George Brunies gave the traditional cry, "Oh, play that thing!" (The solo and the shout are still performed today.) Joe Oliver was Louis Armstrong's mentor, the man who brought him north to Chicago.

Spanier blew with power and sensitivity, as did clarinetist Rod Cless in his re-creation of the original Johnny Dodds solo. Pianist Joe Bushkin and the others played with great drive. These "Great Sixteen" sides helped to spur an interest in the early compositions which led, in a few months, to what would be called "The New Orleans Revival."

Spanier was much in demand as a trumpeter in this period, and he recorded often. He had resisted starting his own big band, but finally gave in. Unfortunately, it didn't succeed.

Around this time, Trombonist George Brunies consulted a numerologist who told him that his last name should have 6 letters, so he changed it. He was Brunis forever after.

13. Billie Holiday & Her Orchestra
THE MAN I LOVE
December 13, 1939
CD 1, Track 13

WIN: The greatest female vocalist in the history of jazz sang one of the best known of the torch songs, accompanied by her musical soulmate, tenor saxophonist Lester Young.

In her phrasing and intensity, her flirtation with the beat, and her interpretation of lyrics, Billie Holiday set the standard for jazz vocalists forever. In *The New Groves Dictionary of Jazz*, James Lincoln Collier wrote, "She always acknowledged her debt to Louis Armstrong for her singing style and it is certainly in emulation of him that she detached her melody line from the ground beat, stretching or condensing the figures of the melody."

On this track she teased new meanings from the sentimental words of George Gershwin's elegant torch song. She was always backed by quality musicians, here drawn primarily from the Count Basie Orchestra. Buck Clayton set the mood at the outset with a few well-chosen notes on trumpet. Pianist Joe Sullivan backs the vocal, and tenor saxophonist Lester Young soloed to provide a velvet pillow of music to show off the vocal gem.

The Billie Holiday-Lester Young musical liaison resulted in some of the greatest moments in recorded jazz. These two artists brought out the very best in each other. (They also gave each other lasting nicknames – "Lady Day" and "Prez," his for president of the tenor sax players.)

In this period, Billie Holiday was nearing the end of over 150 recordings she had made with small groups. They have to be considered some of the finest vocal and instrumental jazz ever put down on wax. They began with the Teddy Wilson and His Orchestra sides on the Brunswick label in 1935 and continued with the Billie Holiday and Her Orchestra titles on Vocalion in 1936. Over the next five years, under both these group names, the greatest musicians of the day accompanied Billie Holiday and added their solos to her artistry. All of these sides are available in a 10 CD box set. (Appendix C lists all of the musicians who played on Holiday's recording sessions.)

Obviously the well-worn record in our photo was played many times. Vocalion was Brunswick's 35 cent label. About this time Columbia bought the company's records but lost the name Vocalion. From then on Columbia's 35 cent records were issued under the Okeh name.

Billy Holiday.

Lester Young.

14. Jimmie Lunceford & His Orchestra
LUNCEFORD SPECIAL
December 14, 1939
CD 1, Track 14

WIN: Arguably the best of all the big bands, Lunceford was admired and imitated by the leaders of the most popular of the white bands. Many adopted his techniques and some hired his players.

With Eddie Durham's arrangement the band made it clear why this music was called "swing." The solos were free and uninhibited and the ensemble work, though precise, really swung. This selection features a graceful solo by the underrated alto saxophonist Willie Smith. Also, there were contributions from trombonist Trummy Young, tenor saxophonist Joe Thomas, and high-note trumpeter Snooky Young.

Many leaders respected and emulated the Lunceford sounds and techniques. This track is typical Lunceford and shows how good the band really was.

British writer Max Harrison wrote of the Lunceford band, "The ensemble playing was superb with finely shaded dynamics, well-matched articulation and attack…hear the saxophone propelling Trummy Young's trombone through 'Lunceford Special.'" (Alto saxophonist Willie Smith later played with Harry James and Duke Ellington. Trombonist Trummy Young became one of Louis Armstrong's All-Stars.)

The band began as a high school group called the "Chicksaw Syncopators." It became a great show band which combined visual tricks with its high-quality music.

Unfortunately, the white general public rarely got a chance to see this group. They played primarily before black audiences.

15. Jelly Roll Morton, piano & vocal
MAMIE'S BLUES
December 16, 1939
CD 1, Track 15

WIN: As a composer, Jelly Roll Morton ranks as one of the greatest in jazz annals. As a pianist and a singer his reputation is not far behind. This record shows him, in the period just before he died, at his contemplative and laid-back best.

Jelly Roll Morton was one of the true giants of jazz – a composer, pianist, and singer who began in New Orleans early in the 20th century. In 1939 Morton was still an effective "tickling" pianist and singer, and still leading small-group recording sessions reminiscent of his Red Hot Peppers classics of the '20s.

Listening to this track one can imagine Morton playing in a New Orleans bawdy-house, rings flashing on his fingers and a diamond in his tooth. His singing is delightful, though sad, and his piano playing is a perfect complement.

The song has the classic, simple twelve-bar blues structure (musicologists call it AAB, i.e., the first four bars – called A— are played twice, followed by a different four bars – called B— that are played once). This structure remains the underpinning of much jazz. Morton says on this record that this was "no doubt" the first blues he ever heard.

Morton biographer James Dapogny emphasizes Morton's "orchestral concept" of writing and playing with whole orchestras in mind; witness the many big band recordings of Morton's "King Porter Stomp." Perhaps this is why Morton is still having an influence on jazz today. Early in the 21st century Dapogny, an active jazz musician, was pressing to get

some of Morton's unused arrangements published and performed.

"Mamie's Blues" was one of the last solo recordings by the man whose calling cards proclaimed himself "The Inventor of Jazz Music." (In actuality, although he had a great influence on jazz, he would have to share the 'inventor' title with many others.) He starts this record out with an autobiographical note; it is a reminder of the hours of recording of both memoirs and music which he did for Alan Lomax, folk music historian, at the Library of Congress in 1938. At long last, that material is all available today on CD.

The General label, on which Morton did this 1939 recording of "Mamie's Blues", was one of the dozens of small record companies that came and went in this period. Commodore Records bought the label and reissued many of their sides.

♪ THINGS TO COME ♪

The last notes of jazz pioneers were blending with the first sounds from youngsters with new ideas about jazz. The careers of Jelly Roll Morton and Dizzy Gillespie spanned the music's first century. In the 1900s, Morton was playing in the bordellos of New Orleans for tips; in the 1990s, Gillespie would be playing with symphony orchestras around the world.

In the 1939-42 period, styles were at a crossroads too. Bob Crosby, Eddie Condon, Lu Watters, and Muggsy Spanier drew inspiration from jazz's early days. Meanwhile, some young African-Americans emerged – Charlie Christian, Dizzy Gillespie, and Charlie Parker – and pushed forward. They would use their Monday nights off from band jobs to explore together in Harlem new ways of playing jazz.

Duke Ellington drew a capacity crowd for a dance at the University of Illinois. Another 1,700 people paid just to sit in the balcony and listen. It was already obvious that his music was headed for the concert stage. (Although Ellington had declined Benny Goodman's invitation to appear at his 1938 Carnegie Hall concert, several of his sidemen did play. The Duke started his yearly Carnegie Hall concerts in 1943.)

On Christmas Eve, 1939, John Hammond produced his second "From Spirituals To Swing" concert in Carnegie, the most prestigious of all American concert halls. The artists ranged from Goodman to obscure black blues singers who were performing before a white audience for the first time.

♪ STORMY WEATHER ♪

An eerie calm settled over Europe in the wake of Hitler's lightning conquest of Poland. Britain and France declared war, but neither country was in a position to stop Germany. Thousands of children were evacuated from London and Paris as all of Europe mobilized for war. Reserve forces were called up and navies bolstered. Meanwhile Great Britain rationed meat, bacon, cheese, fats, sugar, and preserves.

Wartime censorships were imposed. In his first encyclical, Pope Pius XII condemned dictators and treaty violators. Recognizing the state of the world, the Nobel Committee decided to award no Peace Prize for 1939.

On November 8, a bomb killed six and injured sixty in a crowded Munich beer hall, but the intended victim was not among the casualties. Immediately after addressing a rally, Adolf Hitler had departed. Had he tarried, history might have been quite different. Meanwhile, the Soviet Union attacked its neighbor Finland. The Finns put up an heroic but futile resistance.

♪ WINTER WEATHER ♪

In the winter of 1939 life grew grim – even on some movie screens. Because the United States was still neutral, Hollywood had treated the threat of war gingerly, the newsreel companies distributing footage provided by the Germans as well as by the Allies. But in *Confessions of a Nazi Spy*, Edward G. Robinson played an FBI G-man on the trail of a pro-Nazi organization. The Warner Brothers movie included newsreel shots of the recent congressional hearings on a "fraternal" organization, the German-American Bund. The Bund officials filed, and then withdrew, a $5 million libel suit against the film. On November 29 Bund leader Fritz Kuhn was convicted of larceny and sentenced to two to five years. That put a stop to the openly pro-German Bund activities.

Not all Hollywood productions were grim. The biggest box-office star was a blonde, curly-haired moppet named Shirley Temple, according to *Motion Picture Herald*. She stole hearts in feel-good movies about the triumph of the human spirit over adversity. And most of the Academy Awards that year went to the dramatic, but clearly escapist, *Gone With the Wind*.

The character *Rudolph The Red-Nosed Reindeer* made his appearance in 1939 in a give-away promotion booklet from Montgomery Ward stores. The song bearing his name, however, would not appear until 1949.

This high point in the popular arts included books. Major novels of 1939 included James Joyce's bewildering *Finnegan's Wake*, John Steinbeck's *The Grapes of Wrath*, Henry Miller's *Tropic of Capricorn*, and Nathaniel West's *The Day of the Locust*. One of the most popular books was the short story collection *Life With Father* with its delightful and humorous stories of a family. The theatrical adaptation opened a record run at New York's Empire Theater in November. The few productions that focused on war fared poorly on Broadway.

♪ WE'VE GOT PLENTY TO BE ♪ THANKFUL FOR

Americans continued their enthusiasm for sporting events. President Roosevelt decreed that Thanksgiving would be celebrated a week early to lengthen the Christmas shopping season. Retailers welcomed the change, but football schedulers found themselves with traditional games scheduled for a work day. For the first time, the NCAA mandated helmets for collegiate football players. Undefeated Tennessee was the top team in college football, and Tom Harmon of the University of Michigan won the Heisman Trophy. Meanwhile, the New York Yankees had copped their fourth straight World Series.

The speed of daily life quickened in many respects. One indication was the public enthusiasm for a five-minute Cream of Wheat product, introduced by Quaker Oats. (The old kind took fifteen minutes.) Birdseye introduced the first pre-cooked frozen foods – criss-cross steak and chicken fricassee. Turkey, stews, and vegetables went into the freezer soon after.

Pan American Clippers began crossing the Atlantic with passengers and freight. They were ready to fly to England but, when war came, they changed their destination to Lisbon in neutral Portugal.

♪ NEW YORK, NEW YORK ♪

On November 1, Rockefeller Center opened in midtown Manhattan, one of the great urban developments of the century. Its fourteen massive office towers were constructed in a mere eight years. One housed RCA, the parent corporation of the NBC radio network and Victor records. The fanciest of its dinner clubs and dance spots was the Rainbow Room, where many orchestras would perform; others would hold forth in the fabulous Art Deco Radio City Music Hall.

NBC-TV was transmitting television programs every day from the top of the Empire State Building to a few hundred sets in the area of New York City. One of the favorite programs featured comedian Pinky Lee. Across the Big Pond, Great Britain's BBC televised a stage play.

The last half of 1939 had been big for popular music. Many musicians were working and their records were selling and playing on radios and jukeboxes. But no one could foresee what would happen should the U.S. be drawn into the war.

September 29 recording
Ray Noble & His (American) Orchestra recorded "Comanche" & "Iroquois," followed a few months later by "Seminole" & "Sioux"- all parts of an American Indian suite. "Cherokee" (Record 1) had been recorded the year before.

October 11 recording
Jimmy McPartland & His Orchestra recorded four tracks for Decca's *Gems of Jazz* series: "Jazz Me Blues," "China Boy," "The World is Waiting For The Sunrise," and "Sugar." Little traditional jazz was being recorded by the major labels and this was an attempt to keep the music alive. McPartland's career dated back to the '20s when he succeeded Bix Beiderbecke in The Wolverines, a midwestern Dixieland band. During World War II McPartland met and married the young English pianist Marian Page who, as Marian McPartland, became a jazz star and a fixture on public radio.

October 19 recording
Jack Jenney & His Orchestra, "Star Dust." Trombonist Jenney recorded a most unusual version of the Hoagy Carmichael standard. There is no straight playing of the melody on the whole record, only improvised variations. Jenney's own solo is a beautiful paraphrase of the melody, and he repeated portions of it a year later when he recorded the same tune as a member of Artie Shaw's band (Record 30).

November 2 recording
Guitarist Lonnie Johnson, "Jersey Belle Blues." Blues player and singer Johnson had recorded with Louis Armstrong's Hot Five and Duke Ellington, and also played duets with jazz guitarist Eddie Lang in the '20s. Now his guitar solos and vocals were being released on the Bluebird label's blues series.

November 2 recording
Gene Krupa & His Orchestra recorded "Drummin' Man," a take-off on Earl Hines' July recording of "Piano Man," including almost-identical words. The label gave no credit to the Hines version. However, Krupa's new band was making a splash.

November 13 first songbook recordings

Singer Lee Wiley recorded four Gershwin tunes for the first songbook album ever (an entire album devoted to the songs of one composer). She was accompanied by top musicians, including Fats Waller. These were the first jazz recordings on the Liberty Music Shop (NYC) label; they were followed the next year by Wiley's Cole Porter songbook.

November 22 recording

An unusual group called "Haitian Orchestra" recorded for the Varsity label. Caribbean rhythms were mixed with improvisations by soprano saxophonist Sidney Bechet and pianist Willie "The Lion" Smith.

November 27 coronation

Time magazine in its issue of November 27 proclaimed Glenn Miller the new "undisputed king of swing," succeeding Benny Goodman. For many aficionados the coronation was premature.

November 30 recording

Mildred Bailey recorded four sides accompanied by the Alec Wilder Octet, a group which included instruments not often heard in jazz. On "All The Things You Are," future TV star Mitch Miller soloed on English horn.

December 24 recording

Kansas City Six, "Good Morning Blues," "Way Down Yonder in New Orleans," and "Paging The Devil" were recorded at the "From Spirituals To Swing" concert. Basie's top players were joined by Benny Goodman's new electric guitarist, Charlie Christian.

December recording

Stuff Smith & His Orchestra recorded four sides for the Varsity label. Smith was one of the era's few jazz violinists. Eddie South continued with small group sessions, but never matched his early work in Europe with Django Reinhardt and Stephane Grappelly. Joe Venuti, although active, did not record from early 1939 until 1946. Ray Nance performed occasional violin solos with Duke Ellington but mostly played trumpet.

Chapter Three

The Last Time I Saw Paris

January 11 Your Hit Parade
"Frenesi" was atop the ratings, according to the network radio program. It was among the top ten tunes for nineteen straight weeks. The best-selling recorded version was by Artie Shaw's Orchestra.

January 17 last recording session
Don Redman & His Orchestra, "Chant of The Weed." Redman's haunting theme is an ode to marijuana. One of the top arrangers, Redman was much in demand by the white bands and was to give up bandleading for freelance arranging.

February 5 recording
Harpist Casper Reardon, "I Got Rhythm," one of four sides for the Schirmer label. The only other jazz-related harp solos in this period were recorded by Adele Girard in a March 1941 session led by her husband, leader-clarinetist Joe Marsala.

February 7 recording marathon
Benny Goodman put in a hard day in Columbia's NYC studios. He recorded seven numbers for Columbia: two with the Metronome All Stars, three with his orchestra and two with his Sextet. His full band recorded "How High The Moon," "The Fable of the Rose," and "Let's All Sing Together," all Eddie Sauter arrangements with Helen Forrest vocals. Count Basie sat in with the small group for "Till Tom Special" and "Gone With 'What' Wind?"

February 10 movie milestone
Cee Dee Johnson, drummer and band leader, became the first black to score a feature motion picture, *Mystery In Swing.*

1940

As the new decade began, the war was getting closer. German U-boats haunted American shores, and on Long Island, the United States was installing its first anti-aircraft guns. President Roosevelt requested $1.8 billion for defense and $400 million in new taxes. On January 30, Hitler threatened "total war." The next month, construction began on the concentration camp at Auschwitz.

♪ PARIS IN THE SPRING ♪

It was more and more difficult for Americans to ignore what was happening in Europe. Opinion polls confirmed that a vast majority still hoped against hope the U.S. would not be drawn into the war, but those hopes faded as Hitler conquered Holland and Belgium, and Norway was to be next. By March, Mussolini and Hitler pronounced the shape of the "New Order" for Europe. By April, the Germans occupied Denmark and invaded Norway. But it took the fall of France on June 21 to shake America. Hitler insisted the French sign the surrender document at the site near Compiegne where Germany had capitulated in 1918. General Charles de Gaulle broadcast from London that he would lead the French Resistance forces, but there was no rush to join him. A popular song of the day was "The Last Time I Saw Paris" by Jerome Kern and Oscar Hammerstein II – a remembrance of the light-hearted Paris of old.

President Roosevelt told Congress the time had come to re-arm: the nation must build 50,000 planes and a two-ocean navy. Congress agreed. The newspapers and radio commentators overwhelmingly endorsed the military buildup. FDR stopped just short of asking for a peace-time draft, and he did not detail his foreign policy goals.

Isolationists (or noninterventionists), who opposed American involvement in the war, went mostly unheard, although organizations such as the America First Committee did attract thousands to their public rallies. They had the support of a few newspapers, such as the *Chicago Tribune*, but the media was carrying mostly pro-intervention messages.

The President authorized a "Neutrality Patrol" and warned German U-boats to stay away from American vessels. Later in the year, Roosevelt gave Great Britain 50 over-age destroyers in exchange for American use of British naval bases in the Caribbean.

♪ THERE'LL ALWAYS BE ♪ AN ENGLAND

On May 10, Winston Churchill became British Prime Minister, replacing Neville Chamberlain, the architect of the appeasement policy toward Hitler. That same month England lost nearly one-fourth of its expeditionary force plus irreplaceable equipment in a desperate evacuation from Dunkirk, Belgium. In all, however, 337,000 British and French soldiers were saved from capture by the advancing Germans. Churchill implored President Roosevelt to send more war supplies.

Londoners, already accustomed to sleepless nights in shelters, suffered their first daylight air raid on July 2. Broadcasting on radio from London, Edward R. Murrow of CBS described the Battle of Britain for millions of Americans. He emphasized the cheerful heroism and sacrifices of ordinary British civilians—working long hours, taking refuge in air raid shelters, and enduring shortages. His voice became one of the most familiar in the world and a model for many broadcasters to come.

The Royal Air Force began night bombings of German targets in July and the Luftwaffe stepped up attacks on Britain. Spitfires, Hurricanes, and anti-aircraft gunners shot down ninety German bombers in one week. On September 4, Hitler declared all-out war on British cities. As bombs hit Buckingham Palace and St. Paul's Cathedral, the Battle for Britain entered its crucial stage.

♪ EAST OF THE SUN ♪

The Russians, after seizing Lithuania, Estonia and Latvia, invaded Romania, afterward installing Communists as heads of their "popular front" governments. Meanwhile, the Japanese extended their control over Asia. In August, the rising sun flag of Japan was hoisted over Shanghai, and a month later Japan invaded Indochina. Americans were horrified by the newsreel footage of the conquests. The U.S. stopped selling scrap iron to the Japanese. The Land of the Rising Sun formally joined a military alliance in which Germany and Italy recognized the "New Order" for the Far East.

By the time Congress bit the bullet and enacted the first peacetime draft in the summer of 1940, pollsters found a remarkable 86 percent of Americans approved. The stream of recruits and draftees would have to be clothed with garments not yet sewn, fed with food not yet grown, equipped with arms not yet manufactured, and housed in camps not yet designed, much less built. Because of these shortages, some draftees had to be sent home temporarily.

In the fall, the Germans invaded Greece and Hungary, and Romania joined the Axis. The Russians and the Germans were still allied with each other and the Japanese resented American hostility to its moves in the Pacific.

♪ BLUE AND SENTIMENTAL ♪

In the United States, "It's A Blue World," the title of one of the top tunes, sounded prophetic. For the 8 million Americans still unemployed, it certainly was. In spite of a generally positive economic picture, nearly 15 percent of the work force was out of work.

The weak state of the economy did not hurt the President's chances for reelection. On June 28, the Republicans nominated Wendell Willkie, a Wall Street attorney from Indiana, to oppose Roosevelt in his bid for an unprecedented third term. FDR won handily in November.

Those Americans who could afford them were buying automobiles at a fast pace; they figured there would be no more if war came. Typical retail prices: Chevrolet coupe, $659; Studebaker Champion, $660; Pontiac station wagon, $1,015. In December, Los Angeles' first freeway was dedicated. In the East, drivers marveled at the new Pennsylvania Turnpike.

For those who preferred flying to driving (and could afford it) the first commercial flight with a pressurized cabin took off from New York's one year-old LaGuardia Airport for California. With a stop at Kansas City, the flight took 14 hours. The Trans-World Airlines Stratoliner carried 33 passengers.

Despite unemployment for many, Americans still had money to go to the movies. Hollywood studios turned out propaganda shorts and wove pro-war messages into feature films. Moviegoers were excited about the lighthearted *My Little Chickadee*, the first pairing of W. C. Fields and Mae West, both stars in their own right by this time. *Lights Out in Europe* opened on Broadway.

In the fall, the Detroit Tigers broke the New York Yankees' stranglehold on the American League pennant, then went on to lose to the Cincinnati Reds in the World Series.

♪ TRYLON SWING ♪

In New York the World's Fair began its second season. Appropriately for an exhibit based on optimism, its sponsors foresaw larger crowds, enough to recoup their losses from the year before. The new edition had a more patriotic tone, its centerpiece an historical spectacle called *American Jubilee*. The loudspeakers carried no war news; folks came to shut out the world of today, and preferred to get lost in the fanciful World of Tomorrow.

The Germans never had been invited to the Fair, and the Russians had removed their building. The Polish and Finnish exhibits did not reopen. The starkly modern Italian building boasted of Mussolini's accomplishments, but the Japanese pavilion, modeled after a Shinto shrine, stressed culture rather than technology. A bomb severely damaged the British exhibit and killed two police officers. (Who set the bomb or why it was set was never determined.) The lake, around which the foreign nations exhibited, had a name change – from Peace Lake to Liberty Lake.

Most commercial exhibitors returned. In the Railroads building a young woman played Kurt Weill tunes on the Hammond Novachord. Powered by 144 vacuum tubes, it could imitate the sounds of piano, harpsichord, trumpet, guitar, and violin. That could not have been very comforting to unemployed musicians, and music newspapers were disappointed that the fair didn't employ more jazz players than it did. But the fair was certainly not devoid of jazz men.

The orchestras of Benny Goodman, Artie Shaw, Jack Teagarden, Eddie Duchin, Ben Bernie, John Kirby, and Hal Kemp all played for dancers at the World's Fair. The bands played not only at the fair but about it. During 1939, Jan Garber recorded the syrupy "World's Fair Waltz" and Cab Calloway the upbeat "Trylon Swing." The fair inspired other recordings: "Wings Over Manhattan" by Charlie Barnet and "Zoomin' at the Zombie" by John Kirby.

In addition to hearing some great jazz, fairgoers had plenty to see. They ogled stripper Gypsy Rose Lee, marveled at explorer Frank Buck's Jungleland, and were thrilled by the architectural designs of Norman Bel Geddes and Raymond Loewy. They were amazed by demonstrations of television, which the Federal Communications Commission hoped was about ready to go commercial. Many employed jazz musicians feared TV would kill off their steady work in radio.

In spite of bargain tickets and lots of promotions (including an amateur swing band competition), the fair drew only 19 million in 1940, about 6 million fewer than the year before. Fair officials had predicted at least 50 million for each season. When the books were finally closed, the fair had cost sponsors and exhibitors $170 million. The city had dropped $48 million and the state $7.5 million.

♪ OVER THERE ♪

Jazz, America's home-grown music, could now be heard around the world, in countries sympathetic to and hostile toward the U.S. To bolster morale, the BBC aired English swing bands during the German air raids. Behind blacked-out windows, British youngsters listened to trumpeter-singer Nat Gonella feature an American hit, "South of the Border." Gonella and His New Georgians also recorded "Hot Dogs" and "Tuxedo Junction" for English Columbia, while Joe Daniels and His Hot Shots did "Spitfire," (a tribute to the British fighter airplane) and "Baton Rouge Blues" for Parlophone. British bands persisted, determined to muddle through. During the height of the aerial Battle of Britain, bandleader Ambrose and His Orchestra recorded "Mood Indigo." The elegant Ambrose long had been king of Saturday night dance music on the BBC, signing off at midnight with "When Day Is Done." Inconvenienced but undeterred, musicians continued to record in London.

In October, the Japanese padlocked public ballrooms and banned jazz as "unfit" for import or radio play. Officials declared jazz "noisy and discordant," but as in Germany, many youngsters continued to listen secretly to Ellington, Armstrong, and Goodman.

American jazz records were still sold throughout Europe until late in the War, often clandestinely. Many German soldiers were music fans and, trying to capitalize on that interest, Glenn Miller and His Air Force Band produced some broadcasts aimed at German soldiers, including Miller speaking in Iowa-accented German. In France in 1943, nearly 200 professional drummers were registered. To obey the curfews the wealthy often hosted all-night jazz parties in cabarets.

Unknown to the German public, who had been told that jazz was a decadent music, Nazi propaganda chief Joseph Goebbels ordered a high-quality swing band put together with the best musicians from Germany, Italy, and the occupied countries. Its objective was to influence British and American listeners. Called Charly (sic) and His Orchestra, the band played standard tunes, e.g., "You're Driving Me Crazy," well-arranged and well-played, but with a twist. A singer would first sing the regular lyrics, then special Nazi lyrics with anti-Churchill, anti-Roosevelt, and extreme anti-semitic themes. (The songs were broadcast to Great Britain, but there's no record that any Americans ever heard them.) After the war, when confronted with the records, the musicians all claimed that they had not heard the lyrics, an unlikely excuse. (CDs are available of all Charly's records now.)

When the Germans conquered France, violinist Stephane Grappelly of the Quintette of the Hot Club of France was in London and he stayed there. His colleague, the guitarist Django Reinhardt, returned to Paris and performed openly throughout the German Occupation for both French and Germans. It was a risky move for Reinhardt who identified himself as a Gypsy (or Roma in modern terms). As Mike Zwerin summarized in his account of jazz in wartime Europe: "Jazz musicians have some outlaw in them if they are serious about their music. Gypsies are defined as outlaws by society. So during World War II, here was a double outlaw (Reinhardt) on the lam from a regime which considered jazz musicians monkeys and shipped Gypsies to unspeakable places." Somehow or another Reinhardt survived.

♪ FAREWELL BLUES ♪

Musicians were among the first 18,700 draftees who took their oaths in November, 1940. A pop song title told the story: "Twenty-One Dollars a Day – Once a Month," a private's pay. And this was just one of the many songs to be influenced by the war that year. In music magazines *Metronome* and *Down Beat* there was a sharp increase in ads for draft-proof musicians. Two songs about the draft were plays on the title of the blockbuster film, *Gone With The Wind.* The Benny Goodman Sextet recorded an instrumental called, "Gone With 'What' Draft?" and the King Cole Trio sang, "Gone With The Draft," wherein an undraftable young man gets all the girls since the healthy types are all in the armed services. Of the nearly one million men called up in the first year, more than 40 percent failed the physical exam. Flat feet were a major reason.

For years there had been a fad for novelty tunes with Japanese themes; now most bands dropped items such as "Japanese Sandman," "Yokohama Mama," and "Nagasaki." (Five years later the latter would be the second city targeted by an American atomic bomb.) Kato, the valet to radio's "Green Hornet," suddenly became a Filipino rather than a Japanese.

Political themes were usually avoided in songs. The lyrics of the 1940 song, "WPA," chided the New Deal's Works Progress Administration for paying workmen to lean on their shovels rather than work. After the musicians' union called the song "un-American," Victor destroyed the master of Glenn Miller's recording while Decca went ahead and released the Louis Armstrong-Mills Brothers version.

"Goodbye Dear, I'll Be Back in a Year" was a jukebox favorite that highlighted the twelve months of service selectees were scheduled to serve. Despite the promise to be back, many of the first draftees didn't return until the war was over in 1945, and many more didn't come back at all. Sixteen million men between 21 and 36 had to register, but most local draft boards passed over married men, at least in the beginning.

♪ SWING PARADE ♪

Mixed in with war-themed songs were love songs and old favorites, which headed the charts as always. In July, 1940, for example, the songs most played on radio were "Sweet Sue," "Devil May Care," and "The Nearness of You," hardly reminders of the real world. What later would be called country-and-western music started reaching larger audiences. Both Bing Crosby and Bob Wills sold over a million copies with "San Antonio Rose." Other million sellers that year were:

Tommy Dorsey's "I'll Never Smile Again," with a vocal by Frank Sinatra, Jo Stafford, and the Pied Pipers.

Johnny Long's novelty, "In A Shanty In Old Shanty Town." Every teen-ager knew the jazzed up, swing-era lyrics to this sentimental old favorite, e.g., "I'd be just as sassy as Haile Selassie."

Three Artie Shaw instrumentals— "Frenesi," "Summit Ridge Drive" (Record 28), and "Star Dust" (Record 30).

Glenn Miller's "Tuxedo Junction" and "Pennsylvania 6-5000" (the phone number of NYC's Hotel Pennsylvania with its prestigious band venue, the Cafe Rouge).

♪ FLYIN' HIGH ♪

The federal government criminalized marijuana in 1937, imposing fines and up to five years in prison. Most states followed suit. There was a good deal of drug use among jazz musicians and there were references to drugs in many song lyrics.

Authorities found marijuana when two members of Charlie Barnet's band died in an auto crash in 1941. After police in Detroit arrested a peddler with fifty pounds of finely ground "loco weed," he claimed he supplied many bandleaders and musicians. The head of the American Federation of Musicians said that the dope-user image was hurting the profession. The Detroit local took the idea seriously and voted to expel convicted drug users.

Of course, marijuana was not the only drug associated with jazz musicians. Billie Holiday, Charlie Parker, and John Coltrane, to name a few, were known to be heavy users of heroin. Alcoholism plagued, and sometimes killed, great musicians such as Bix Beiderbecke and Bunny Berigan. Perhaps the link with alcoholism was inevitable, given that jazz was most played in places where alcohol was readily available.

Ironically, radio nixed overt references to sex and alcohol. Both were present in the original lyrics of Duke Ellington's, "I Got It Bad." The Duke's own recording used the words, "But when the fish are jumpin' and Friday rolls around, my man and me we gin some, we pray some, we sin some." To be accepted by radio stations, later recordings skipped the weekend with some new lyrics - "But when the weekend's over and Monday rolls around, I end up like I start out, just crying my heart out."

♪ LET ME OFF UPTOWN ♪

In the top music magazine, *Down Beat,* musicians were cautioned to expect no favors when it came to being drafted. Some leaders rushed to sign older or physically-handicapped "draft-proof" musicians. *Down Beat's* chief competitor, *Metronome,* warned that it certainly was no time to think about forming a new band.

Musicians shifted constantly from band to band, causing headaches for the bandleaders. Ozzie Nelson advertised via a 1940 recording, "I'm Looking For a Guy Who Plays Alto and Clarinet and Doubles on Baritone And Wears A Size 37 Suit." And, he might have added, one who would be exempt from military service.

Top bands filled the big halls, even at premium prices. On Halloween night, 1940, more than 6,500 fans paid $3 at the Palladium Ballroom in Los Angeles to see and hear Tommy Dorsey. The admission charge was three times the normal amount. Also, there was little grousing about the new federal tax on admissions as it was considered part of the war effort.

On January 7, Ellington drew 4,200 dancers to Harlem's Savoy Ballroom. The Ella Fitzgerald and Teddy Wilson orchestras followed him there. But white bands played the famed dance spot, too. Glenn Miller drew large crowds in early 1940, as did Jan Savitt. Not all black dancers wanted their music hot. At the Cotton Club, Noble Sissle's sweet band played, augmented for a couple of weeks in March by the band that Louis Armstrong was fronting.

Another premier uptown booking was the Apollo Theater. Bands there early in the year included Count Basie, Earl Hines, Fats Waller, Erskine Hawkins, Cab Calloway, and the white band of Harry James. A black weekly praised James' "sensational swing orchestra."

♪ YOU'RE THE TOP ♪

Benny Goodman, Glenn Miller and Tommy Dorsey headed the *Metronome* band poll, but there were plenty of new names. Charlie Barnet and Woody Herman moved up in the Swing category. Two Goodman alumni, trumpeter Harry James and drummer Gene Krupa started new bands and headed the newcomers on the Swing list. James said one reason he left Goodman was because he got tired of playing "Sing, Sing, Sing" at every performance; whatever the reason, his departure left a gaping hole in the band as did Krupa, whom Goodman always insisted was his favorite drummer.

Down Beat also had its band poll and it's interesting to compare the two magazines' choices (see opposite page).

Notice that the *Down Beat* list had two black bands, Basie and Ellington, and the *Metronome* list had just Basie. Artie Shaw was on the *Down Beat* list only, but Harry James and Tommy Dorsey didn't make it.

Blurring of the categories was evident; four bands placed in both Sweet and Swing lists. In fact, by this time, many bands defied categorization since some sweet bands were trying to become hotter. There were exceptions, of course, and a few bands hung on to the stodgy old sweet style. For example, in his thirty-ninth year as a bandleader, Ted Lewis admitted to *Down Beat*, "My style is plain corny now."

At about the same time, *Down Beat* magazine solicited votes from its readers to choose an All-Star Band. The opposite page shows the selections made by the votes of 19,000 readers.

Harry James told the black *Pittsburgh Courier* that, while he appreciated the honor of being selected for the All-Star Band, Louis Armstrong was still the greatest trumpeter. *Metronome* put together its All Star Band too. Note that the fans chose white pianists Bob Zurke and Jess Stacy, ignoring such exceptional black players as Earl Hines, Art Tatum, and Teddy Wilson. Within a few years many black players would make these all star lists including many members of the Ellington and Basie orchestras.

Note that the *Metronome* band had the same clarinet, guitar, bass, and drums as *Down Beat's* but different personnel in the other sections.

March recording
Art Hodes, piano solo, "A Selection From The Gutter" for Commodore Records. The title came from pianist Hodes' column in *Jazz Record* magazine. He felt that the public's attitude had placed jazz musicians "in the gutter."

March 11 recording
Harlan Leonard & The Rockets. "I Don't Want To Set The World On Fire." The Kansas City band recorded this new tune at a fast tempo; the record went nowhere. Later in the year a sweet band waxed it as a slow ballad and it became a big hit. ("The Rockets" was an unfortunate name for this group. Actually, it was a modern and serious group with Tadd Dameron as one of its arrangers.)

March 29 recording
Al Cooper's Savoy Sultans, "Frenzy." This unheralded band recorded several sides for Decca. It took on many famous groups which ventured onto its turf at the Savoy Ballroom in Harlem. The band's style became the basis for many of the later rhythm-and-blues groups.

Comparison of Metronome's and Down Beat's band polls.

	SWING		SWEET	
	Metronome	**Down Beat**	**Metronome**	**Down Beat**
1.	Benny Goodman	Benny Goodman	Tommy Dorsey	Tommy Dorsey
2.	Glenn Miller	Glenn Miller	Glenn Miller	Glenn Miller
3.	Tommy Dorsey	Bob Crosby	Glen Gray	Glen Gray
4.	Gene Krupa	Artie Shaw	Benny Goodman	Hal Kemp
5.	Bob Crosby	Count Basie	Sammy Kaye	Kay Kyser
6.	Charlie Barnet	Duke Ellington	Kay Kyser	Guy Lombardo
7.	Woody Herman	Jimmy Dorsey	Jimmy Dorsey	Sammy Kaye
8.	Harry James	Gene Krupa	Guy Lombardo	Wayne King
9.	Count Basie	Jan Savitt	Hal Kemp	Jimmy Dorsey
10.	Jimmy Dorsey	Charlie Barnet	Dick Jurgens	Horace Heidt

Comparison of Down Beat's and Metronome's All Star Bands.

	Down Beat	**Metronome**
Trumpet:	Harry James, Ziggy Elman, Bunny Berigan	James, Elman, Charlie Spivak
Trombone:	Jack Teagarden, Tommy Dorsey	Jack Teagarden, Jack Jenney
Sax:	Charlie Barnet, Jimmy Dorsey, Coleman Hawkins	Benny Carter, Eddie Miller, Toots Mondello
Piano:	Bob Zurke	Jess Stacy
Clarinet:	Benny Goodman	Benny Goodman
Guitar:	Charlie Christian	Charlie Christian
Bass:	Bob Haggart	Bob Haggart
Drums:	Gene Krupa	Gene Krupa
Arranger:	Fletcher Henderson	
Vocals:	Bing Crosby, Ella Fitzgerald	

16. Duke Ellington
& His Famous Orchestra
KO-KO
March 6, 1940
CD 1, Track 16

WIN: The greatest composer in the jazz idiom displays his superb talents as an arranger also. In ensemble portions and on solos, his players turn this chart into a masterpiece of big band jazz.

It was said that Duke Ellington played the piano but used the orchestra as his instrument. And what an instrument it was! On this record, after his musicians perform precisely in the ensemble passages, he brings them on for their inventive solos.

"Ko-Ko" features the uncanny voice-like "wah-wah" trombone of Joe "Tricky Sam" Nanton. Also, notice the string bass sounds. Young Jimmy Blanton was promoting the bass to a melody instrument equal to the horns, even though he was playing an unamplified one.

The entire performance is marked by a low-pitched, exotic dance feeling. At one time Ellington considered using the number in an African suite. Its original title was "Kaline."

The "Ko-Ko" session marked the beginning of the Duke's greatest creative surge. He had just split with Irving Mills, his long-time manager, and this was the beginning of a five-year association with Victor records. The '40-'42 period would produce some of his best recorded work ever and many call "Ko-Ko" the best of the best. Writer Martin Williams considered it the top big band instrumental by any group.

Portraits & Concertos

At the same session in which "Ko-Ko" was recorded, Ellington also waxed "Jack The Bear," a tribute to a legendary Harlem pianist. He had already paid tributes to such black entertainers as singer Florence Mills ("Black Beauty"), pianist Willie "The Lion" Smith ("Portrait of The Lion"), vaudevillian Bert Williams ("Portrait of Bert Williams"), and dancer Bill Robinson ("Bojangles").

Ellington had early training as a painter and many writers have noted that his musicians had become the tonal colors on his palette. He often wrote concertos tailored to their talents. Early examples were "Echoes of Harlem" for trumpeter Cootie Williams, "Clarinet Lament" for Barney Bigard, and "Boy Meets Horn," for the distinctive half-valve effects of cornetist Rex Stewart. Two Ellington concertos recorded in 1940 became jazz standards – the magnificent "Concerto For Cootie," the second he wrote for Williams, became "Do Nothing 'Til You Hear From Me" when words were added. The other, the high-voltage "Cotton Tail," was written for tenor saxophonist Ben Webster.

RCA Victor reissues referred to the '40-'42 Ellington orchestra as the "Blanton-Webster Band" in recognition of the addition of the bassist and the tenor saxophonist to Duke's "instrument" that already included alto saxophonist Johnny Hodges, clarinetist Barney Bigard, and trumpeter Cootie Williams. But another newcomer, composer-arranger-pianist Billy Strayhorn, deserves equal billing; it really should be called the Strayhorn-Blanton-Webster Band.

In these same years Ellington also composed and recorded "In A Mellotone," "C Jam Blues" (later called "Duke's Place"), and "Main Stem," which became standards. There also were the Strayhorn works, notably "Take The 'A' Train" and "Chelsea Bridge." The former was literally a subway direction, the New York system having recently extended the route of the "A" train north to the heart of Harlem. Interestingly, "Chelsea Bridge" was mistitled. It was inspired by a painting, the subject of which was another bridge over the Thames, the Battersea.

Ellington and Strayhorn collaborated so closely and thought so much alike it was difficult to know who wrote what. Strayhorn was Duke's alter ego as composer, arranger, and pianist. Ellington was appreciative: "It was like going out with your armor on instead of going out naked."

Although his orchestra could swing with the best of them, Ellington was wary of being seen as just another swing band. Swing would pass, he told newspaper reporters, but "Negro music" would endure. He was thinking of the body of music he had already created and was looking forward to the longer works which lay ahead.

At the age of 41 Edward Kennedy Duke Ellington was on a creative roll. He had a new manager and a new recording contract; *Metronome* magazine called his 1940 records the best of all the bands. White audiences finally had come to know him, both with his records and in the previously closed-to-blacks white venues. The Boston Symphony had just premiered one of his compositions. All of these factors contributed to making the 1940-1942 period the most productive of his career.

17. Cab Calloway & His Orchestra

PICKIN' THE CABBAGE

March 8, 1940

CD 1, Track 17

WIN: This is a good recording by a first-class band. Mature and serious, it's an early effort by one of the greatest figures in jazz history.

John Birks "Dizzy" Gillespie composed and arranged this instrumental. It features bassist Milt Hinton and drummer Cozy Cole and, like Ellington's "Ko-Ko," places great emphasis on the low sounds of the orchestra, in particular the string bass and the baritone saxophone.

Gillespie was on his way to becoming a major figure; his trumpet solo on this record is confident and well constructed. (The down-home title is misleading. This composition is actually a sophisticated modern melody without a trace of novelty touches.)

Calloway was not a musician himself but knew good jazz when he heard it. In his autobiography he refers to this band as the best he ever had and, like Ellington's, there were many compositions featuring his top players. However, Calloway and Gillespie had a falling out over some on-stage horseplay, and Dizzy left the band. Fortunately, Calloway had hired trumpeter Jonah Jones. So the Calloway band, which once had existed mostly to back its singer-leader, now played first-rate jazz.

This track showcases Dizzy Gillespie. Charlie Parker will be heard on Record 40. Miles Davis was playing with a territory band in St. Louis and wouldn't appear on records for a few more years. But in many ways the next generation was in place to move jazz into its next phase.

18. Jam Session at Commodore No. 3

A GOOD MAN IS HARD TO FIND

March 23 & 24, 1940

CD 1, Track 18

WIN: These four 12" 78rpm sides contain over 16 minutes of relaxed and imaginative Dixieland jazz featuring one of the fine standard tunes.

Because of space limitations, CD 1 - Track 18 contains only side 3 of the 4-sided 12" 78rpm issue. Side 3 prominently features trombonist Miff Mole. All four sides can be heard on "Eddie Condon, The Classic Sessions: (JSP-CD 906)."

Milt Gabler ran the Commodore Music Shop in New York. He decided that not enough jazz was being recorded and set up his own label, Commodore Records. At first he specialized in Dixieland or Chicago-style or Eddie Condon style music and saw himself as a source of support for the struggling musicians who played this kind of music.

Gabler soon had a reputation for the high technical quality of his records and for producing more 12" 78rpm records than the major labels. In those days most records were on 10" 78s but the 12" size, with over 60% more time, allowed the musicians much more freedom. Gabler had to charge more for his records than the major labels did, but they still sold fairly well. (Managing the Commodore shop at this time was Milt Gabler's brother-in-law, Jack Crystal, who was comedian Billy Crystal's father. Billy says he spent a lot of time in the shop.)

For these 4 12" 78rpm sides, Gabler pulled off a technical feat not surpassed until a few years later. He

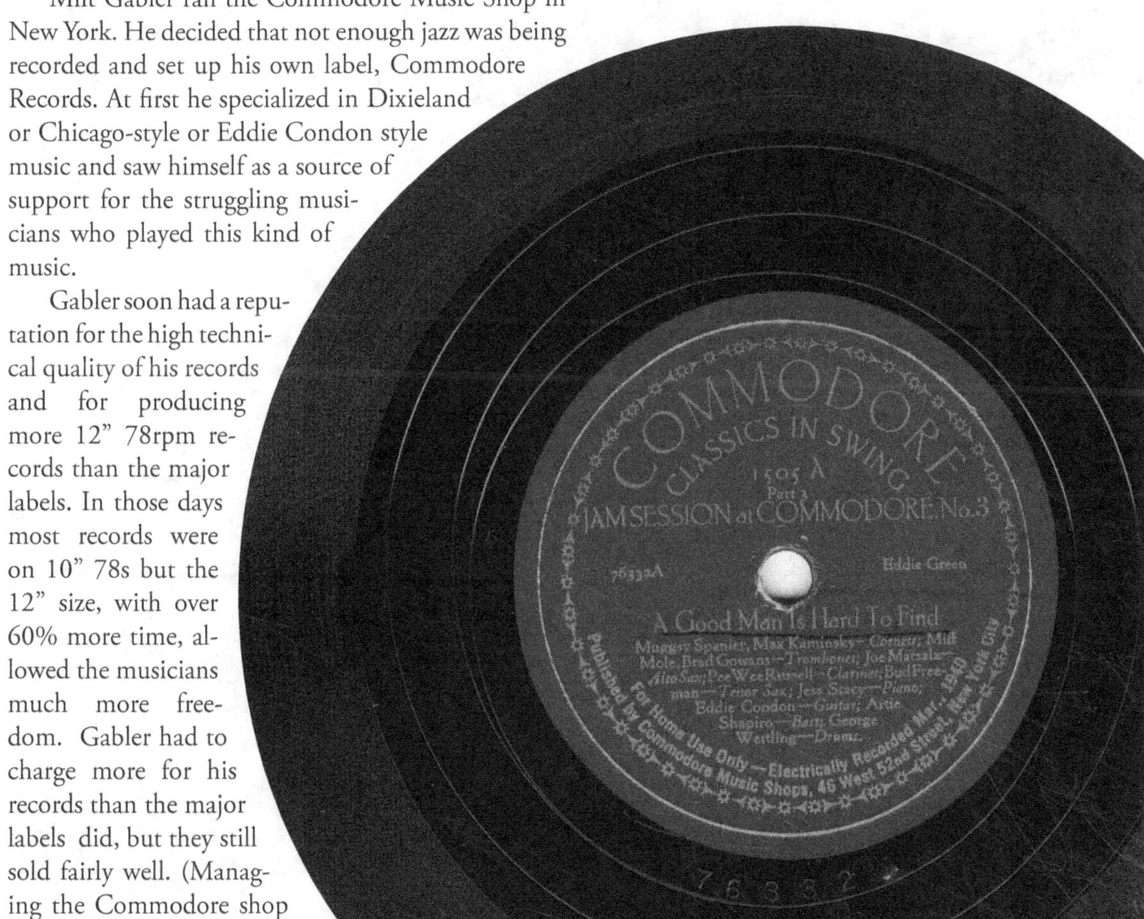

got some of the best Dixieland players of the day into the studio, then had them just go at it for hours on "A Good Man Is Hard To Find." It wasn't completely ad-lib– there was a little bit of arranging plus a predetermined order of solos. Gabler took the resulting music, edited it, and then pressed it on 4 12" 78rpm sides. The results were musically and technically excellent.

It's hard to pick one outstanding soloist on these discs; they were all so good we'll just list them all: trumpet, Max Kaminsky; cornet, Muggsy Spanier; slide trombone, Miff Mole; valve trombone, Brad Gowans; clarinet, Pee Wee Russell; clarinet & alto sax, Joe Marsala; tenor sax, Bud Freeman; piano, Jess Stacy; guitar, Eddie Condon; bass, Artie Shapiro; and drums, George Wettling.

Several of these players were in on Jam Session No. 1, Commodore's first recording session on Jan. 17, 1938. It was the morning after Benny Goodman's Carnegie Hall concert, and they recorded "Carnegie Drag" and "Carnegie Jump" as thanks to Goodman for allowing them to use his pianist, Jess Stacy.

Milt Gabler also worked for Decca Records in this period and produced a lot of jazz for that label. Certainly he deserves the thanks of fans of recorded jazz, then and now.

Muggsy Spanier playing cornet.

19. Bechet-Spanier Big Four
FOUR OR FIVE TIMES
March 28, 1940
CD 1, Track 19

WIN: The chemistry of this recording session produced superb results from the four players. The two hornmen, Bechet and Spanier, show why they are in that exclusive circle of some of the very best instrumentalists in jazz history.

Fresh from the Commodore session just a few days before, Muggsy Spanier recorded with Sidney Bechet, one of the few figures in the history of jazz whose reed sounds are immediately identifiable (on soprano saxophone) and one of the major players in the history of the music. These two powerful, inventive musicians chase each other as they play, alternating the lead. We hear Bechet on both soprano saxophone and clarinet.

Spanier, the white Dixieland (or Chicago-style) player and Bechet, the Creole from New Orleans, are joined by former Ellington bassist Wellman Braud and former Tommy Dorsey guitarist Carmen Mastren. This unlikely combination from diverse backgrounds creates some breathtaking music.

This track is one of eight sides that the group recorded for a small jazz label, The Hot Record Society. The Society originally specialized in re-releasing '20s jazz classics, but then started organizing new sessions such as this one on their HRS label. All of this Bechet-Spanier session originally was released on 12-inch 78s. Unfortunately, even the LP and CD reissues were unable to compensate for the original sub-standard technical quality of the recordings.

The Jazz Labels

The Commodore and Hot Record Society releases of 12-inch discs were unusual since Victor, Columbia, and Decca usually reserved that size for classical music or special items. For example, Benny Goodman's original studio recording of "Sing, Sing, Sing" was issued as a double-sided 12-incher, but when it started selling well, Victor cut portions and issued it as a 10-inch "dub." Apparently they did it because that smaller size fit jukeboxes and was easier to play on home phonographs.

Once in a while, a major company released a jazz performance on several 10-inch records. For example, Duke Ellington's "Reminiscing In Tempo" was issued in 1935 on four sides. (By this time, on many home record players you could stack up several records at a time, but the phonographs couldn't accommodate both 10" and 12" in the same stack.)

The small jazz companies were trying to free their artists from the tyranny of the three-minute limit imposed by 10-inch recordings. The best of them, like Commodore and Blue Note, paid well and maintained high technical standards. Blue Note began in 1939 as a specialist in blues and boogie-woogie. Pianist Meade Lux Lewis improvised on the blues at the very first Blue Note session, which was released on four 12-inch sides (recorded consecutively and not edited).

Some of the jazz labels couldn't afford high technical quality and so, even today, their output is sub-standard. World War II made it even more difficult, because the big companies could get recording materials that they couldn't. Also, because of their limited distribution outlets, the specialty labels had to charge premium prices. Many jazz buffs, however, felt the artistic quality was worth the extra cost. Another feature of these jazz labels was that they often listed the full personnel on their records, something the major companies rarely did.

The Blue Notes, Commodores, and the later Keynotes, including all of the alternate and misplaced takes, were reissued in the '80s and '90s on vinyl and CDs. These collections not only present the listener with new performances of old jazz, but they also extend the privilege of second-guessing the original producers on their choice of issued takes!

20. Mildred Bailey
I'M NOBODY'S BABY
April 2, 1940
CD 1, Track 20

WIN: Mildred Bailey had all of the attributes of a good jazz singer – a distinctive sound, a good feeling for the lyrics, and the ability to sing all around the beat. On this record she was accompanied by some of the best jazz musicians of the day.

This song is perfectly suited to Bailey's light, sweet voice as she pleads for someone to love. On the other hand, the up-tempo arrangement makes it clear that she isn't too desperate. "The Rocking Chair Lady" (she received that title for her recording of the tune) was the first female to sing regularly with a big band (Paul Whiteman's in the early '30s). By this time she was a polished professional. Producer John Hammond considered her the best white jazz singer of them all.

Like Billie Holiday, Mildred Bailey had only the best accompanists. Pianist Teddy Wilson provides a lilting solo on this side. The lovely restrained trumpet solo is by Roy Eldridge, the man often called the stylistic link between Louis Armstrong and Dizzy Gillespie.

After her stint with Whiteman she married xylophonist Red Norvo and made many fine records with his band. Also, in the '30s she recorded with the Dorsey Bros. Orchestra, Casa Loma, John Kirby, and other groups. She recorded a couple of excellent sides with Benny Goodman in 1939 and he wanted her to join his band. But her health wouldn't allow her to travel so she remained a freelancer the rest of her short life (she died at the age of 44).

21. Tommy Dorsey & His Sentimentalists
EAST OF THE SUN
Vocal: Frank Sinatra & Chorus
April 23, 1940
CD 1, Track 21

WIN: Perhaps the greatest of all the popular male vocalists, Frank Sinatra is accompanied here by Tommy Dorsey, the smoothest trombone of all, followed by a trumpet solo by Bunny Berigan, one of the masters.

This track features three of the best sounds of the period – the trombone of Tommy Dorsey, the voice of Frank Sinatra, and the trumpet of Bunny Berigan. The arrangement is similar to those that Dorsey recorded for the tunes "Marie," "Who," and "Blue Skies," with the vocalist singing a straight chorus while the band responds with swing-era slang, e.g.,

SINGER: East of the sun
BAND: Babe, in the brightness
SINGER: And west of the moon
BAND: We'll be diggin' the glow

After Dorsey's smooth trombone introduction, Sinatra sings his chorus with great concentration and articulation, making every word count. The band's last words are, "Well, all right then, take 'em, Bunny" to introduce Berigan's short but fiery trumpet solo, reminiscent of his classic solo three years earlier on Dorsey's recording of "Marie."

When "East of the Sun" was recorded, Berigan was back with Dorsey for a few months. He is considered by many critics to be the best white trumpeter of the '30s, but he had an alcohol problem. He died in June of 1942 at the age of 33.

Busy Joe Bushkin

Tommy Dorsey's small groups usually recorded Dixieland and novelties, but for "East of the Sun" they chose an arrangement of the kind the big band usually played. In addition to Berigan and TD, this group, "The Sentimentalists," had Buddy Rich on drums, Joe Bushkin on piano, and clarinetist Johnny Mince.

Bushkin was an example of how much in demand a first-class musician was in those days. Here are some of his activities. Early in 1939 he recorded with Bunny Berigan's big band and played piano duets with his mentor, the stride pianist Willie "The Lion" Smith. Later in the year, he was in on two classic recording sessions – the Muggsy Spanier "Great Sixteen" (Record 12) and the Lee Wiley Liberty Music Shop "first songbook" sessions.

Early in 1940 Bushkin left Joe Marsala's band to begin a two-year stay with Tommy Dorsey. (Marsala lost so many sidemen to Dorsey that he once sent a telegram to Dorsey, asking TD to hire him so that he could play with his band!)

Bushkin fit well with the Dorsey organization, called by writer George Simon "the best all-around big band of them all." Bushkin played the arrangements of Sy Oliver alongside other top big band players. The versatile Bushkin sounded equally at ease tinkling the delicate celeste on "I'll Never Smile Again" and banging out two-fisted piano on his own composition, "Oh, Look At Me Now." Somehow or another, he found time also to record piano solos for Commodore Records.

May 21 recording
Will Bradley and His Orchestra, "Beat Me Daddy, Eight To The Bar." This jazz-talk tune was released on two sides of a 10-inch record and featured drums and vocals by Ray McKinley and piano by Freddie Slack. When the record became a hit, the band featured more boogie-woogie numbers.

June 5 Dodds' farewell recording session
Johnny Dodds & His Orchestra, "Red Onion Blues" and "Gravier Street Blues." This was Dodds' last session; he died on August 8. New Orleans-born Dodds set the standard for the clarinet's role in the jazz ensemble and was an important player in Louis Armstrong's early records. On Sept. 6, Sidney Bechet & His New Orleans Feetwarmers recorded a tribute to Dodds, "Blues For You, Johnny" with brother Warren "Baby" Dodds on drums and a vocal by Ellingtonian Herb Jeffries. (Moviemaker Woody Allen plays clarinet as a hobby and sometimes appears at clubs in New York. He says that his style of playing is modeled on Johnny Dodds.)

22. The Chocolate Dandies
I CAN'T BELIEVE THAT YOU'RE IN LOVE WITH ME
May 25, 1940
CD 1, Track 22

WIN: Benny Carter on alto sax, Coleman Hawkins on tenor sax, and Roy Eldridge on trumpet display their considerable skills at improvisation, showing why they deserve their places in the jazz pantheon.

"Carter delivers a solo that is at times highly active and, at other times, contemplative."

This is the prototypical hard-swinging, free-improvising track of the era. Three of the hottest horns – the trumpet of Roy Elridge, the tenor saxophone of Coleman Hawkins, and the alto saxophone of Benny Carter– indulge in a four-minute jam session on one of the fine popular songs.

After Hawkins states the melody in his best up-tempo style, Eldridge kicks in with his high-speed, high-energy trumpet, and then Carter delivers a solo that is at times highly active and, at other times, contemplative. The rhythm section does its supportive part.

This is another 12" 78rpm Commodore produced at a reunion for alumni of the Fletcher Henderson Orchestra. The group name, Chocolate Dandies, was taken from a 1929 studio band in which Carter and Hawkins had played. This track is included in the definitive *Smithsonian Collection of Classic Jazz.*

Victor Records had their "Swing Classics," Commodore their "Classics in Swing."

23. Louis Armstrong
& His Orchestra with Sidney Bechet
COAL CART BLUES
Vocals: Louis Armstrong
May 27, 1940
CD 1, Track 23

WIN: Louis Armstrong created the jazz of this triennium, and he shows that he has kept up with the times. Bechet exhibits the extraordinary skills that allowed him to play at Armstrong's level.

It's hard to believe that in 1940 people were already looking back at the history of jazz. This recording was part of a successful effort by Decca Records to capture the music of early New Orleans. Armstrong, not yet 40 years old, plays with his usual power and sings with deep feeling. (He had pulled a coal cart as a child.) Bechet's soprano saxophone matches Armstrong note for note. A veteran of the jazz scene, Bechet had just turned 43.

Armstrong and Bechet both play with the same free-wheeling approach they used in the '20s. Even though by 1940 both musicians had been recording for almost twenty years, their playing still sounds fresh.

Armstrong shows why he was still an influential player in the game of jazz. His singing is serious and reveals his deep feeling for the blues. His trumpet playing is powerful, imaginative, and beautiful.

Bechet was jealous of Louis and quibbled with him over such things as the order of solos on this record.

Satchmo's Rise, Fall, And Rise

If Louis Armstrong had hung up his horn in 1930, he still would rank as one of the jazz greats. By then he had nothing else to prove. His Hot Five and Hot Seven recordings had transformed a rigid ensemble music into a soloist's art form. As Dizzy Gillespie marveled, "Louis influenced every jazz trumpeter and singer."

Armstrong refused to be stereotyped. In the early '30s the reeds in his band sounded like Guy Lombardo's, to the despair of the hard-core jazz buffs who detested sweet music. He even liked to sit in and play with Lombardo on occasion. There's a photo from Armstrong's funeral in Ken Burns' book, *Jazz: A History of America's Music.* In it, sitting next to each other, are an unlikely pair, Guy Lombardo and Dizzy Gillespie, both Satchmo fans!

By 1940, Louis had become a popular celebrity with prudent managers who protected him from exploitation. He had the luxury of being the figurehead leader of a big band without the drudgery of managing its details. The Armstrong band didn't compare with those of Ellington, Lunceford, and Basie, but it had great moments. One was its excellent 1941 recording of Joe Garland's "Leap Frog," a selection which became more famous later when Les Brown adopted it as his band's theme.

Traditionalists who despaired that Louis was wasting his talent on the popular tunes of the period overlooked the fire and inventiveness in Satchmo's solos. One critic even wrote an article called "The Apostasy of Louis Armstrong," chastising him for neglecting the parent style. For many years critics disparaged Armstrong's work in this period, but most finally conceded that even if, for example, his 1940 recording of "Sweethearts on Parade" fell short of the 1930 version, it still sounded good.

In 1947 he abandoned the big band format, and for the rest of his career led a series of All-Star small groups. Pianist Earl Hines and trombonist Jack Teagarden were members for several years. Singing and clowning more, Louis seemed to be having fun again; certainly he was acclaimed more widely than ever. He even had hit records which helped his financial situation, e.g., "Mack The Knife" and "Hello, Dolly."

In the '60s Louis toured the world as a U.S. "unofficial goodwill ambassador." He died in 1971, admired and beloved by musicians and the public. The Louis Armstrong International Airport in New Orleans is a tribute to him as are numerous buildings, streets, schools, etc., around the world.

Some of Armstrong's letters were published after his death and reveal a depth of intelligence and feeling that was not apparent during most of his life. He never forgot his New Orleans' beginnings, signing his letters, "Red beans and ricely yours."

Duke Ellington said of Louis, "Louis Armstrong was born poor, died rich, and never hurt anyone on the way."

24. Lee Wiley
SUGAR
July 10, 1940
CD 1, Track 24

WIN: Lee Wiley has one of those unusual voices that is at once smoky, sensual, and swinging. Here she is backed up by two outstanding players on trumpet and piano.

The singing voice of Lee Wiley is among the best-kept secrets of the whole era. Because she refused to compromise her high standards in the areas of song selection and musical styles, she never became a commercial success. Her jazz feeling made her a great favorite among musicians and she attracted the best accompanists. She was one of the few singers admired by bandleader Eddie Condon.

There are several tunes with the title "Sugar." (A song title cannot be copyrighted.) This one is sometimes subtitled "That Sugar Baby Of Mine." A number of jazz singers have recorded it, but it is perfectly suited to Wiley's style and husky voice. After singing the clever but rarely-heard verse, she snuggles up next to the song, cuddles it for a while, then, with her sexiest tones, pronounces the verdict about her man's lips: "they're granulated!"

Jess Stacy plays piano and Muggsy Spanier is on cornet. (Spanier certainly got around in those days! He's also on Records 12, 18, & 19.) Both men provided solid background for the singer, and Spanier's muted solo is a perfect counterpart to Wiley's voice. The original release was on a 12-inch Commodore disc.

Leonard Feather called her records "timeless and memorable...due to her unique characteristics."

25. Bud Freeman
& His Famous Chicagoans
JACK HITS THE ROAD
Vocals: Jack Teagarden
July 23, 1940
CD 2, Track 1

WIN: The best trombonist of the day shows off his big sound, his improvisational skills, and his wonderful singing voice with a group of top Dixielanders.

The short vocal on this humorous blues reflects Jack Teagarden's disenchantment with leading a big band. (His first band had recently failed, but he would try again, and fail a second time.) On this track "Big T's" Texas-sized trombone and voice are backed by some of the best Dixieland players.

Bud Freeman's stringent, freewheeling tenor sax style sounds very different from Lester Young or Ben Webster, both of whom acknowledged Freeman's high quality. British writer Albert McCarthy wrote: "The rolling quality of Freeman's solos is the result of his phrasing, which frequently governs the nature of his melodic line."

The rough-sounding clarinet solo on this record is vintage Pee Wee Russell. At that time, Freeman and Russell played in the house band at Nick's in Greenwich Village, the mecca of traditional jazz.

Teagarden was held in high esteem by fellow musicians because of his vocal and trombone-playing abilities. He certainly was the top jazz trombonist of this period. Even Tommy Dorsey refused to play jazz when "Big T" was around. On an All-Star recording session when both were present, a compromise was reached by having Dorsey lead off with a straight playing of a blues with Teagarden improvising around him.

This label notation (C40-3) indicates that the side was the third in an album of the day. Note also, "fox trot blues," suggesting the proper dance step to the music and its structure. Such instructions were a throwback to the '20s and were dropped by many companies during this period.

The Chemistry of Recording Sessions

At some recording sessions everything seemed to come together just right – players, tunes, studio, ambience, recording director, and technicians. This was certainly true of the Bud Freeman session above: musicians who played together every night were joined by old buddy Jack Teagarden. In addition to "Jack Hits The Road," the group dug back into the repertoire and jammed on five standards for the rest of the recording session.

Typical of this period, guest Teagarden is given extra solo time. Then the others are given their chances. Few recorded solos ran more than one minute. However, in the two-star Armstrong-Bechet and Bechet-Spanier sessions the solo time was longer with the producers making sure that each jazz "star" received adequate time. Of course the longer 12-inch 78s increased solo time too, as in the Bechet-Spanier, Chocolate Dandies, and Lee Wiley sessions.

Since many small-group sessions brought together horn players not familiar with each other, a solid rhythm section (some combination of piano, guitar, bass, and drums) was especially important. The names of the players in such rhythm sections were seldom known by the public. For example, the Armstrong-Bechet session had guitarist Bernard Addison (who also played on the Chocolate Dandies date) and bassist Wellman Braud, of the Bechet-Spanier session.

Because it seemed important for musicians be compatible in both style and personality, critics of that day doubted that the Metronome All-Star sessions could work. Even though the players all had different backgrounds, the records were made and sound fine today. This is a tribute to the organizing and persuasion skills of producer George Simon.

Some sessions jelled and some didn't. Not every producer knew how to create the right climate or how to coax the best performances out of the musicians. Milt Gabler of Commodore inspired his players as did John Hammond of American (later Columbia), although Hammond did forbid drugs and alcohol in the studio. At Commodore, Gabler was as interested in keeping his artists working as in capturing their music. He looked at his recording sessions as part of a musician's total compensation package.

Some studios, producers, and technicians had not embraced the new sounds of improvisational jazz. Many musicians were intimidated by a sign in the Decca studios which warned, "Remember The Melody." In a '20s session, a producer heard the musicians imitating "corny," out-of-tune playing during a rehearsal break and said, "That's it, that's what I want," so the musicians recorded one number that way. In 1939, at what was to be Benny Goodman's last Victor recording session, the embarrassed technicians had to ask Goodman to repeat several tunes since their equipment hadn't operated properly.

Studios were expensive, but because his manager owned a recording company, Duke Ellington enjoyed the luxury of unlimited studio time for a while. Independent producers like Milt Gabler of Commodore and Harry Lim of Keynote sometimes rented radio studios. To ensure technical quality, they had to control the whole process from recording to pressing the records.

On big band recording sessions, the efficiency of the leader was a factor. Could the leader get the players into the studio, cut four to six sides, then get them on their way to their next assignment? Not all leaders were efficient taskmasters like Glenn Miller and Benny Goodman. In one chapter of his autobiography, Artie Shaw gave an excellent picture of a big band rehearsal, with tired musicians trying new arrangements late at night, giving us a rare peek into the creative process.

Count Basie at the piano, Benny Goodman with his clarinet, and singer Ethel Waters.

26. Art Tatum, Piano solo
BEGIN THE BEGUINE
July 26, 1940
CD 2, Track 2

WIN: A jazz version of the Cole Porter composition is played by the man considered the greatest pianist in the history of jazz.

Dazzling embellishments at high speed marked the piano artistry of Art Tatum. Considered by many to be the best of all jazz pianists, Tatum never allowed his impressive virtuosity to overwhelm his jazz feeling.

He opens this record with a statement of the long chorus, then starts to romp, complete with trills and runs aplenty. Tatum never had a hit record, and it's hard to believe that pianist Eddie Heywood would have one with this same tune a few years later since Tatum's recording is such a tour-de-force.

Tatum said that his original inspiration was Fats Waller, but by this time each one played the piano very differently, Waller with his striding bass and trills and Tatum with his incredible runs and decorations. (Tatum attended Waller's 1943 Carnegie Hall concert and Waller said to the crowd, "I'm a good piano player, but God is in this house tonight.")

Tatum was one of the first jazz players to win praise from classical musicians. Pianist Vladimir Horowitz was so impressed with Tatum that he took conductor Arturo Toscannini to hear him. Another of his devout followers was Oscar Peterson who jokingly compared him to a lion; you want to get close enough to hear him roar, but not too close because he's dangerous!

Tatum was almost totally blind but this disability didn't seem to affect his playing at all.

27. Will Bradley Trio
JUST DOWN THE ROAD A PIECE
Vocal: Ray McKinley & Don Raye
August 12, 1940
(Not included on CD, see note)

WIN: This small group boogie-woogie record became a popular success. The rhythm section gives us a rollicking ride and the singing of Ray McKinley shows how jazz can be fun.

This side is not included on the accompanying CDs because of space limitations. It is available on Columbia CD CK 46151, "Will Bradley & Ray McKinley Orchestra."

Ray McKinley was underrated as one of the good rhythmic singers in jazz. On this side he catches the spirit of boogie-woogie in his vocal. A percussionist, McKinley had a successful big band career before and after WWII, as well as a stint with Glenn Miller's Army Air Force Band during the war.

The Bradley band was billed as Will Bradley & His Orchestra featuring Ray McKinley. They had many numbers highlighting the leader's trombone virtuosity. However, after the success of a few boogie woogie records, the band emphasized that style more often.

This record is a delightful exercise, an example of the sense of humor which jazz musicians bring to their work. The song was inspired by the legendary pianist, Peck Kelly, who was said to be a great boogie-woogie player but who never recorded.

The pianist is Freddy Slack, who later led his own band.

Humorist Robert Benchley clowning with Artie Shaw and his clarinet.

July 12 recording
An English band with the bizarre name of Felix Mendelssohn and His Hawaiian Serenaders recorded "Japanese Sandman," "Tiger Rag," "Lady Be Good," and "Goodbye Blues" in London for English Columbia. (English critic Brian Rust later called the sides "truly exceptional.")

August 3 Your Hit Parade
"I'll Never Smile Again" was in the coveted number one spot on the popular Saturday night program. It was at or near the top through the fall. The big record was by Tommy Dorsey with Frank Sinatra and The Pied Pipers.

August 21 Revival recordings
Henry "Kid" Rena and his band recorded eight sides for the Delta label in New Orleans. These were the first on-the-spot recordings of the New Orleans Revival, an attempt to bring jazz's parent style back to life in its original setting with some of the older musicians.

September 11 unnoticed recording
Clarence Profit Trio, "Azure." This obscure, beautiful Ellington composition and three other tracks were recorded for Decca. In this period of musical plenty these tasteful sides went unnoticed and the group never recorded again.

28. Artie Shaw & His Gramercy 5
SUMMIT RIDGE DRIVE
September 3, 1940
CD 2, Track 3

WIN: This small group record displays Artie Shaw's creative ability to develop new and different ensemble sounds, his managerial skill to engage good sidemen, and his talent as a great swing soloist himself.

This group was Artie Shaw's answer to Benny Goodman, Count Basie, Tommy Dorsey, Bob Crosby, etc. and their small groups, and a unique answer it was. It featured the sound of a harpsichord as played by the fine jazz pianist Johnny Guarnieri of the violin-making family. (The harpsichord was a predecessor to the piano. Its strings are plucked, rather than being struck by hammers as on a piano.) Shaw had suggested that they use it for this session, and it helped to make this record a million-seller, rare for small-group jazz.

The tune is a simple blues with good solos by Guarnieri, Shaw on clarinet, Billy Butterfield on plunger-muted trumpet, and bassist Jud DeNaut. The ensemble playing is both swinging and distinctive with the harpsichord sound. Shaw's good taste and jazz feeling show throughout. (Gramercy 5 was his telephone exchange and he lived on Summit Ridge Drive.)

Shaw was often compared to Benny Goodman in this period. Years later composer, arranger, and clarinetist Shaw said, "Benny was a better clarinetist, but I was a better musician."

This was one of eight Gramercy Five sides in 1940. In 1945, Shaw revived the name for a group which featured the great trumpeter; Roy Eldridge; and the brilliant young bop pianist; Dodo Marmarosa.

29. Meade Lux Lewis, Piano solo
HONKY TONK TRAIN BLUES
October 4, 1940
CD 2, Track 4

WIN: A top boogie-woogie piano player does an energetic performance of his own train-influenced composition. It is still a standard in the repertoire of pianists of this genre.

This is one of the classic compositions in the boogie-woogie repertoire and it is played by its composer, one of the greatest players. Meade Lux Lewis uses his powerful left hand with great precision at fast tempos. The repeating boogie bass and the catchy melody of this track give a perfect musical imitation of a train. Lewis' two-fisted playing is a reminder that boogie-woogie was originally played for dancers by pianists who worked alone.

Lewis recorded the tune for Paramount Records in 1929, and then disappeared from public view. In the '30s producer John Hammond found him working in a car wash and brought him back to a musical world that was just rediscovering boogie-woogie. "Lux" became a favorite in New York night clubs. In addition to piano, he also recorded on harpsichord and celeste in this period.

Blue Note has to be one of the longest lasting of labels that featured jazz exclusively. It was started in 1939 by Alfred Lion and Francis Wolff, two German emigres, and is still going strong today. This side was only their 15th record and Meade Lux Lewis had recorded their first sides the year before.

The first Blue Notes featured mostly pianists and traditional jazz but later branched out to all kinds of jazz. In some periods it was *the* major jazz label.

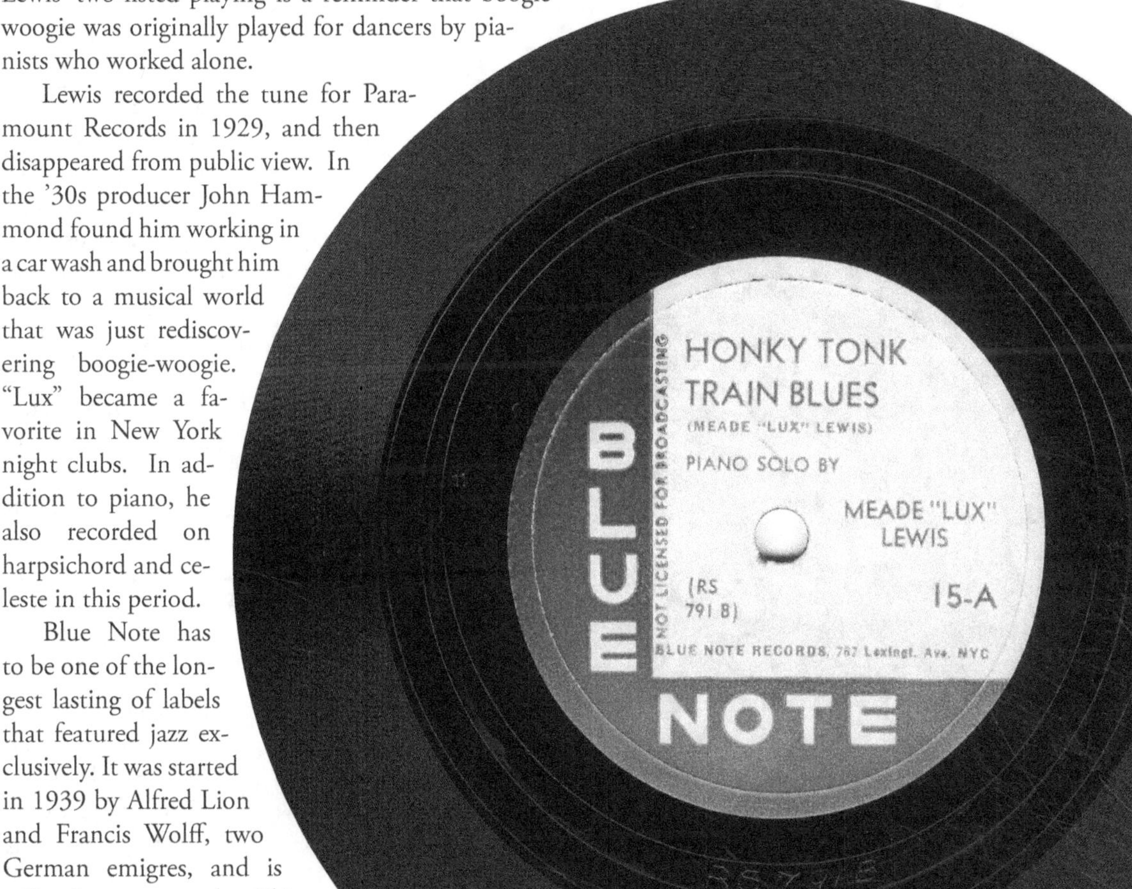

30. Artie Shaw & His Orchestra

STAR DUST

October 7, 1940

CD 2, Track 5

WIN: This arrangement is a perfect mixture of strings, brass, and reeds, with excellent solos by trumpet, trombone, and clarinet. It is a demonstration piece, showing how to arrange for a large dance band with a result both beautiful and swinging.

This may be the best big band ballad recording of them all. It is a romantic tune played at a slow tempo but with jazz feeling and without cloying sentimentality. There are three superb solos: the lyrical opening trumpet of Billy Butterfield, the relaxed, imaginative trombone of Jack Jenney, and the soaring clarinet of the leader. The solos are backed by brass, reeds, and strings. Shaw's version of "Star Dust," plus 1940 recordings by Tommy Dorsey and Glenn Miller, helped the song on its way to becoming one of the most-recorded popular songs in history.

Unlike other leaders who felt that a string section dragged the beat, Shaw used the strings well. His early experiments with a string section in his band in 1936 had not been popular, so he dropped the idea for a while. But now he and other leaders were traveling and recording with string sections.

Billy Butterfield's beautiful opening solo recalls a similar job he did in 1938 on Bob Crosby's "What's New?" He was later featured with Benny Goodman and, still later, led his own band.

Notice the Spanish subtitle on the disc. This was a carryover from the '20s which was eventually discontinued.

31. Johnny Hodges & His Orchestra
DAY DREAM
November 2, 1940
CD 2, Track 6

WIN: The leading alto saxophone player of the '30s plays a composition that perfectly matches his style. Johnny Hodges and other Ellingtonians do justice and more to this beautiful melody by Billy Strayhorn.

Duke Ellington's alter-ego Billy Strayhorn wrote this tune specifically for Hodges' insinuating and sensual alto-saxophone style. Writer James Lincoln Collier compares the sound to "poured honey." Hodges probes the emotional depths of his horn in this moving interpretation.

This track is from one of dozens of small-group recording sessions involving members of the Ellington orchestra; sometimes, these sessons were used to try out new Strayhhorn or Ellington compositions. (Notice that this one is credited to both.) The Duke himself often sat in, and he provides a short piano introduction on this track. The original disc credits Hodges as leader of this session, but with the subscript "an Ellington unit."

After the piano intro this record is all Hodges with his exquisite sounds. Backing him up are some of the Ellington standbys– trumpeter Cootie Williams, baritone saxophonist Harry Carney, bassist Jimmy Blanton, and others. These Hodges-led sessions produced some of the best small group jazz of the period.

As with many Ellington and Strayhorn compositions, words were later added to "Day Dream" and some bands recorded it with the vocal.

This label is a Canadian Bluebird. Notice that it has a slightly different layout than the U.S. version and not as many words.

32. Benny Carter & His Orchestra

ALL OF ME

November. 19, 1940

CD 2, Track 7

WIN: An exciting selection by Benny Carter who was considered an outstanding arranger of reed instruments. The record is a classic of its kind, taking one of the best American popular songs and presenting it with the wide variety of the instruments available in a dance band.

"...the entire first chorus is played by the saxophones in unison, with swooping variations on the melody."

In the liner notes for the Classics CD reissue of this track, Anatol Schenker wrote, "'All of Me' must be among the most impressive big-band arrangements ever written." It certainly is; the entire first chorus is played by the saxophones in unison, with swooping variations on the melody. Hearing this arrangement, it's easy to understand why musicians just loved to play in this band.

Although Carter's first instrument was the alto sax (Records 7, 22, and 36), he played all the reeds well. On this side he solos on clarinet. Actually, Carter's second instrument was the trumpet and he played it beautifully on many records.

Carter's band of this period was an artistic success, and he even had a few minor hits. But Carter lacked the charisma of an Ellington or a Basie, so his bands were never successful commercially. Others had the hits and Carter had his reputation – it was great among musicians. This record shows why they respected him.

The Versatile Benny Carter

A quiet, unassuming man of many talents, Benny Carter was best known as a big band arranger, and many experts feel that none was better, particularly in the blending of the reeds. He had written arrangements for Fletcher Henderson, McKinney's Cotton Pickers, Charlie Barnet, Chick Webb, and Tommy Dorsey, and he was one of the few outsiders to write for the orchestra of Duke Ellington.

During this period, he led his own band and did occasional arrangements for Gene Krupa, Cab Calloway, Louis Armstrong, and Glenn Miller. He was the first black to arrange for the "Your Hit Parade" radio show. His charts still sound fresh and tasteful today. In October, 2007 the Jazz at Lincoln Center Orchestra presented a "Benny Carter Centennial" concert. Among the Carter arrangements Wynton Marsalis chose to play was "All of Me" (Record 32). The City of New York proclaimed October 19 as "Benny Carter Day."

In September, 1939 *Down Beat* magazine named Carter's its Band of the Month. As a leader, Carter attracted the best musicians, some of whom sacrificed higher salaries with other bands to play the rich Carter arrangements. Sidemen wanted to play for Carter, leaders sought his arrangements, and singers such as Ethel Waters, Billie Holiday, and Maxine Sullivan requested him as an accompanist. (Note in Appendix C, Carter is on both lists, the Hampton and the Wilson/Holiday sessions.)

Not only was Benny Carter one of the top alto saxophonists of the period, but he excelled on trumpet and on tenor and soprano saxophones, clarinet (Record 32), piano, and trombone. He even sang on a few records.

In 1939 Carter was at three all-star recording sessions, and during 1940 he recorded with the Metronome All-Stars, Coleman Hawkins, Freddie Rich's Orchestra, the Chocolate Dandies (Record 22), and Buster Bailey's Sextet (the group which evolved into John Kirby's Orchestra). A few years later he showed his versatility by playing with groups at both ends of the jazz spectrum of the day– the Dixielanders at Nick's in Greenwich Village and Dizzy Gillespie's beboppers on 52nd Street. Thoughtful and articulate, in 1942 he was a guest lecturer at the New School for Social Research. Many years later, he taught jazz at Princeton.

Carter's composing credits include "Melancholy Lullaby" (his big band theme), the lovely standard "When Lights Are Low" (Record 7), and "Malibu." It's ironic that this musical sophisticate's only hit is a novelty song, "Cow Cow Boogie." (The irony was compounded by the fact that he was sued by "Cow Cow" Davenport for stealing his work. Carter lost the case!)

Carter took care of himself, surviving to do some excellent playing in the 1980s, continuing composing and playing well into his nineties. (He died in 2003 at age 96.) Carter never became a popular star, but he did live long enough to become a celebrated and much-loved figure among jazz musicians and fans. Many accomplishments, both in arranging and playing, have earned Carter a place in the pantheon of jazz greats.

33. Big Joe Turner
CARELESS LOVE
November 26, 1940
(Not included on CD, see note)

WIN: There were few who sang the blues as well as "Big Joe" Turner, and few who could accompany them as well as Willie "The Lion" Smith. Together they make this W. C. Handy tune a blues delight.

This side was not included on the accompanying CDs because of space limitations. It is available on some collections of Turner's works, including JSP 7709.

"Big Joe" Turner sang with abandon, using his full voice. He breathed new life into this W.C. Handy blues. Turner began his career as a singing bartender in Kansas City, where his reputation grew; on this track, it's easy to picture him in that raucous setting. (He was called "Big" to distinguish him from a pianist of the same name.) The rolling stride accompaniment on this record is by Willie "The Lion" Smith, not to be confused with saxophonist Willie Smith (Record 14).

At this time, in Harlem, renters would sometimes hire a pianist and invite people to their apartments to listen and dance. The guests at these parties would contribute money that would help pay the rent. Smith was a Harlem rent-party buddy of such fellow pianists as Duke Ellington and James P. Johnson, and was much admired by musicians.

Smith wrote some lovely piano pieces which are still studied by jazz musicians. A colorful character, he was seen often wearing his signature derby and smoking a cigar. He earned his nickname during field artillery duty in WWI. Of Negro and Jewish parentage, his full name was William Henry Joseph Berthol Bonaparte Bertholoff Smith.

34. King Cole Trio

SWEET LORRAINE

Vocals: Nat "King" Cole

December 6, 1940

CD 2, Track 8

WIN: From the beginning, with their very first records, this group was able to swing fast numbers and yet play ballads with intelligence and feeling.

At this time this group hadn't yet had a hit record, but they were playing fine jazz. The piano and voice of Nat Cole and the inventive guitar of Oscar Moore infuse "Sweet Lorraine" with smooth urbanity and jazz feeling.

Years later, when he had such success as a popular vocalist, many forgot what a fine pianist Nat Cole was, a nimble-fingered disciple of Earl "Fatha" Hines. Oscar Moore, too, is considered one of the best players at a time when the electric guitar was becoming popular.

The King Cole Trio recorded sixteen sides for Decca from December, 1940 to October, 1941. Along with a lot of "hip talk" songs and instrumentals, they included "Honeysuckle Rose" and "Sweet Lorraine." Dropped by Decca, the trio went on to small jazz labels until 1943, when Capitol signed them. Their hits started rolling, beginning with "Straighten Up and Fly Right" on their first session for Capitol.

Cole was a reluctant singer. Early on he had to be coaxed to sing. It's ironic that in later years, when he wanted to play more jazz piano, he had become a really popular singer. He was the first black to have his own TV show.

Der Bingle

The King Cole Trio, Stan Kenton, and Woody Herman were all recording at this time for Decca records. Then they all left and joined other labels just before they had their big successes. Decca, meanwhile, didn't need them; their cash cow was Bing Crosby. By 1940 Crosby was a superstar in recording, radio, and films. His big-time career began as a fresh-faced boy crooner with Paul Whiteman, both as one of the three "Rhythm Boys" and then as a solo singer. Whitney Balliett wrote, "Crosby, cutting the silver cord to Europe, almost by himself invented American popular singing; (he) did it by listening to jazz musicians." Crosby worked with Bix Beiderbecke, the Dorsey Brothers, Duke Ellington, and others to develop an easy, laid-back style and on-stage persona.

Jazz writers have had difficulty categorizing Crosby (as they did later with Frank Sinatra). Leonard Feather wrestled with it in his *Encyclopedia of Jazz*: "Though the Rhythm Boys were considered a 'hot' trio…and Crosby certainly has had jazz associations, he is, of course, basically a pop music figure." Roger Kinkle called Crosby, "jazz-influenced, especially by Louis Armstrong and Bix Beiderbecke." But the *British Illustrated Encyclopedia of Jazz* went further: "…Crosby's singing was much influenced by jazz – in fact, there is little doubt that he could be classified as a jazz singer." Certainly he was the most imitated. Almost every male vocalist of the 1930s was trying to sound like Crosby, just as those in the '40s and '50s would try to imitate Sinatra.

In this 1939-1942 period Crosby recorded a number of sides accompanied by jazz groups, and they show him off at his rhythmic best. He recorded two duets with singer Connee Boswell, backed up by his brother Bob's Bob Cats. He also recorded with the big bands of Woody Herman and Jack Teagarden, sharing duets with each of those bandleaders.

In 1942, he recorded the Irving Berlin tune, "White Christmas," as part of a holiday album. It became the biggest-selling record of all time. (A great trivia question: Who played drums on that record? The answer: Spike Jones, who later became famous for his wacky novelty band.) The song was featured in two films: *Holiday Inn* (released in 1942) and, much later, *White Christmas* (1964).

Bing Crosby was known and loved all over the world. Even the Nazis knew it was hopeless to fight the success of the man to whom the Germans gave the affectionate nickname, "Der Bingle."

In later years Crosby appeared frequently with Louis Armstrong. Crosby aged gracefully, adapting his singing and acting to the times. An avid golfer, he died in 1977 while coming off the 18th hole of a course in Spain.

♪ WHEN THE LIGHTS ♪ GO ON AGAIN

By the end of 1940, Europe was firmly entrenched in war. More than 4,500 Britons were killed in November air raids, but Hitler's expected cross-channel invasion never came. His eyes had turned eastward. One week before Christmas, Hitler issued the order for Operation Barbarrosa, the invasion of Russia – perhaps the turning point of World War II. Hitler would not believe the warnings of his staff, who knew the risks. Military historian John Keegan wrote that invading Russia had dominated Hitler's "world outlook" from the day he set out to take power in Germany, nearly two decades earlier. The non-aggression pact between Germany and Russia meant nothing to him. The ill-starred offensive was launched the next June.

Hitler's actions made it hard for movie-goers in the U.S. to laugh at Charlie Chaplin's *The Great Dictator.* If they found Hitler too real, too scary, they found *Fantasia* too high-brow, a lesson that Walt Disney never forgot. (The animated film attempted to visualize a number of classical compositions.) Before its release, Disney had predicted, "This movie will make Tchaikovsky!" (whose 'Nutcracker Suite' was featured). *Fantasia* did not recover its production costs until it seventh re-release.

By the end of 1940 there were 23 television stations and 10,000 television sets in the country. Within a few months the Federal Communications Commission authorized the use of the medium for commercial purposes. Soon, when the U.S. entered the war, all but six stations would fold. Material shortages would stop all further growth until 1945.

Pessimists detected in the title of a new Eugene O'Neill play a summary of world events. It did seem like the world was headed on *A Long Day's Journey Into Night.* But ticket buyers preferred musicals, revues, mysteries, and comedies to the serious and depressing *Long Day.* The hottest ticket on Broadway remained the light-hearted *Life With Father.* Other hit comedies included *The Male Animal* and *My Sister Eileen. Panama Hattie* with Ethel Merman was the most popular musical, and *Johnny Belinda* won the Pulitzer Prize for drama.

Among the noteworthy novels was Ernest Hemingway's *For Whom the Bell Tolls.* His tale of the Spanish Civil War was high on the best-seller list, but trailed *How Green Was My Valley*, *Kitty Foyle*, and *Mrs. Miniver.* John Steinbeck's *Grapes of Wrath*, Edmund Wilson's *To the Finland Station*, and Richard Wright's *Native Son* did not make the list. Novelist F. Scott Fitzgerald died in December of 1940, but the world of the 1920s he had described seemed as remote as the court of Louis XIV.

February 11 radio debut

NBC launched *"The Chamber Music Society of Lower Basin Street,"* a spoof of high-brow musical shows. Studio musicians played in a pseudo-Dixieland style, but guests such as Sidney Bechet, Jelly Roll Morton, and Lionel Hampton gave the show legitimacy. Vocalists included "Mademoiselle" Dinah Shore and Lena Horne. Victor produced some recordings under the Chamber name.

February 26 recording

Earl Hines, "Body and Soul" and "Child of A Disordered Brain." These solos were recorded on a Storytone piano, probably the first electronic keyboard instrument. Hines gave it his best, but the Storytone just could not produce the rich sounds and sustained tones of the standard acoustic instrument.

April 18 Cab wows 'em

Cab Calloway opened at Boston's Southland. It was the start of a six-month tour during which the "Hi-Dee-Ho Man" broke ballroom attendance marks from coast to coast.

April 27 Your Hit Parade

For the fourth straight week, "When You Wish Upon a Star," the theme from Walt Disney's film *Pinocchio*, was the most popular song in the U.S., according to the Saturday night radio program. Several swing bands adapted it to their books.

May 9 recording

Fred Astaire with Benny Goodman & His Orchestra, "Who Cares" and "Just Like Taking Candy From A Baby." Astaire sang and tap danced, Goodman and Lionel Hampton soloed.

June 10 recording

Erskine Hawkins and His Orchestra, "After Hours." This slow blues, written and played by pianist Avery Parrish, became a great favorite of black teenagers, and often was the last selection of the night at their dances.

June 14 recording
Leadbelly (Huddie Leadbetter) with the Golden Gate Quartet, "Rock Island Line." Guitarist-singer Leadbelly defies category, fitting into the jazz, folk, and blues catalogs.

August 8 recording
Larry Clinton recorded his own composition "Bolero in Blue," not a big-seller. In 1981, Andrew Lloyd-Weber's Show, "Cats," featured a beautiful melody called "Memories." Some noted an amazing resemblance to the Larry Clinton tune.

October 4 recording
Eddy Howard, "Star Dust," "Old Fashioned Love," "Exactly Like You," and "Wrap Your Troubles in Dreams." This would be a forgettable session by a popular vocalist of the day except for excellent solos by the accompanists– pianist Teddy Wilson, trombonist Benny Morton, guitarist Charlie Christian, saxophonist Bud Freeman, and trumpeter Bill Coleman.

November 7 historic dance
Duke Ellington and His Orchestra played a dance at the Crystal Ballroom in Fargo, North Dakota. A state-of-the-art disc recorder preserved thirty-six of the tunes played. The Book-of-The-Month Club won a Grammy Award in 1978 for their LP of much of the music, and in 1991 a CD of the entire "Fargo Dance Date" was released.

November 11 recording
"Hot Lips" Page & His Band, "Lafayette" and "South." With these two tracks, trumpeter Page recalled his stint a decade earlier with Bennie Moten's Kansas City Orchestra. Boogie-woogie pianist Pete Johnson and future star saxophonist Don Byas also are featured.

December recordings
Bing Crosby recorded six sides accompanied by Bob Crosby's Orchestra and by the Bob Cats. Two tracks were duets with Connee Boswell.

Chapter Four

Things Ain't What They Used To Be

February 8 Wilson Won't Return
Pianist Teddy Wilson denied rumors he was returning to Goodman after breaking up his own big band. He told the *Pittsburgh Courier* he was busy organizing small-group sessions.

February 15 Record crowds
Louis Armstrong's band broke house records at Chicago's Oriental Theater, while Earl Hines was doing the same at the Royal Theater in Baltimore.

March 10 recording
Una Mae Carlisle, "Blitzkrieg Baby, You Can't Bomb Me." The war-lingo lyrics included not-yet-familiar words, such as "hand grenade," "propaganda,""TNT," etc . The excellent quintet accompanying Carlisle was assembled by tenor saxophonist Lester Young after he left Count Basie. Four tracks with Carlisle were its only recordings.

March 11 recording
Slim Gaillard & His Flat Foot Floogie Boys, "The Slim Slam Boogie." Vocalist-guitarist Gaillard combined funny lyrics and jazz. With him on this session were bassist Slam Stewart and drummer Kenny Clarke, both serious and later, influential, jazz musicians. In 1945, Dizzy Gillespie and Charlie Parker would make some of their first joint recordings with Gaillard.

March 15 house records
Cab Calloway set a new attendance mark at Pittsburgh's Stanley Theater. Erskine Hawkins eclipsed Count Basie's attendance record at Chicago's Regal Theater.

1941

In the spring of 1941, Bulgaria joined the Axis and the Nazis overran Greece and the Balkans. Simultaneously, Hitler was moving ahead with plans to attack Russia. In May, Rudolf Hess, one of Hitler's top aides, flew to Scotland in an apparent attempt to negotiate peace. He crash-landed, but was never able to explain why he came. Hess remained a prisoner of the Allied powers until his death forty years after the war.

Americans expected their nation to be drawn into the conflict "sometime," but President Roosevelt still had to steer a wary course toward preparedness. In early 1941 he asked Congress to authorize shipment of virtually unlimited war materials to England. "We want to be the arsenal of democracy," he said. He argued that instead of inciting a war with Germany, the measure would forestall that danger. There followed a titanic two-month struggle in rallies, in the press, and in Congress. With the passage of the Lend-Lease Act, American factories started turning out war goods.

American forces went to Iceland, at the invitation of the Icelanders, after Hitler had taken over its parent country, Denmark. When Hitler invaded Russia that summer, Josef Stalin assumed virtually complete power in Russia and soon would become commander-in-chief. The White House promised aid to the Soviets. At about the same time, FDR froze Japanese assets in the United States. In Asia militant Japanese were advancing through Indo-China. Vichy France sent 5,000 Parisian Jews to labor camps.

After a secret meeting in Newfoundland with Prime Minister Churchill, FDR ordered American destroyers to "shoot to kill" German submarines found in the North Atlantic. Since the destroyers were to accompany convoys carrying arms to England, encounters were inevitable. An incident would likely bring the United States formally into the war. Although the Royal Navy sank the largest German surface warship, the 40,000-ton Bismarck, German submarine attacks were becoming increasingly effective.

♪ KEEP YOUR SUNNY SIDE UP ♪

By mid-1941, the Germans occupied Poland, Denmark, Norway, Belgium, Holland, France, Yugoslavia and Greece. The BBC urged the occupied countries to continue their resistance, making the first four notes of Beethoven's Fifth Symphony the musical symbol. (Dot, dot, dot, dash - which sounded like the four ominous opening notes of Beethoven's Fifth -- was Morse Code for "V" for victory.) Glenn Miller recorded the melancholy "Spring Will Be So Sad (When She Comes This Year)."

Winston Churchill toured the bombed-out ruins of London flashing the two-finger V-for-victory signal, but he had little reason to be optimistic. The only bright spot was that the British and Free French had driven the Vichy French forces from Syria. Meanwhile, Hitler's armies were racing across Russia. As Japanese troops flooded Thailand and Cambodia, FDR placed the Filipino defense forces under the command of General Douglas MacArthur.

America's relations with Germany were so tense that each nation withdrew its diplomats. In the U.S., Hitler's picture in newsreels drew boos, and Americans of German descent were worried about hostility from their neighbors – as had happened in WWI.

By September, Jews in Germany were ordered to wear a prominent Star of David at all times. Gradually they would be stripped of all civil rights, and before long came extensive use of the concentration camps and gas chambers. Gypsies (ordered to wear black triangles or green patches) and homosexuals (wearing black or pink triangles) were also singled out for systematic persecution.

♪ TOGETHER ♪

In the summer of 1941, President Roosevelt and Prime Minister Churchill issued the Atlantic Charter, promising joint efforts to destroy the Nazi regime. Secretary of State Cordell Hull warned the Japanese not to interfere with American ships in the Pacific. These moves drew shudders among the remaining isolationists.

Scripps-Howard columnist Ernie Pyle (soon to be a famous war correspondent) was opposed to entering the war, reflecting the views of most Americans. How could anyone believe, as some were claiming, that under-trained U.S. kids could lick ten times as many militant Germans?

♪ THINGS ARE LOOKING UP ♪

While, on the other side of the globe, Chinese troops showed temporary signs of halting their Japanese invaders, German U-boats sank two American destroyers in October. All summer the German army had rolled across the Soviet Union, but, as Napoleon's forces had before them, they fell victim to the Russian winter and to the heroism and tenacity of Soviet soldiers and civilians. (Stalin had dropped the Communist rhetoric and urged his people to save "Mother Russia.") By late November, just two years and three months after invading Poland, the Thousand-Year Reich had reached the high tide of its conquests. Barely twenty miles from Moscow, the Germans were repulsed.

On November 10, Churchill promised Britain would enter immediately on the side of the U.S. if the Japanese attacked. On November 26, a Japanese carrier fleet headed east, a fact unknown to the Allied Forces.

Meanwhile, solemn Japanese diplomats were sent to Washington to confer with State Department officials. When Tokyo made the final decision to bomb Pearl Harbor, these diplomats were to deliver a declaration of war before the attack. Due to bureaucratic delay, they were late in their delivery, thus continuing a Japanese reputation for surprise attacks on an enemy and leading to a severe rebuke from Secretary of State Cordell Hull.

♪ LET'S REMEMBER ♪ PEARL HARBOR (AS WE DID THE ALAMO)

On December 7, Japanese aircraft achieved almost complete surprise in an early morning attack on the U.S. fleet anchored at Pearl Harbor, Hawaii. The effect was devastating. Five battleships and fourteen smaller warships sank. One mitigating factor was that there were no aircraft carriers in the harbor; they were out on maneuvers.

In declaring war on Japan the next day, President Roosevelt said that December 7, 1941 would forever be "a day that will live in infamy." Within a week the U.S. was also at war with Germany and Italy. Hitler decided to support his Japanese ally by declaring war on the U.S., hoping that Japan would return the favor and declare war on Russia. Japan never did, and thus the Russians could concentrate on fighting the German army on its western borders.

While almost every American can remember where they were when hearing the news about Pearl Harbor, bandleader Jimmy Dorsey had more reason to recall than most. He was broadcasting a one-hour program from the Meadowbrook Ballroom, and the station interrupted his program forty-two times with war bulletins. There were six interruptions during "Fingerbustin'" alone. Finally he signed off with the National Anthem.

Time magazine (December 15) declared: "The war came as a great relief, like a severe earthquake that in one terrible jerk shook everything disjointed."

Four days after the attack on Pearl Harbor, Japanese planes sank the British heavy cruiser *Repulse* and the pride of the fleet, the new battleship *The Prince of Wales*. Winston Churchill said remorsefully, "I do not remember any naval blow so heavy or so painful." A British Battleship Admiral, thinking air cover unnecessary, had sailed out in Malayan waters, hoping to scare the Japanese invaders away. Within four days,

Japanese planes had sunk seven large ships of the Allied fleet and proven that small maneuverable aircraft could sink large ships.

On May 17 a committee from the National Academy of Sciences reported that "atomic bombs can hardly be anticipated before 1945." Still, concerned that German scientists were working on such a bomb, U.S. officials continued to sponsor nuclear weapon research.

Although not prepared for war, neither were Americans pessimistic. Young men flooded enlistment centers. Songsmiths exploited every rhyme with "Japs" and "Nips" – derogatory names for Japanese citizens. "Remember Pearl Harbor" became a big hit. By coincidence Hollywood had just released *Sergeant York*. Gary Cooper won the Academy Award for his portrayal of the pacifist-turned-hero of World War I. Reluctant combatants, like *Sergeant York*, was exactly how most Americans saw themselves in 1941.

♪ TOOTIN' THROUGH ♪ THE ROOF

In April, in an effort to head off inflation, President Roosevelt created the Office of Price Administration (OPA). While limits on profits, prices, and wages would be controversial, the government did contain prices far better than in World War I.

Despite the fact that food store prices in December were 60 percent higher than the year before, Americans did not hold back as consumers. Total retail sales exceeded the previous year by $10 billion.

The public spent three times as much on radios, phonographs, and records as they did in 1933. Total record sales for 1941 matched the population total of 110 million. Victor sold nearly half the total and most of them were the 35-cent Bluebirds.

Although expensive cars, such as the Packard or the Lincoln, cost more than a year's salary for the typical worker, Americans bought new cars twice as fast as they had the year before. Production for the year topped three million cars. Meanwhile, Henry Ford relented and, for the first time, signed a contract recognizing the CIO-affiliated United Auto Workers Union.

♪ WORKING MAN'S BLUES ♪

Although there had been difficulties converting peacetime factories into plants producing war materials, American plants were producing a steady stream of war goods. Planes were being built at the rate of 25,000 a year. One plant was turning out 100 tanks a week. Many factories ran twenty-four hours a day, with three shifts of workers.

Most Black Americans could not take advantage of the new jobs created in wartime, as job opportunities often were closed to them. In 1940 only 240 of the 100,000 workers in one aircraft firm were black, and all of them were janitors. The Marines accepted no blacks, and initially the Navy used them only as messmen. The United States Employment Service, a federal agency, continued until July 1942 to fill "whites only" requests for defense labor. It was late in the war before there were any black airmen. Even the Red Cross blood supply was segregated by race.

Black leaders were tired of discrimination in defense industries and in other government jobs. After A. Philip Randolph called off a threatened protest march by 50,000 people in Washington, the President created a Fair Employment Practices Commission on June 25.

♪ NICE WORK IF YOU ♪ CAN GET IT

As usual, jazz was slightly ahead of the times when it came to jobs for blacks. The black *Pittsburgh Courier* noted in January singer Lena Horne's success with Charlie Barnet's band. She was only the third black vocalist with a white band. (June Richmond with Jimmy Dorsey and Billie Holiday with Artie Shaw were the others.) The same month Ella Fitzgerald led her orchestra to the stage of the Paramount on Broadway. According to *Down Beat*, the former Chick Webb orchestra had lost its distinctive sound. One record reviewer complained: "the Fitzgerald outfit sounds more white with every new release."

Most musicians were at the mercy of their bandleaders. The federal government ruled that leaders were not employers and, therefore, not responsible for withholding Social Security from the wages of their musicians. Most sidemen worked without contracts and by the week. They had virtually no job security. But even musicians were shocked by the July 1 headline in *Down Beat*: "Goodman Changes Half the Band." Many veterans had been replaced without any compensation. The most notable addition was a drummer, "Big Sid" Catlett, who came over from Louis Armstrong's band.

The musicians' union insisted that its members not be required to travel more than 400 miles for a one-night engagement. The policy was designed to increase safety on the band buses. There had been several recent accidents and even more close calls.

♪ YOU OUGHTA' BE ♪ IN PICTURES

In the world of arts, young Orson Welles stunned the film world with his *Citizen Kane*. Critics liked the thinly disguised roman a clef of publisher William Randolph Hearst better than did ticket buyers. Only later was it accepted as one of the greatest – if not the greatest – movie ever made. Welles' Mercury Theater group earlier had alarmed the country with its "War Of The Worlds" radio broadcast. Thousands of listeners believed that the U.S. actually was being invaded by Martians.

By midyear the movie box office perked up. Even before Pearl Harbor, filmmakers debated about what kind of movies would further the war effort. Early in 1941 *Variety* reported that the studios were planning a few war films "to aid national preparedness." More people praised high-minded films than went to see them. Deciding the nation needed escapist fare, Hollywood ground out mostly musicals and comedies, e.g., *Babes on Broadway*; *No, No, Nannete*; *Ziegfeld Girl*, etc. By November 10, Americans lined up to see *The Maltese Falcon*.

Not all films released in 1941 were escapist, however. The very week in August that *A Yank in the RAF* (Britain's Royal Air Force), starring Tyrone Power opened, the Germans revealed they had captured two American fliers after a bombing raid.

Like Hollywood, Broadway offered mostly escapist shows, such as *Arsenic and Old Lace* and *Hellzapoppin*. After eight years the decidedly more serious *Tobacco Road* finally closed.

♪ I COULD WRITE A BOOK ♪

Despite the imminent entry into war, only two war-related books were selling in 1941. Correspondent William Shirer's *Berlin Diary* was among the year's popular books and Hemingway's *For Whom the Bell Tolls* continued to be near the top of the best-seller list all year.

But other war novels did not sell well. This was to be "the summer of the paperback." In 1941 mass-marketed paperback books first appeared on racks in drugstores. These pocket books– mostly fiction– would prove immensely popular.

♪ JOLTIN' JOE DIMAGGIO ♪

Also in the summer of 1941, Joe Dimaggio had a remarkable 56-game hitting streak. Dimaggio, called "The Yankee Clipper," was the toast of baseball. But soon enough, he would trade his Yankee pin stripes for military khaki. In a subway Series, the Yankees downed their cross-town rivals, the Brooklyn Dodgers, four games to one. Yet the talk of the baseball world was young Ted Williams of the Boston Red Sox, who batted an astounding .406 for the season. (No player has hit that well since.)

♪ UP A LAZY RIVER ♪

In 1941 jazz was like a great river, fed by many rivulets and meandering currents. The mainstream was the music of the dance bands, which itself was a blend from many sources. But the river had many tributaries.

Two January sessions make the point. First, a fan lugged an awkward, desk-sized disk recorder up to Harlem in a taxi to capture some of Charlie Christian's improvisations. Next, Sidney Bechet and His New Orleans Footwarmers recorded "Baby, Won't You Please Come Home," a number that had been in the standard jazz repertoire for decades. Released on the Vox label, Christian's amazing swing-era jazz guitar improvisations were very different from Bechet's equally skillful, but New Orleans-rooted, music.

Benny Goodman still led the *Down Beat* swing band poll, but Duke Ellington was closing in. "For ten years a favorite with musicians, Ellington nonetheless has been unable to show better than fifth in any poll," the magazine commented. The critics consistently honored Ellington for turning out excellent records.

Glenn Miller edged Tommy Dorsey in the sweet band category. The favorite small group was again Goodman's, followed by John Kirby's, and then the Crosby Bobcats. Most promising new bands were Raymond Scott, Tony Pastor, Claude Thornhill, Charlie Spivak, and Teddy Powell. Readers voted Guy Lombardo the "King of Corn" for his outdated, corny music. He beat out Clyde McCoy for the dubious honor and Glenn Miller placed third.

The *Metronome* poll also indicated that the mass audience finally was getting to know about the black bands and their players. After choosing two blacks for the 1940 All-Star Band, *Metronome* readers elected six in 1941. Within a few years all-star groups would be predominately black, certainly a more accurate reflection of the jazz talent pool of the day. *Metronome's* 1941 All-Star Band recorded two excellent sides, the Fletcher Henderson arrangement of "Bugle Call Rag" and the Count Basie arrangement of "One O'Clock Jump" (Record 36).

As the popularity of jazz and recognition of black artists was peaking around the world, the composer and jazz pioneer Jelly Roll Morton died on July 10, 1941. At the time he was looked upon as a braggart and an eccentric, but as the years went by his contributions to jazz were recognized as seminal and immense.

♪ THEY CAN'T TAKE THAT ♪ AWAY FROM ME

Jazz was about to take a sharp turn because of an organization that controlled the playing of music. The American Society of Composers, Authors and Publishers (ASCAP) had been formed in 1914 in an effort to compensate composers for performances of their music. (Victor Herbert and Irving Berlin were among the founders.) ASCAP registered a composer's work, then charged users each time a tune was played. In the late '30s when ASCAP increased the fees to radio stations and networks for playing their tunes on the air, the radio industry set up a rival organization, Broadcast Music Incorporated (BMI). Although BMI managed to attract a few young composers, ASCAP dominated licensing.

As the financial negotiations between the radio networks and ASCAP became stalemated, the bands worried about what might happen. They began to rehearse BMI tunes and to look for compositions in the public domain, i.e., those too old to have been licensed or items never licensed. Suddenly "Annie Laurie," "Swanee River," and "Loch Lomond" were popular. They also exploited "longhair" music – symphonic airs, sonatas, arias and concertos. Les Brown reported on that trend with a ditty called "Everybody's Making Money But Tchaikovsky," and Xavier Cugat chose as a title for an Offenbach melody, "Let's Steal a Tune." Arranger Larry Clinton made so many of these transformations that one wag suggested that classical music went in his ear and out his pen.

ASCAP-radio network negotiations eventually broke off, and from January until October, 1941, ASCAP tunes were not allowed to be heard on commercial radio programs. The hassle did not affect recordings, live performances, or sustaining (non-commercial) radio programs. Actually, there is some ambiguity about the whole prohibition. Off-the-air recordings seem to indicate that some bands paid no attention to it.

Jazz musicians, who often interpolate portions of other tunes in their improvisations, had trouble avoiding ASCAP music. Bandleader Eddie Condon remembered assuring an ASCAP detective that clarinetist Pee Wee Russell would play his on-the-air solos exactly the way he had during the rehearsals. However, Condon knew full well that Russell couldn't do that if his life depended on it, since his forte was to spontaneously pick tunes out of the air as he played.

Some bands resorted to subterfuge. A few instrumentals written for Glenn Miller during the dispute sound suspiciously like the work of Billy May, an ASCAP member, but they are credited to May's wife.

Almost all the bands lost the theme songs, primarily written by ASCAP members, by which radio listeners identified them. They tailored their new BMI themes to sound as much as possible like their ASCAP themes. Charlie Barnet's "Redskin Rhumba" was very close to "Cherokee" (Record 1) and Woody Herman's "Furtrappers' Ball" closely resembled "Woodchoppers' Ball." Duke Ellington switched to "Take The 'A' Train" for his theme; it was written by Billy Strayhorn who had not yet joined ASCAP. It became, of course, one of the most popular compositions of the period. (The bands were not the only ones who lost their themes. The popular night-time radio show, "Mr Keen, Tracer of Lost Persons" lost its perfectly-titled theme, "Someday I'll Find You.")

Glenn Miller's beautiful "Moonlight Serenade" was converted into "Slumber Song," which, according to one musician, "used every other note" from his ASCAP theme. On October 30, his first CBS program after the settlement, Miller returned to "Moonlight Serenade." On that same broadcast he played all ASCAP tunes, including one he had recorded five months earlier but had been unable to play on the air. With the on-air boost, "Chattanooga Choo Choo" zoomed to the top of the charts.

The ASCAP dispute left few swing legacies. Tommy Dorsey's "Swanee River," Ellington's "Frankie and Johnny," and Wingy Manone's "Annie Laurie" are exceptions. Goodman recorded a good "Caprice XXIV Paganini," and Lunceford's "Chopin Prelude" is still worth a listen. Most of the 1940 BMI tunes disappeared like an April snow, but the organization did find a niche and is still a major player in the music business.

The music licensing dispute between ASCAP and the networks had barely calmed down when there were rumblings from another quarter. The American Federation of Musicians (AFM), the musicians' labor union, was demanding a larger share of recording profits, and all musicians would stand by their union and its aggressive leadership. Both of these controversies indicated that there was a lot of money being made in music and all of the parties, i.e., the musicians, the radio networks, the record companies, etc., wanted their pieces of it.

Woody Herman.

35. Benny Goodman & His Sextet
I FOUND A NEW BABY
January 15, 1941
CD 2, Track 9

WIN: Benny Goodman's record comes out swinging, bringing out the very best from all the participants. This is one of his outstanding small-group gems.

The Benny Goodman small-group recordings must be counted as some of the very best in jazz history. On this track, the sextet turns what had been a Dixieland standard into a swing-era classic. Goodman's clarinet is confident and swinging, as it always was when he played with quality musicians. Charlie Christian provides cool and clever improvisations on the electric guitar, which his playing had promoted to solo status equal to the horns. Count Basie's minimalist piano solo consists of a few perfect notes, Cootie Williams' muted trumpet punctuates, George Auld blows a big-toned tenor sax solo, and Jo Jones pitches in with a classy drum break. None of these solos runs longer than 45 seconds, but each contributes to the overall sound of three-minutes of superb small-group jazz. (One advantage of the 10" 78rpm record was that it forced the musicians to put their very best efforts into the short time they had for their solos.)

Basie recorded a number of sides with Goodman in this period and some thought he might even join the Goodman band, but he went back to full-time bandleading. Basie's name is prominent on the first issues of this record but, sic transit gloria, was dropped from the labels on later releases.

Goodman's Charlie Christian and Ellington's Jimmy Blanton (Record 16) were both in their mid-twenties. Both were black and both played stringed instruments used in the rhythm section, Blanton the string bass and Christian the guitar. Of Blanton, British critic Eddie Lambert wrote, "During his brief and tragic career he revolutionized the jazz bass." Guitarist-writer Marty Grosz credited Christian with "utterly transforming" jazz guitar. Electricity helped with this transformation, too. Both made all of their recordings in this 1939-1942 triennium, and both died in 1942 of tuberculosis, a scourge of the black community in that day.

Notice the rather formal listing of names on this label. Bernstein was usually known as "Artie," Christian as "Charlie," and Auld as "Georgie."

In The Hall Of The Swing King

At heart Benny Goodman, unlike many of his fellow leaders, was a jazz musician and really enjoyed his small-group sessions. He loved playing with the best players – veterans and modernists, black and white – in the small-group setting, and it showed, with musicians responding with great imagination and energy. Like Duke Ellington and Artie Shaw he was more than equal to the talents of his players, and all three of these leaders enjoyed playing in their small groups.

By mid-1939, only Lionel Hampton remained with Goodman from the classic trios and quartets of 1935-38. Soon Hampton would follow pianist Teddy Wilson, drummer Gene Krupa, and trumpeter Harry James into the bandleading business. As great as all of those players were considered to be, many observers feel that Charlie Christian was the best soloist Goodman ever had. His first Sextet recordings, "Rose Room" and "Flying Home" (October 2, 1939), mixed the new sounds of Christian's amplified guitar, the swing-era styles of Goodman and Hampton, and the stilted '20s-style piano playing of Fletcher Henderson. (These "Sextet" sessions might include seven or eight musicians.) Christian's last Sextet recording session was March 22, 1941, a year before his untimely death. Later, John Guarnieri replaced Henderson as pianist, and Count Basie sat in for some classic sides, such as "I Found A New Baby."

During 1940-41, the addition of trumpeter Cootie Williams and tenor saxophonist George Auld produced some of Goodman's finest small-group jazz. Goodman could pick his sidemen – which is fortunate since he had to pick so many. Pianist Mel Powell and trombonist Lou McGarity sparked his next small group, recording many fine sides such as "The Wang Wang Blues." This group also backed Peggy Lee on three sides, including "Blues In The Night." Powell and Goodman were in on two excellent versions of "The World Is Waiting For The Sunrise." Powell led the first (Record 50) and Goodman the second.

Goodman, foremost a jazz musician, found that to be a successful leader he had to be a disciplinarian, businessman, and promoter also. He had to keep a bunch of young prima donnas in line while maintaining musical standards. On the bandstand and over the air, Goodman seemed to enjoy himself and indulged in some showboating. He courted the press. Goodman seemed colorful, but not offensive. The public took to him in a way it never did to "dull" leaders, such as Teddy Wilson and Benny Carter, or to the irascible Artie Shaw.

Under producer John Hammond's tutelage, Goodman had hired first-class arrangers, beginning with Fletcher Henderson who wrote the classic charts. Benny freely acknowledged his debt to Fletcher in his autobiography. Henderson continued to contribute in this period: "Stealin' Apples," "Honeysuckle Rose," and a swing version of Mendelssohn's "Spring Song," among others.

In 1939, Eddie Sauter became Goodman's key arranger. Sauter came from Red Norvo's orchestra; his adventuresome charts mixed well with the Henderson arrangements. Sauter's originals included "Benny Rides Again," "Clarinet a la King," and "Superman" (yet another concerto for Cootie Williams). Among his striking arrangements were "Time On My Hands" and "The Hour of Parting." (The last was a most unusual Goodman recording because it featured another reed player, alto saxophonist Toots Mondello.) Sauter was especially good at arranging for the band's vocalists: "Darn That Dream" for Mildred Bailey, "I Found A Million Dollar Baby" for Helen Forrest, and "How Deep Is The Ocean?" for Peggy Lee. Goodman admired the advanced work by Sauter, but he maintained it was easier to dance to the Henderson charts.

When Goodman hired 18-year-old pianist Mel Powell in 1941, he gained an all-around musical genius. In addition to playing fine jazz piano in the orchestra and small groups, Powell's composing credits included "Mission To Moscow," and he arranged "Jersey Bounce," "Why Don't You Do Right" (Record 55), and many other tunes.

Even though he was working with the talent-laden Henderson-Sauter-Powell combination, Goodman engaged other arrangers as well. On March 27, 1941, the band recorded Jimmy Mundy's arrangement of still another concerto for Cootie Williams, "Fiesta In Blue," and "Cherry." (Goodman nixed the release of the latter which he found uninteresting compared to Harry James' record. Later, during the LP era, the first release of "Cherry" received critical acclaim.)

"When Goodman was playing music – and a good deal of the time when he wasn't," wrote James Lincoln Collier, "he was totally concentrated. He was always trying to play as well as he could: there were to be no letdowns." Because he expected the same intensity from others, he was constantly looking for replacements. Over this three-year period his files indicate that he employed nearly 100 different musicians and arrangers; in the same time span, Ellington used 21.

Goodman didn't think much of vocalists. Unlike Glenn Miller or Tommy Dorsey, he usually carried only one singer (female) at a time. Helen Ward and Martha Tilton had been succeeded briefly by an old friend, Mildred Bailey, who didn't feel well enough to travel so had to leave the band. Then came Helen Forrest, who had been with Artie Shaw before coming to Goodman's band. Many experts consider Forrest the consummate swing-band vocalist, although she was a little too controlled to be considered a jazz singer. Her voice was pleasant and the listener heard every word, but she didn't have the feeling for jazz that Mildred Bailey or Billie Holiday did.

When Forrest jumped to Harry James (she later said that it bothered her to have Goodman's clarinet noodling behind her!), Goodman's wife discovered a perky 19-year-old blond from North Dakota named Norma Deloris Egstrom. Renamed Peggy Lee, she was an instant success. George Simon wrote that while she looked sophisticated and sensuous, she really was "rather insecure, extremely sensitive, and terribly sentimental." After her twenty months with Goodman she went out on her own to become a super-star. Multi-talented, she wrote a number of songs herself. Unlike some other leaders, Goodman never was linked romantically with any of his singers.

Goodman and Ellington both held out against baritones, but at about the same time, Goodman added Tommy Taylor, then Art London (later "Art Lund") and Ellington hired Herb Jeffries. When the Army got London, Dick Haymes joined Goodman. Unlike many other bandleaders, neither Goodman nor the Duke ever featured a singing group.

Goodman was equally at ease playing for dancers at the posh Waldorf-Astoria, jamming up in Harlem, or playing classical recitals. He recorded compositions by Aaron Copeland and Morton Gould and even commissioned a piece from classical composer Bela Bartok, which he later recorded. (His ventures into the classics drew mixed reviews.)

Benny Goodman's contributions to American music were monumental. Gunther Schuller summed it up this way: "For one fine moment in American musical history there was an alliance between national popular taste and a creative music called jazz. For that we are deeply grateful to Benny Goodman."

Duke Ellington with three of his trumpeters: Artie Whetsol, Cootie Williams, and Rex Stewart.

A Big Year For Cootie Williams

Cootie Williams joined Duke Ellington in 1929 and was the featured growl and plunger-mute trumpeter on many of the Duke's major recordings of the '30s. In 1936 the Duke honored Williams with his own concerto, "Echoes of Harlem," subtitled "Cootie's Concerto." In March of 1940, Ellington wrote and recorded a second Williams-centered composition, "Concerto for Cootie." (When words were added it became, "Do Nothin' 'Til You Hear From Me.") The record featured Cootie at his growling, muted-trumpet and open-trumpet best– one of the great all-time jazz recordings. It brought Williams to a larger audience than the small group of jazz buffs who had appreciated him before.

In 1940 the Ellington band was beginning what most experts believe was the Duke's most productive period (with the Strayhorn-Blanton-Webster orchestra referred to earlier). The band was truly an all-star group of experienced players, e.g., Johnny Hodges, Barney Bigard, Sonny Greer, and others, and all of them appeared to be happily ensconced in the organization. Then, later in the year, Williams announced that he was leaving Ellington...to join Benny Goodman.

Personnel changes in a band regularly are mentioned in the pages of *Down Beat*, not in styles and titles from the recording studios; this was not the case when Cootie Williams departed the Ellington orchestra. First, Rex Stewart, Cootie's colleague in the Ellington trumpet section, led a small-group recording session in which the Duke himself played. One number from that session, "Mobile Bay," featured Stewart in an approximation of Cootie's growling style. (The song referred to Williams' hometown in Alabama.) Second, the Raymond Scott Orchestra recorded an even more direct statement of the jazz event – "When Cootie Left The Duke." Scott's trumpet soloist did a creditable imitation of Williams' style.

Meanwhile, Cootie had joined Goodman and began recording with the Sextet on November 7, 1940. (An historic date for the Ellington band also – the Fargo Dance Date recordings, with Ray Nance replacing Williams in the trumpet section.) In December of 1940, Williams recorded "Superman," a number written for him by Eddie Sauter. On March 27, 1941 with Goodman, there was yet another concerto, "Fiesta in Blue," originally titled, "Cootie Growls."

So in just over five years, Cootie Williams had six recordings devoted to him – Ellington's "Echoes of Harlem" and "Concerto for Cootie," Rex Stewart's "Mobile Bay," Raymond Scott's "When Cootie Left The Duke," and Benny Goodman's "Superman" and "Fiesta in Blue." Not bad for the big-band sideman Cootie, whose name, though catchy, was hardly a household word.

After leaving Goodman, Williams led his own big band for a while. It featured Eddie 'Cleanhead' Vinson's vocals and introduced pianist Bud Powell. Williams returned to Ellington intermittently over the years.

36. The *Metronome* All Star Band
ONE O'CLOCK JUMP
January 16, 1941
Not included on CD, see note

WIN: This record settles the argument: Can a bunch of all-stars come together in a big band setting and make good music? Here, many cream-of-the-crop musicians play Count Basie's arrangement of his own tune, doing it more than justice, with tight ensembles and good short solos.

This side is not included on the accompanying CDs because of space limitations. It is available on FA5050: "Summit Meetings, Metronome All Stars/Esquire All Stars, 1939-1950."

This arrangement is a variation on the one written by Count Basie for Benny Goodman's band. The composition is always credited to Basie, but most of it was actually a blues that had been recorded under other names.

There were questions about whether a group of all-stars selected by the readers of *Metronome* magazine could play together well enough to make good music, but they certainly did on this side. (It compares well with Goodman's recording of "One O'Clock Jump" as well as Basie's two tries in this period.)

The *Metronome* readers, who choose the all-stars, still weren't "with it," however. A photograph from this session shows the tenor sax star Coleman Hawkins sitting next to Tex Beneke from Glenn Miller's band. Maybe the readers weren't aware of great black tenor players such as Ben Webster or Chu Berry, but they should have known about other white players such as Bud Freeman and Eddie Miller who were both superior to Beneke. (Beneke, an average saxophone player, was popular because of his engaging vocal style for Glenn Miller.)

The All Stars managed to squeeze a number of solos in on this side, with first honors going to Goodman's guitarist, Charlie Christian. Also soloing were Harry James, Goodman himself, and the ubiquitous Benny Carter.

Both 78rpm sides from this session turned out very well (the other was "Bugle Call Rag"), so *Metronome* continued to select and record their All-Star bands. The later ones were better representations of all the jazz talent available at the time.

Meanwhile, *Esquire* magazine jumped into the fray with all-star bands chosen by a panel of experts. At last black players like Louis Armstrong, Roy Eldridge, and Art Tatum were presented in an all-star setting and some fine sessions resulted.

The term 'all-star' was loosely applied to many jazz groups over the years. In many cases, such as Louis Armstrong's bands, the name was well-deserved, but often not. However, the Metronome and Esquire recordings from the '40s still stand out as first-class jazz.

Count Basie.

1941 trend

Many boogie-woogie piano players emerged out of poverty and obscurity to star in posh New York clubs. Tommy Dorsey's recording of "Boogie Woogie," only a modest seller when released in 1938, reached the million mark in 1941. (The tune had been recorded by Pine Top Smith in 1928 as "Pine Top's Boogie Woogie," considered the first boogie-woogie record ever. On this record Pine Top recalls the early days of solo piano by giving a young woman directions on how to dance to his music as he plays)

37. Woody Herman & His Orchestra

BLUE FLAME

February 13, 1941
CD 2, Track 10

WIN: A lovely tune played by a band which featured the blues. The dramatic qualities of the melody led the band to adopt it as their theme song.

The Herman band's first theme song was "Woodchopper's Ball," which, during the music licensing hassle (see p. 93), was changed to "Furtrapper's Ball." Over time, however, Herman changed the theme to "Blue Flame," arranged for the band by Joe Bishop. This haunting melody was perfect for the Herman group, then billed as the "Band That Plays The Blues." As the band evolved into the boppish First Herd in the mid-'40s it still kept "Blue Flame" as its theme song.

On this first recording of the theme, Herman, only an average clarinetist, solos to good effect. Neil Reid's trombone solo matches the "after-hours" mood of this track. Reid was yet another of those hightly capable, but almost anonymous, professionals who played in the big bands.

The Herman band, like some others of the day, had evolved out of an earlier group, the band of songwriter-leader Isham Jones. The handsome Herman, who sang and played clarinet and sax, was a perfect choice as leader and he performed that function for the rest of his long life. He stuck with it through wars, drug use by musicians, and changes in public taste. Although he died in poverty, he left a legacy of pleasing several generations of jazz fans.

38. Count Basie and His Orchestra

9:20 SPECIAL

April 10, 1941

CD 2, Track 11

WIN: The blues-influenced Basie orchestra had top arrangers, first-class horn players in each section, and the best rhythm section in jazz. This quality side is one of dozens the Basie band turned out in its first years.

It is said that Count Basie reminded his arrangers that "less is more," and this track is one of the dozens of minimalist gems that the Count recorded. It is simple, great for dancing, and swings like crazy.

Alto saxophonist Earle Warren wrote this number and contributes a good solo. He intended it as a tribute to his favorite radio station that was at 920 on the AM dial, but the record company thought it was a train song and inserted the colon.

Basie gives us one of his sparse but elegant solos, and he and the rest of the rhythm section propel the band at a fine pace. The muted trumpet solo is by one of the best, Harry "Sweets" Edison. "Sweets" did great work with Basie and then went on to an even more successful career. He played with small jazz groups and in large studio orchestras where he was much in demand. (Frank Sinatra requested that "Sweets" be in his accompanying groups.)

Near the end of the record comes a surprise, the big sound of tenor saxophonist Coleman Hawkins, who was sitting in with Basie for a couple of numbers. "The Hawk" solos, then plays the last few notes of the record. (Hawkins is also on Records 9, 22, and 36.)

This composition was recorded by a number of groups at the time and became a jazz standard.

39. Teddy Wilson, Piano solo
CHINA BOY
April 11, 1941
CD 2, Track 12

WIN: Of all of the pianists in the history of jazz Teddy Wilson must be listed near the top. His light touch and imaginative improvisations influenced many of the next generation of jazz piano players.

Teddy Wilson's delicate, floating style demands less of the listener than the intensity of Earl Hines or Art Tatum, but he ranks with them as one of the finest original jazz pianists. "China Boy," an instrumental from the '20s, is a fine vehicle for Wilson's sprightly playing. He is ably backed up by Al Hall on bass and J.C. Heard on drums.

Wilson's short-lived big band had just broken up when this record was made (it was an artistic, if not a financial, success). But Wilson's place in jazz had been earned already for dozens of excellent recordings with small groups, including Benny Goodman's, and the ensembles that backed Billie Holiday and Mildred Bailey.

"China Boy" contained no Oriental effects; it was just one of those '20s tunes with exotic titles. "When Buddha Smiles," "Japanese Sandman," and "Limehouse Blues" are other examples of tunes still played by traditional jazz musicians.

In 1938 and '39 Wilson was involved in a project called "The Teddy Wilson School for Pianists," which issued an instruction book and some special instructional recordings on which Wilson played standards. Later, someone issued the records seperately, without Wilson's approval. Wilson tried to stop this because he felt they were not his best work. Actually, they sound pretty good, even today!

40. Jay McShann & His Orchestra
HOOTIE BLUES
Vocals: Walter Brown
April 30, 1941
CD 2, Track 13

WIN: This track presents the composing, arranging, and alto sax creations of the next major innovator in jazz – Charlie Parker.

Popular during this period, at least among black audiences, McShann's Kansas City-based orchestra is remembered now primarily for introducing Charlie "Yardbird" (or just "Bird") Parker. Parker is the composer, arranger and one of the soloists on this track.

Parker's alto saxophone already sounds assured and powerful and he shows a great feeling for the blues which is the hallmark of all of the great jazz soloists. Soon he would assume his position as the next great alto player and, along with Gillespie, create the next phase of jazz – bebop.

After his big band days, "Hootie" McShann was much sought after as a solo pianist, playing into the '90s.

Decca listed this record as a "Blues Dance," a term rarely used. It was included in their "Sepia Series," a classification apparently used to indicate that the record was made by black musicians and intended for black audiences.

Even though they never played together, one historian has said that you can sum up the history of jazz in four words – Louis Armstrong, Charlie Parker. Here begins the second phase, the period when the two great innovators were both active players.

Bird, Diz & Bebop

In its beginnings, Louis Armstrong had turned jazz into a soloist's art and loosened up its rhythms. In the future, Charlie Parker would expand its harmonic and rhythmic parameters, creating the music that would be known as "bebop" or "bop." Pianist Lennie Tristano wrote: "There is quite a sizeable gap between (be)bop and previous phases of jazz. Charlie Parker not only provided the life-giving force, which is the essence of (be)bop, but also adequately expressed the music – the creator and the performer" wrapped up in one. Unlike the swing music before it, bebop did not rely heavily on melodies and was not conducive to ballroom dancing. It was complicated and intellectual where swing often was simple and emotional.

With Jay McShann's Orchestra, Parker's recorded solos already sound much like his later work. Meanwhile, in live meetings, he was collaborating with Dizzy Gillespie in creating a new music. Gillespie's boss, Cab Calloway, called it "Chinese music," apparently because it sounded foreign to him and he didn't like it. The Parker-Gillespie experiments flowered when they came together in the Earl Hines band, which evolved into the Billy Eckstine Orchestra.

Gillespie and Parker were joined in their early musical explorations by pianist-composer Thelonius Monk and drummer Kenny Clarke. These men got together on Monday nights (musicians' nights off) to jam in Harlem at Minton's Playhouse, (run by ex-bandleader Teddy Hill). Minton's is still pointed out by guides on tour buses in Harlem. Originally the dining room of the Hotel Cecil, Minton's opened again in 2006 as a jazz venue.

Few musicians could keep up with Gillespie's and Parker's complex harmonies and high-speed, multi-note playing. However, the new music was rooted in the old. Parker said that his first bebop ideas came while he was improvising on the Ray Noble standard, "Cherokee," and his later classics were based on such standards as "I Got Rhythm," "Whispering," and "How High The Moon." The beboppers, like the later "cool" and "fusion" innovators, also played the blues, the one style common to all jazz musicians.

Bebop thrilled some, appalled others. Vibraphonist Red Norvo said that Bird and Diz were "dirty words" among his friends, but personally he thought their music was exciting. Norvo recorded with the two of them on the obscure Comet label.

When critics accused the beboppers of being fast-playing exhibitionists, Parker and Gillespie showed that they could play ballads beautifully, too. For an example, compare Gillespie's "I Can't Get Started" to Bunny Berigan's early classic treatment of the same tune.

Others dismissed the beboppers for their use of drugs. Bird's heroin arrests were publicized widely, and despite his insistence that his creativity did not depend on chemicals, a few of his disciples began to emulate his drug habit.

The originators of bebop were all African-Americans, and some of them wanted to keep it exclusively black music. However, Parker and Gillespie had played with whites in their early groups, and the music eventually influenced all of jazz, including big bands. Once controversial, bebop now is one of the standard ways of playing jazz.

41. Pete Johnson & Al Ammons

CUTTIN' THE BOOGIE

May 7, 1941

Not included on CD, see note

WIN: Two-piano boogie-woogie played by top practitioners. The music is fast, swinging, and inventive.

This track is not included on the accompanying CDs because of space limitations. It is available on ASV5305, "Albert Ammons, Boogie Woogie Man."

Victor Records jumped on the boogie-woogie bandwagon by pairing two of its finest players for some four-handed two-piano jazz. In 1939. Johnson and Ammons had joined Meade Lux Lewis as a trio on Blue Note records. Now they waxed eight sides in duet for Victor. "Cuttin' The Boogie" is typical of the fine work they did for this 78rpm album.

Both of these men played all styles of piano, but on this album they confined themselves to boogie-woogie, very popular at the time. Ammons was the father of saxophonist Gene who came to public attention later in the Billy Eckstine Orchestra.

These records were full of life and great fun. The album was surprisingly popular for a two-piano jazz work, probably because it was advertised as music for dancing. Boogie-woogie's origins in the turpentine camps in the South and its travels on the freight trains coming North, ended when it settled in the juke joints of Harlem. By 1941 however, boogie-woogie was a hot item in the posh clubs of Manhattan.

Victor commissioned original artwork for the cover of this album. Many artists designed the covers of jazz albums, well into the LP era, with many of their works reaching the level of fine art.

42. Gene Krupa & His Orchestra

LET ME OFF UPTOWN

Vocals: Anita O'Day and Roy Eldridge

May 8, 1941

CD 2, Track 14

WIN: Backed by the powerhouse Krupa band, Anita O'Day and Roy Eldridge conduct a jazz dialogue, and then show off their considerable vocal and trumpet skills on this big band jewel.

After leaving Benny Goodman, drummer Gene Krupa formed his own group. It reached a creative peak in this period, when singer Anita O'Day and trumpeter Roy Eldridge joined the band.

With Krupa's drums providing the rhythmic force, the honors on this track belong to O'Day and Eldridge, whose vocal and trumpet solos propel this swing-era classic.

The hottest of the white female singers, O'Day influenced a whole generation of vocalists. She later sang with Stan Kenton and then as a single. She was considered, in the mid-'40s, to be the "most hip," i.e., up-to-date and savvy, of the female singers.

In a film about her, critic Will Friedwald said, "When you think about the great jazz singers, I would think that Anita is the only white woman that belongs in the same breath as Ella Fitzgerald and Billie Holiday and Sarah Vaughan."

As a black player with white bands, Eldridge endured many humiliations on the road, particularly in finding food and lodging. At some theaters, where his name was on the marquee, "Little Jazz" had to enter through a rear door. Undaunted, Eldridge played with Krupa and Artie Shaw and then led his own band in this period.

43. Claude Thornhill & His Orchestra
SNOWFALL
May 21, 1941
CD 2, Track 15

WIN: Jazz, as heard on this record, can be beautiful. This lovely orchestral velvet curtain is set off by Thornhill's solo piano, creating an impressionistic musical picture of a winter scene.

Although Thornhill's background was in jazz, he borrowed heavily from modern classical music and its instruments. On his gorgeous theme, "Snowfall," against the entire orchestra's wall of sound, he provides a sensitive and unadorned piano solo. Gunther Schuller called this tune an "hypnotic, impressionistic tone 'poemlet.'"

Thornhill's lush sounds, and his use of instruments rarely heard in dance bands, were imitated often by other bands of the day. Before forming his own band, Thornhill had been much in demand, as a pianist for big bands and small jazz groups, and as an accompanist for some of the major singers.

He played piano on many of Billie Holiday's recordings. In 1937, he had a big hit with his arrangement of a swing version of "Loch Lomond" for Maxine Sullivan. It started a trend of swinging folk tunes.

Thornhill did most of his own arranging until Gil Evans joined him in early 1942. After a few years with Thornhill, Evans went on to collaborate with Miles Davis. The historic "Birth of the Cool" and other important sessions followed.

Claude Thornhill and his music were "laid-back" and "cool" before those terms were in common usage. "Snowfall" was a prime example.

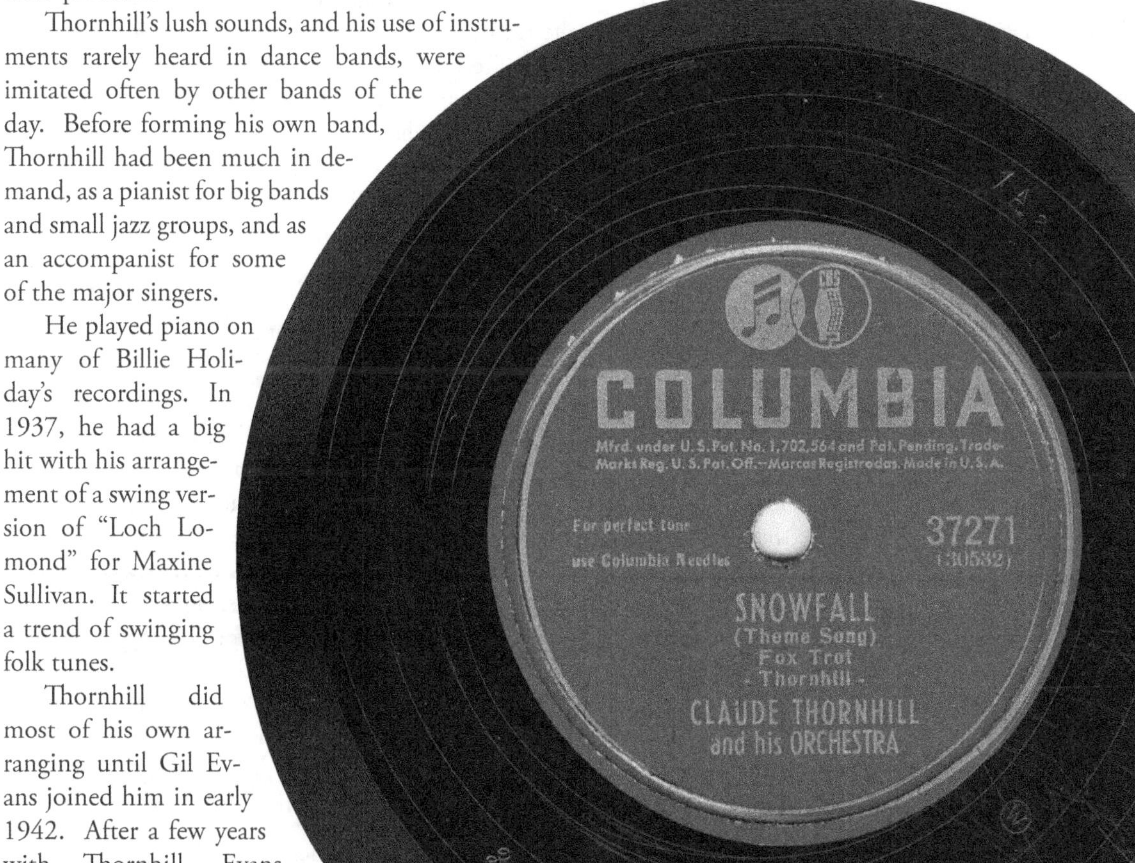

The Repertoire

When Thornhill, Basie, Shaw, and Miller composed their own theme songs, these compositions became part of everyone's rich and varied repertoire. Dozens of big band instrumentals were created every month. One problem was to find titles for them all.

Many original instrumentals were dedicated to the pace-setting bands, particularly to their "royalty." In France Alix Combelle recorded "Rock-A-Bye Basie," and composer Mary Lou Williams honored "The Count" with her composition for the Andy Kirk band. Sonny Burke contributed "The Count Basically," while Charlie Barnet gave a nod to his two heroes with "The Count's Idea" and "The Duke's Idea." Burke introduced Lunceford to Basie in "Jimmie Meets The Count," and Erskine Hawkins, "the Twentieth Century Gabriel," introduced himself to Ellington on "Gabriel Meets The Duke." Mel Powell saluted Earl Hines with "The Earl," which he arranged for both the Goodman and Hines bands.

Compositions sometimes referred to the places where the bands played. Ellington did the "Sherman Shuffle" (Chicago hotel) and Jan Savitt the "Meadowbrook Shuffle" (New Jersey ballroom). Charlie Barnet recorded "Leapin' At The Lincoln" (New York hotel), and Fats Waller "Pantin' In The Panther Room" (Chicago hotel). Nor did the bands forget their radio friends who spun the records. Glenn Miller toasted Martin Block with a 1940 recording of "Make-Believe Ballroom." Meanwhile, Barnet saluted the fictional "Stay Up Stan, The All-Night Record Man;" Lionel Hampton recorded "Jivin' With Jarvis" for Al Jarvis, a West Coast record spinner.

They paid homage also to the jukeboxes. George Auld recorded "Juke Box Jump," Sonny Dunham "The Nickel Serenade," and Jimmy Dorsey "Hep-Tee-Hootie, The Juke Box Jive." But Glenn Miller came up with the biggest of the coin machine hits, "Juke Box Saturday Night."

Ellington wasn't the only one who wrote concertos for his players. Many instrumentals were written for particular musicians. "Solo Flight" (originally "Chonk, Charlie, Chonk") was written for Benny Goodman's Charlie Christian and "Clarinet a la King" and "Clarinade" for Goodman himself.

Often a sideman or arranger in a band would contribute compositions. Buck Clayton, Harry Edison, and Herschal Evans wrote numbers for Count Basie that became standards for other bands. Edgar Sampson penned "Blue Lou," "Stompin' At The Savoy," and "Don't Be That Way" for Chick Webb, all of which were recorded by many other bands. Arranger Jerry Gray wrote "String of Pearls" for Miller (Record 46). Many of the early Fletcher Henderson originals, such as "Down South Camp Meeting" and "Wrappin' It Up," were rearranged for Goodman. Sy Oliver did the same for Tommy Dorsey with "Blue Blazes" and others that he wrote originally for Lunceford.

The bands and combos also dug back into jazz literature. Jelly Roll Morton's "King Porter Stomp," W.C. Handy's "St. Louis Blues," and Scott Joplin's "Maple Leaf Rag" were in the books of many bands. Miller converted Lucky Roberts' piano specialty, "Ripples of The Nile," into "Moonlight Cocktail" and turned the traditional song "Long, Long Ago" into "Don't Sit Under The Apple Tree."

The Dixielanders— Muggsy Spanier, Eddie Condon, and Lu Watters— mixed '20s tunes with New Orleans and Chicago standards. (The same tunes were sometimes played in widely different styles. In this period, for example, there were two excellent recordings of "Mandy, Make Up Your Mind:" one by Spanier's small group and the other a superb Sy Oliver arrangement for Tommy Dorsey's big band.)

As mentioned earlier, the ASCAP-BMI dispute intensified the search for traditional music, but the hunt had begun before that and continued afterward. New Orleans Revival groups loved such spirituals and hymns as "Just A Closer Walk With Thee" and "When The Saints Go Marching In." The big bands adapted "Swing Low, Sweet Chariot" and others. Some unlikely tunes from early in the century entered the jazz repertory, notably Victor Herbert's "Indian Summer" and Franz Lehar's "Lover Come Back To Me." As war clouds gathered, bands recorded patriotic marches such as "The Caissons Go Rolling Along," "The Marines' Hymn," and "American Patrol."

Most bands had their rhumbas and sambas; Xavier Cugat played little else. Ellington, Shaw, and Krupa incorporated Latin themes, and Jimmy Dorsey scored with Latin vocals. Still others recorded satires on Latin themes, such as "Six Lessons From Madame Lazonga."

Broadway and Hollywood musicals and Tin Pan Alley provided quality songs for vocalists Billy Holiday, Lee Wiley, Peggy Lee, Mildred Bailey, and others. Bailey's records over just a few months indicate a rich variety of sources and composers: a spiritual; "Sometimes I Feel Like A Motherless Child;" "All The Things You Are," by Kern & Hammerstein; "Easy To Love," by Cole Porter; "Fools Rush In," by Bloom & Mercer; "Rockin' Chair" and "Georgia On My Mind" by Hoagy Carmichael; "Lover Come Back To Me" by Franz Lehar; "It's So Peaceful In The Country" by Alec Wilder; "All Too Soon" by Duke Ellington; "Sometimes I'm Happy" and "More Than You Know," by Vincent Youmans; and a Rachmaninoff theme was turned into "I Think Of You."

Benny Goodman once doubted that Cole Porter's sophisticated music would be accepted in small-town Altoona, Pennsylvania. But jazz musicians had long relied on his fellow songwriting giant, George Gershwin. Gershwin's "I Got Rhythm" was a great favorite, both in its original form and in rearrangments such as "Lester Leaps In" and "Cotton Tail." It later appeared as "Apple Honey," "Red Cross," and "Olio." (Even today, leaders often kick off their group's play by saying, "Rhythm changes," which calls for variations on the Gershwin tune.)

In the '30s, "Honeysuckle Rose" had been the national anthem of jazz; in the mid '40s the new choice became "How High The Moon." The lyrics to these and many other showtunes might be forgotten, but jazz musicians improvised on the melodies.

An occasional item from abroad crept into the repertoire. The Irish contributed "Londonderry Air" ("Danny Boy") which became leader Bobby Byrne's theme song. A Swedish folk ditty, "The Hut Sut Song," was a novelty hit in 1941. Many bands had arrangements of the Russian folk song, "Dark Eyes."

Adaptations of the Italian folk song "Sorrento" were recorded, with a couple of sets of lyrics. Artie Shaw and Paul Robeson both recorded "Gloomy Sunday," a Hungarian song so depressing that it was blamed for suicides. Surely the most unusual imports were the four Shapearean sonnets recorded by Bob Crosby in 1939. During one of these, "Blow, Blow, Thou Winter Winds," one of the Bob Cats cries out, "Oh, blow that thing!," echoing the famous shout from "Dipper Mouth Blues." (The 78rpm labels credit these sonnets to Arthur Young and William Shakespeare, in that order!)

Another source was Jewish folk music. "Bei Mir Bist Du Schoen" was the first hit from this source. Others followed– Ziggy Elman's "Fralich in Swing" became "And The Angels Sing" (with lyrics by Johnny Mercer, former Episcopalian choir boy from Savannah). "Yes, My Darling Daughter" and "My Little Cousin" are other examples of Jewish music.

Many popular songs were transformed to instrumentals; many instrumentals were later given words. This happened to many Ellington works, such as "Concerto For Cootie" and "Never No Lament;" they became the hit songs "Do Nothin' Till You Hear From Me" and "Don't Get Around Much Anymore." "String of Pearls," "Jersey Bounce," and "Opus One" were other instrumentals belatedly given lyrics. Often songs got new titles as well. After crooner Bing Crosby heard his brother Bob's band instrumental recording of "I'm Free," he commissioned lyrics. The new creation became "What's New?"

Johnny Mercer with composer Harold Arlen contributed "Blues In The Night" to the jazzman's repertoire. It did not follow the blues structure, but it became a jazz standard. In 1942 Billie Holiday recorded Mercer's salute to his own daughter, "Mandy Is Two." Columbia must have forgotten about this little gem since they didn't release it until the real Mandy was 22!

Bands selected compositions that fit their own styles or that could be improvised upon. Because jazz is a performer's art, the composition is usually secondary. The players drew freely on the blues, spirituals, folk tunes, classical compositions, Broadway and Hollywood songs, and the originals from their own bands. They needed them all to meet the demand. However, each band had its own emphasis:

- Ellington favored his and Billy Strayhorn's compositions, some of the best of which were produced in this period, e.g., "In A Mellotone," "Take The A Train," "Cotton Tail," "C Jam Blues," "Just A Sittin' and A Rockin."

- Basie played the blues – old, new, fast, slow, vocal, instrumental, original, big band, small group: "Jump The Blues Away," "Goin' To Chicago," "Harvard Blues," "Sugar Blues."

- Tommy Dorsey played many Tin Pan Alley tunes, making them sound mellow. He admitted in *Down Beat* in June 1941 that, like many other bands, he was trying to sound more like Jimmie Lunceford. Hiring Lunceford arranger Sy Oliver brought him closer to that objective.

- Artie Shaw concentrated on high-quality Broadway, Tin Pan Alley, and semi-classical compositions: "Oh, Lady Be Good," "Temptation," "April In Paris," "Dancing In The Dark," "It Had To Be You." Apparently he'd developed enough clout with these to avoid recording the thin pop tunes of the day.

- Goodman's sources were often the black bands and the black composers: "Jumpin' At The Woodside," "Stealin' Apples," "Honeysuckle Rose," "Why Don't You Do Right."

By 1940, jazz musicians had a rich and varied musical spectrum to draw from. Of course, this contributed to the successes of this period. It contrasts greatly with the short list of novelties and originals that the Original Dixieland Jass Band had to draw on for the first jazz recordings in 1917. In just 23 years American music had increased in quantity, quality, and diversity, and jazz had grown with it. Jazz musicians today still rely heavily on the compositions from this period and the myriad ways of playing the music.

April 9 legal note
Boogie-woogie pianist Meade Lux Lewis recorded "Yancey Special" as a tribute to fellow pianist, Jimmy Yancey. Yancey sued Lewis for stealing his material. The judge asked Lewis where he got the tune; he replied, "It came to me in a dream."

April 17 war victim
Singer Al Bowlly died from a bomb dropped during an air raid on London. A handsome South African with a rich, virile baritone voice, he made hundreds of records and sang with Ray Noble's orchestras both in England and the U.S. Bowlly's records still show one of the few male singers of the period who sang with intelligence and feeling.

April 18 recording
Sidney Bechet & His One Man Band, "The Sheik" and "Blues of Bechet." A remarkable technical feat for this period, Bechet played six instruments – clarinet, soprano sax, tenor sax, piano, bass and drums. He had to record one instrument, then overdub the next, then the next, etc., an awkward process compared to today's use of electronic mixing technology. The sound quality of the final recording is fuzzy, but it does show off the virtuosity of this jazz giant.

June movie role
Ella Fitzgerald played a maid in "Ride 'Em Cowboy," an Abbott and Costello comedy. She sang two numbers and made the most of a small role, according to *Down Beat*. During the filming her band played the Orpheum Theater in Hollywood.

44. Ella Fitzgerald
& Her Famous Orchestra
I GOT IT BAD (AND THAT AIN'T GOOD)
July 31, 1941
CD 2, Track 16

WIN: Ella Fitzgerald sings a composition by Duke Ellington. Two of the most famous names in American music bring us a delightful treat.

Bandleader Chick Webb died in June, 1939. A fine drummer (musician-writer Gunther Schuller says he was "without doubt" the best big-band drummer), Webb headed a band that had been featured since 1933 at the Savoy Ballroom in Harlem. His are the first recordings of such jazz standards as "Blue Lou," "Stompin' At the Savoy," and "Don't Be That Way." Upon his death in 1939, a young singer he had discovered was chosen to be the nominal leader of the band; Ella Fitzgerald and Her Famous Orchestra picked up where Webb left off and traveled and recorded for two years. This recording is from their last session.

On this side Ella sings the poignant lyrics; her reading is earthy, but dignified, and perfect for the beautiful Ellington melody.

Ella Fitzgerald was billed as the "First Lady of Song," and she carried that title with grace and dignity into the 1990s. In her personal appearances she was charming and modest. She sang with the emotion appropriate to the song, whether tenderness, sorrow, humor, or authority. She did fine uptempo and scat (wordless vocal) turns. The "first lady" indeed.

45. Stan Kenton's Orchestra

ADIOS

September 11, 1941

Not included on CD, see note

WIN: Stan Kenton's first nationally-distributed work, a Latin-American tune of the day converted into a staccato classic, shows a musical style which will soon make him a major figure in jazz.

This track is not included on the accompanying CDs because of space limitations. It is available on Jazz Archives 159182, "Stan Kenton."

Kenton's West Coast-based band was two years away from a hit record, but this track shows that his affinity for Latin-American tunes and his distinctive staccato-arranging style are already in place. He does not yet have the top soloists he would hire later. While "Adios" is somewhat repetitive, the piece compares favorably with other big band recordings of the composition.

Kenton was a fine pianist in the Earl Hines tradition and his playing, arranging, and outgoing personality had been attracting attention in southern California. His big breakthrough came in late 1943 with recordings of "Artistry in Rhythm" and "Eager Beaver" for Capitol Records.

In later years, Kenton was an evangelist for what he called "progressive jazz," a term which never did come into general usage ("modern jazz" was the term used more often at the time). Traditionalists resented his references to their "more primitive forms." Dixielander Eddie Condon compared Kenton's group to a Prussian marching band, i.e., too big and too brassy! Notice that Decca bills Kenton as "Stanley."

46. Glenn Miller & His Orchestra
STRING OF PEARLS
November 3, 1941
CD 2, Track 17

WIN: The most popular big band of the period shows off with a hot instrumental piece. The track's simple melody, tight ensembles, and inventive solos make it a model of big band jazz at its best.

Here the most popular of all the dance orchestras is hard-swinging and loose. This track is an up-tempo adaptation of the familiar Miller reed blending– a clarinet leading alto saxophones, while a tenor saxophone plays the melody an octave lower.

"String of Pearls" is not a complex composition. In their liner notes for the *Smithsonian Collection of Big Band Jazz*, Gunther Schuller and Martin Williams noted: "This piece has a main melody that is virtually no melody, barely even a riff, and is for most people absolutely memorable once it is heard."

Jerry Gray's arrangement of his own composition features two short exchanges, or "duels," between the saxes, but solo honors belong to Bobby Hackett, whose brief (less than thirty seconds) improvised cornet solo is still regarded as a classic. Whitney Balliett put it this way: "The most famous solo ever played on a Glenn Miller recording is this exquisite twelve-bar statement on cornet in 'String of Pearls.'" (On radio broadcasts in this period, Miller alerts the audience to listen for Hackett's solo.)

In addition to Hackett, Miller had added other good jazz musicians to his band. Billie May brought his trumpet and arranging skills, and Ernie Caceres played baritone saxophone, an instrument which broadened the ensemble sound. This is the Miller band at its very best.

47. Jimmy Dorsey & His Orchestra
TANGERINE
Vocals: Bob Eberly & Helen O'Connell
December 10, 1941
CD 2, Track 18

WIN: Two of the best big band vocalists sing two versions of a catchy pop tune. In addition, the bandleader's alto sax interlude and the clever lyrics by Johnny Mercer stand out.

This track was a sampler of Jimmy Dorsey & His Orchestra during the playing of one tune. It followed the format used on his radio shows to introduce the singers and the leader. "Tangerine" starts with a slow vocal chorus featuring the rich baritone of Bob Eberly, then an up-tempo alto saxophone solo by the leader, followed by the sexy voice of Helen O'Connell doing an alternate set of lyrics. This formula scored on several earlier records including "Green Eyes," one of three Dorsey million sellers in 1941.

The lyrics to "Tangerine" were written by Johnny Mercer for the Dorsey band's appearance in the film, *The Fleet's In*. (In this period, no major musicial was complete without the appearance of a big band.) Mercer applied the formula developed in "Green Eyes," "Yours," and "Amapola." His lyrics topped them all. (To Eberly's straight line, "And I've seen toasts to Tangerine raised in every bar across the Argentine," O'Connell responds, "And I've seen clothes on Tangerine where the label says from Macy's Mezzanine.")

Years later Jimmy and brother Tommy joined together to introduce a new singer– Elvis Presley.

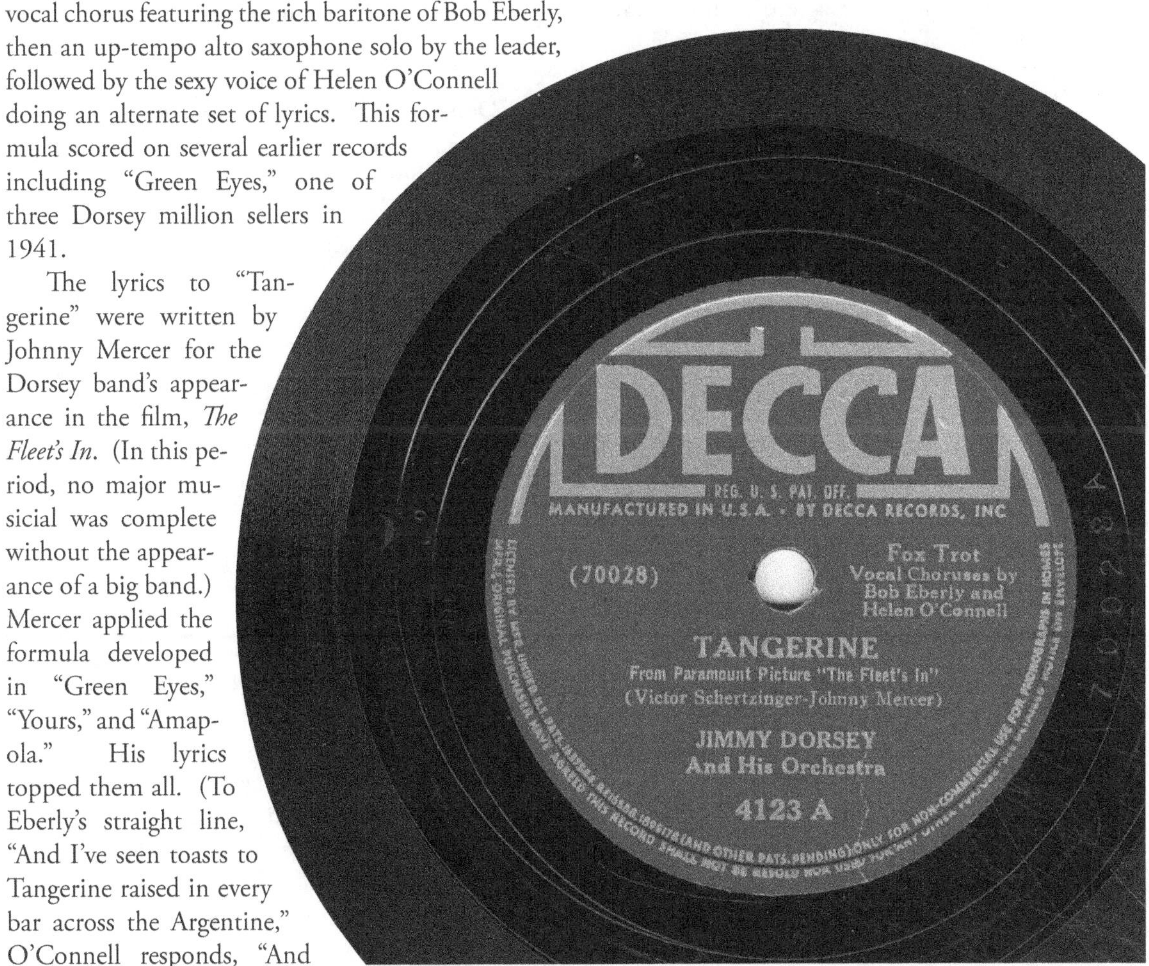

The "Boy" Singers

During 1941, Bob Eberly sang on three one-million-selling records with Jimmy Dorsey: "Green Eyes," "Amapola," and "Maria Elena." He was the top male vocalist of the day, although in that year, he had a challenger. Frank Sinatra, singing then with Tommy Dorsey's band, admired Eberly's singing, but he was worried that Bob would go out as a single before he could, and thus corner the "boy" singer market. (No matter how old they were, vocalists were called "boy" and "girl" singers.)

In 1935 Eberly had replaced Bob Crosby as the male vocalist in the Dorsey Brothers Orchestra, and he stayed with the band when Tommy left and the band became Jimmy's. For the next couple of years Eberly was virtually unnoticed, since the Dorsey band backed Bing Crosby on his radio show and Bing did all the vocals.

Among others, former Dorsey Brothers arranger Glenn Miller remembered Eberly's rich voice and good looks. When Miller was forming his own band he asked Bob, in effect, "Are there any more at home like you?" Bob said he had a brother, Ray, who didn't sing, but Miller hired him anyway as his male vocalist. The critics who reviewed Miller's early band agreed with Bob about his brother's singing. (Ray used the regular spelling of the family name – Eberle.)

In the 1939-42 period both brothers were great favorites with the fans. Critics praised Bob's big, deep voice and tasteful phrasing. Dorsey's accompaniments and tempos made Eberly sound even better. Brother Ray wasn't as lucky; on most records, his higher voice strained to overcome Miller's "businessman's bounce" tempos. In his last few recordings before Miller fired him, with tempos slowed and backgrounds subdued, he sounded more relaxed and confident, e.g. "Elmer's Tune," "Moonlight Cocktail," "Serenade in Blue," and "At Last."

Neither of the brothers had much of a career after the Big Band era– only occasional appearances on Big Band-nostalgia TV shows. Other "boy" singers fared much better, with Frank Sinatra as the prime example. He benefited from the superb settings Tommy Dorsey provided for singers, and from the lessons he learned from TD's sound and phrasing. In the introduction to George Simon's *The Big Bands*, Sinatra is quoted as saying that his big band experience provided him with an on-the-road college education.

Probably the best-trained "boy" singer, and the one with the best natural voice, was Dick Haymes. He replaced Sinatra in both the Harry James and Tommy Dorsey bands, with a brief stint with Benny Goodman in between. He had some success with radio, recordings, and films, but later succumbed to the tangled life of a celebrity with multiple marriages and self-abuse. (The movie star Rita Hayworth was one of his many wives.) After his band days Haymes signed with Decca records around the same time that Sinatra went with Columbia. This left Victor without a major singer, so they searched for a refugee from the big bands and found a gem. Perry Como had been the singer in the sweet Ted Weems band. With this gimmicky band he had had no chance to apply his deep, rich baritone voice to the slow ballads which became his trademark while at Victor. Later he became one of the top stars of television.

One of the few black band singers to achieve later popular success was Billy Eckstine (Record 53). (Nat "King" Cole was an even bigger star, but he had not come from one of the bands.) Eckstine sang with the Earl Hines orchestra, which became Eckstine's and later evolved into the "incubator of be-bop." As "Mr. B," Eckstine was a popular vocalist and in the '50s his records often topped the charts.

The singers and the leaders attracted some of most beautiful women of the day. Sinatra, Haymes, Harry James, Artie Shaw and Charlie Barnet were married a total of 25 times to these glamorous women and more: Rita Hayworth, Betty Grable, Lana Turner, Evelyn Keyes, and Kathleen Windsor. Ava Gardner was married to Shaw and then Sinatra. In many ways, these men lived as rock stars do today.

Brothers Tommy (l) and Jimmy Dorsey.

48. Lu Watter's Yerba Buena Jazz Band
MUSKRAT RAMBLE
December 19, 1941
Not included on CD, see note

WIN: This brassy, swaggering side is a wonderful example of the skills of the group who led the New Orleans Revival on the West Coast.

This track is not included on the accompanying CDs because of space limitations. It is available on Living Era CD AJA 5550, "Lu Watters and his Yerba Buena Jazz Band Play Good Time Music, San Francisco Style."

These young San Franciscans re-invigorated this old tune by jazz pioneer Kid Ory. The two-trumpet front line of Bob Scobey and Watters recalled both the early brass bands and the Joe "King" Oliver-Louis Armstrong collaboration. The group also included future stars Turk Murphy on trombone, Wally Rose on piano, and Clancy Hayes on banjo. Together they give this old tune a rousing ride through the polyphonic thickets. Characteristic of New Orleans Revival groups, they are much freer with the beat and do not stick to the rigid two-beat and four-beat rhythms of old.

The composition's original title was "Muscat Ramble" (for the grape from which muscatel wine is made), evolved to "Muskat," and then to "Muskrat." Early records have the second word as both "Ramble" and "Scramble." It is periodically revived, including efforts to add or change lyrics and/or the title.

This group is often credited with leading the New Orleans Revival, and they certainly were the West Coast leaders. They played with great skill and energy, and they left an exceptional group of high-quality recordings.

49. Harry James & His Orchestra
THE MOLE
December 30, 1941
CD 2, Track 19

WIN: Harry James' band performs his own composition. This elegant arrangement, with the string section carrying the melody and backed by the prominent sounds of a baritone saxophone, is a big band classic.

Trumpeter Harry James had left Benny Goodman in 1938 and now led one of the top big bands. James' big selling records gave little indication of his jazz ability. Realist that he was, he cashed in on syrupy tunes, virtuoso trickery, or pretentious instrumentals. He had paid his jazz dues, however, playing hot trumpet on records with Goodman, Lionel Hampton, Teddy Wilson, and on many of his own big band instrumentals.

This record's unusual arrangement occurs during the first chorus, in which the strings carry the melody and the horns play behind them. Also, the low sounds of the baritone saxophone are very prominent and, mixed with the strings, make a fine combination. Unlike some leaders, James believed that strings could swing!

"The Mole" was chosen by Martin Williams and Gunther Schuller for their select *Smithsonian Collection of Big Band Jazz*, an honor indeed. They bemoaned the later loss of strings in the big bands, "...strings in bands had to go, because after the mid-'40s few could afford them."

The James band was playing very well and, at Glenn Miller's suggestion, it replaced his group on the popular Chesterfield radio program when Miller entered the Army.

♪ SONGS OF OUR TIMES ♪

Jimmy Dorsey, Glenn Miller, Artie Shaw, and Harry James all recorded million-sellers in 1941; Dorsey had three. (Benny Goodman, for all his success, wouldn't record a gold record until the next year.)

Dorsey's mega-hits all had a Latin flavor and featured Bob Eberly; Helen O'Connell joined him on "Amapola" and "Green Eyes," but he sang "Maria Elena" alone. All were 35-cent blue label Deccas. Victor scored with Miller's "Chattanooga Choo Choo," Vaughan Monroe's theme, "Racing With The Moon," and Freddie Martin's version of a Tschaikovsky piano concerto, all on 35-cent Bluebird. Shaw's winner, "Dancing In The Dark," was released on the 50-cent Victor label.

Harry James soared to the top of the charts with the syrupy and sentimental "You Made Me Love You," and Ray Noble scored with an update of "By The Light of The Silvery Moon." Both were released by Columbia. Rounding out the honor list were two hillbilly (later called country-and-western) records and a Kate Smith novelty vocal.

The Academy Award-winning song in 1941 was "The Last Time I Saw Paris," the Kern-Hammerstein memory of Paris before the German Army entered. Also nominated were "Blues In the Night," "Boogie Woogie Bugle Boy," and "Chattanooga Choo Choo." 1941 has been called the year America held its breath. With the attack on Pearl Harbor the waiting was over. The war would change everything, including the music.

October 6 many versions
Time magazine reported jukeboxes were playing more Tchaikovsky than ever. Played by a classical pianist in a Mary Astor movie, his "Piano Concerto in B Flat" had drawn praise. Freddy Martin and Woody Herman next recorded it without lyrics. Guy Lombardo called his record "Concerto" and Tony Martin made his vocal version, "Tonight We Love." Finally, Claude Thornhill adapted it as "Concerto for Two."

October 18 Your Hit Parade
"I Don't Want to Set the World on Fire" was the most popular song in the nation, according to the radio program, "Your Hit Parade." It was certainly a popular hope. The tune remained atop the poll for four weeks and among the top ten through the end of the year.

December 30 recording
Xavier Cugat & His Waldorf-Astoria Orchestra, "Brazil." Cugat dressed his band in colorful costumes and featured pretty vocalists. In spite of the show-biz glitter, the band recorded a number of tasteful arrangements and this track is one of them.

Glenn Miller playing trombone.

March 25 recording
The Three Deuces, "Deuces Wild." Clarinetist Pee Wee Russell, pianist Joe Sullivan, and drummer Zutty Singleton recorded four first-class sides in the congenial setting of Commodore Records.

April 23 recording
Lil Green, "Why Don't You Do Right" released on Bluebird's blues label. Singer Peggy Lee heard the record and convinced Benny Goodman to record the tune in July 1942; it became Goodman's first million-seller (Record 55). Lil Green's version was later paired with her 1940 record, "Romance In The Dark," another tune made famous by other artists, including Billie Holiday.

May 7 tradition continued
Cootie Williams & His Orchestra, "West End Blues." Recorded with a group from the Benny Goodman band, Williams honored Louis Armstrong's 1928 classic recording with a note-for-note reproduction of Louis' introduction.

May 26 recording
Bing Crosby and Jack Teagarden recorded with a young Mary Martin, a Broadway newcomer. In 1939, *Variety* speculated that Martin might be just a "one-record star;" she'd had a hit with "My Heart Belongs To Daddy!" Yet she went on to dominate Broadway musicals and made many more hit records.

June 19 Americans abroad
Willie Lewis and His Negro Band, an American group which spent the '30s leading the good life in Europe, continued to record in Zurich for the Swiss Elite label – "Old Man River," "Body And Soul," and "Christmas Night in Harlem."

July 3 recording
Two Ellington small bands tried some new compositions. Johnny Hodges led a group in the first recording of "Things Ain't What They Used To Be." Rex Stewart waxed "Subtle Slough," which, with words, became "Just Squeeze Me" (not to be confused with Fats Waller's "Squeeze Me").

July 5 novelty hit
"The Hut Sut Song," the year's top novelty song, reached the number one spot on "Your Hit Parade."

July 7 recording
Jack Teagarden led the final session of his debt-ridden big band. Appropriately, the last number recorded was "Nobody Knows The Trouble I've Seen!"

July 17 last session
Pianist Mary Lou Williams made her last recordings with Andy Kirk & His Twelve Clouds of Joy. As a composer and an arranger she was the most influential woman in jazz. In addition to her job with Kirk, she arranged for Ellington, Goodman, and others. Her compositions included 'Roll 'Em," "Little Joe From Chicago," and, in 1945, her "Zodiac Suite," which is still played today. Williams later composed additional longer works, including at least one Mass, and served as mentor to younger players such as Errol Garner and Thelonius Monk.

August 2 song hit
"Daddy" began a six-week reign at the top of radio's "Your Hit Parade." The "Swing and Sway with Sammy Kaye" band had the top recording.

September 26 Andy Kirk scores
Andy Kirk and his Twelve Clouds of Joy were held over after filling 52nd St.'s Famous Door for four weeks. The hot band was making four network broadcasts a week and drawing critical attention. In Harlem, at the Savoy, the feature was the International Sweethearts of Rhythm, one of the few all-female jazz bands.

October 1 recording
Fats Waller & His Rhythm, "Buck Jumpin'." This track showcased the considerable talents of guitarist Al Casey. Featured on numerous Waller sides, Casey continued to play the acoustic guitar at a time when many players were switching over to amplification. Casey was yet another example of the dozens of fine musicians who only occasionally came to public attention.

October 1 unusual pairing
Count Basie and His Orchestra, "King Joe." This two-sided salute to heavyweight boxing champion Joe Louis featured vocalist Paul Robeson. A former Phi Beta Kappa and football All-American at Rutgers, Columbia law graduate, then Broadway actor and concert singer, it was unfortunate that Robeson's magnificent voice couldn't break out of its classical restraints to sing this number as the blues should be sung.

December 6 Your Hit Parade
"Tonight We Love" reached number one on "Your Hit Parade." Runners-up were "Elmer's Tune," "Chattanooga Choo-Choo," and "Shepherd's Serenade."

Chapter Five

Don't Sit Under the Apple Tree

January 19 recording
Frank Sinatra was still with Tommy Dorsey but made four recordings under his own name: "The Lamplighter's Serenade," "Night and Day," "The Song is You," and "The Night We Called It A Day." The accompanying group, including strings, was led by arranger Axel Stordhal, who went with Sinatra when he left Tommy Dorsey later in 1942. Sinatra didn't leave for another six months, but this session was his first step in gaining control over every aspect of his career. (See Appendix D for other singers, instrumentalists, and leaders who were starting their careers.)

January 21 recording
On the same day that Basie made his second recording of "One O'Clock Jump," Duke Ellington continued his string of outstanding sides with "Perdido," "C Jam Blues," and "Moon Mist." The latter featured the violin of Ray Nance, an unusual sound on an Ellington disc. At his next session the Duke recorded "What Am I Here For," the theme used on the NPR radio program, "Jazz Revisited."

January 24 Your Hit Parade
"The White Cliffs of Dover" was tops, according to "Your Hit Parade." It would retain the spot for six of the next seven weeks. The sentimental lyrics expressed hope for the end of the war.

January recording
Les Hite & His Orchestra, "Jersey Bounce." Because of Dizzy Gillespie's trumpet solo, some writers cite this as the first recorded bebop. Gunther Schuller wrote, "Dizzy Gillespie was the first to break the sixteenth-note sound barrier on trumpet, as can be heard on (this) recording."

1942

As historian Geoffrey Perrett put it, "The war came as a surprise that was expected." Gone now were the pretenses of undeclared war. In 1942, President Roosevelt called for production of 60,000 planes, 45,000 tanks, 20,000 anti-aircraft guns, and six million tons of merchant ships. The $58 million national budget included more than $52 million for the war effort.

The news from abroad was disturbing. The White House took months to reveal the extent of the naval losses at Pearl Harbor, but the newspapers told of Japanese conquests of Singapore, Manila, and the Dutch West Indies. Australia was bombed. When the Philippines surrendered in March, General Douglas MacArthur escaped and promised to return.

Patriotic Americans rushed to buy War Bonds and Stamps. Yet, in spite of early predictions, bond sales fell far short of "financing the war." The drives did more for civilian morale than for the Treasury. By July the government was spending $150 million a day on the expenses of war.

The war brought about many changes. On January 1 the Rose Bowl football game was not played in Pasadena, California, for fear of Japanese attack on the West Coast. It was the only time, before or since, that it has not been held in its home stadium. For the 1942 Rose Bowl, Duke University hosted Oregon in Durham, North Carolina, and the visitors won.

♪ FOR THE GOOD OF YOUR COUNTRY ♪

British "Desert Rats" and their tanks attacked Italian troops in North Africa, forcing Germany to come to the aid of their Axis partner. In February the brilliant German General Erwin Rommel took command of the Afrika Korps in Tripoli and drove the British back. Later in the year, Americans showed up in Tripoli to reinforce the British.

FDR urged the American people to sacrifice. To win the war, everyone would pay in "hard work, sorrow, and blood." Indeed, many consumer goods were in short supply. For example, nylon stockings, introduced in October, 1939, were very scarce. Sugar was the first item rationed; before long coffee, shoes, gasoline, and tires were added to the list. Meat and canned goods would follow. Most grumbles centered on gasoline (most drivers were allowed just three gallons a week with a standard "A" card).

On February 10 the last automobile rolled off the Ford assembly line and all car production came to a halt. Owners babied their 34 million cars, knowing there wouldn't soon be replacements. One week after Pearl Harbor, on his popular network radio show, comedian Jack Benny was telling his chauffeur, Rochester, to conserve gas and tires on his ancient Maxwell. Yet even late in the war, nearly two-thirds of civilians admitted they were living better than they had during the 1930s. There were plenty of jobs, and savings were at an all-time high.

In addition to rationing gas and other supplies, Americans had to practice blackouts and air raid precautions amid reports of impending air attacks. (Glenn Miller even suggested undrafted bandsmen serve as air raid wardens, but no one picked up on this idea.) Civilian defense plans were in such a shambles that many felt Laurel and Hardy's movie called *Air Raid Wardens* – a slapstick comedy – was hardly an exaggeration.

Americans did do more for the war effort. Four of ten Americans did volunteer war work – collecting tin cans and kitchen grease, planting Victory gardens, scanning the skies for enemy aircraft, rolling bandages. *The Red Cross Handbook on First Aid* sold more than 8 million copies, mostly to people wanting to prepare for war injuries. Such ubiquitous activity was reflected in comic strips as well as in books and movies. Orphan Annie led scrap drives and organized junior spy chasers, while in the black *Chicago Defender*, Bungleton Green gave his wife coveralls instead of an Easter bonnet.

♪ WHY WAS I BORN? ♪

On January 29 in the *San Francisco Examiner*, columnist Henry McLemore urged the immediate removal of every Japanese-American from the West Coast. "Herd'em up, pack'em off, give'em the inside room in the Bad Lands. Let'em be pinched, hungry and dead up against it…Let us have no patience with the enemy or anyone whose veins carry his blood. Personally, I hate the Japanese. And that goes for all of them." He was not alone – many Americans wanted revenge for the attacks on Pearl Harbor.

In February, the government incarcerated 110,000 Americans of Japanese descent (two-thirds of them U.S. citizens). They went first to temporary quarters in places such as fairgrounds, and then to relocation centers further inland. Fears of sabotage spurred the removal. The evacuees could not return to the West Coast until 1945. (Despite this treatment, many young Japanese-American men enlisted in the U.S. armed services, some in the Army's "most decorated" division, others as interpreters in the Pacific, and in many other roles.) Pollsters found that 60 percent of Americans approved of jailing Japanese-American citizens, and 93 percent supported jailing those born in Japan. Forty years later Congress formally apologized to the victims and paid them modest reparations. But in the meantime, many lost homes, businesses, family, and friends that could never be replaced.

Black Americans still were frustrated by the government's reluctance to allow them to enlist in the military in any but menial positions. On May 9, an editorial in the *Baltimore Afro-American* demanded: "Give us a chance to fight!" It requested removal of all policies that restricted entry to jobs for the military. The *Pittsburgh Courier*, another prominent black paper, soon launched its "Double V" drive, signifying victory at home, over discrimination, as well as victory abroad.

♪ COLD IN HAND BLUES ♪

Once they overcame the spring mud, German soldiers resumed their Russian campaign, sweeping eastward all summer, only to be halted by winter weather in front of the city of Stalingrad. The weather was nearly as hellish across the United States that first spring of the war. Floods, tornadoes, and hailstorms lashed the country.

General James Doolittle led a daring air raid on Tokyo on April 18 using sixteen B-25s launched from an aircraft carrier. (The Japanese couldn't figure out where the planes came from; President Roosevelt would only say they came from "Shangri-la.") Three U.S. flyers died in crash landings and eleven others were captured by the Japanese. Their bombs did little damage but helped bolster American morale after 36,000 American defenders were captured in the Philippine Islands. Many died during forced marches; photos fueled American hatred for the Japanese.

On May 7 and 8, U.S. and Japanese forces fought the Battle of the Coral Sea, the first naval conflict in history in which the ships never sighted each other. Clearly, naval warfare after this would be airplanes against ships. The battle thwarted Japanese designs on Australia. How lucky for the U.S. that the aircraft carriers had not been in Pearl Harbor on December 7, for clearly these huge launching bases had replaced the battleship as the primary naval weapon.

Later that month, Cologne felt the wrath of the first massive Allied bombardment. On May 30 more than 1,000 RAF bombers rained bombs on the industrial center.

On June 4, at the Battle of Midway, the U.S. handed the Imperial Japanese Navy its first defeat in history, sinking four of their aircraft carriers. The Japanese never recovered from their loss at Midway, even though the bitter island-by-island struggle in the Pacific would last three more years.

Axis forces did come close to the United States, but only once. On June 28, the FBI captured eight German agents after they were landed by a U-boat on Long Island. All were swiftly tried and executed. It was the only "invasion" of American soil, although a Japanese submarine shelled the Oregon coast and a few balloon-bombs launched from Japan did make it across the Pacific to land in uninhabited U.S. forests.

♪ A WOMAN'S PREROGATIVE ♪

Because the war spurred a sense of shared national purpose and unity, many of the changes were accepted "for the duration." For the first time women drove buses, operated rivet guns, and poured molten steel. Women began wearing slacks in public; meanwhile, men's trousers lost their cuffs to save material.

The Women's Auxiliary Army Corps (WAAC) was established in May, the WAVES (Women Accepted for Voluntary Emergency Service) two months later. The Marines and Coast Guard soon added women's corps. Interestingly, no heroines from the radio soap operas ever donned a uniform, although the fictional Sallie Farrell and Stella Dallas went to work in war plants and the radio son of Ma Perkins was killed in the infantry.

♪ TAKE ME OUT TO ♪ THE BALL GAME

Deciding that baseball was vital to civilian morale, President Roosevelt granted teams travel concessions; however, enlistments and the draft were depleting the rosters. Familiar names were missing from the All-Star Game in New York on July 6. The next night, the American League team edged a team of former major leaguers in a benefit for the Army-Navy Relief Fund in Cleveland. That fall the St. Louis Cardinals would dethrone the New York Yankees as world champions.

Although in the early months of war the news was gloomy, civilians told pollsters they wanted accurate news, no matter how bad. Commentators like Gabriel Heatter, H.V. Kaltenborn, and Lowell Thomas tried to explain to listeners the meaning of battles in far-off places with unpronounceable names. Although there was no formal news censorship, print and broadcast media cleared war-related matters with Washington before broadcasting.

Broadcasters stopped weather reports, although no one seemed quite sure what threat they posed. The ban on amateur operators ("hams") made more sense since their equipment could be used by the enemy or by saboteurs to transmit sensitive information. On the commercial networks, comedies and variety shows were still the main network fare. Bob Hope and many of the bands on these shows originated their broadcasts from military bases and hospitals. Crime shows frequently focused on black marketers or ration book counterfeiters.

Americans hungered for entertainment in all media. They bought more books than ever. Each month they purchased nearly 2 million paperback books – and six times that many comic books. Even some newspaper comic strip heroes went to war. When Joe Palooka, the heavyweight champion of the funnies, entered the army, the public debated about whether he should go to Officer Candidate School. (He didn't.) Only a few readers protested when Pvt. Palooka shot a Nazi. Although Superman volunteered, he flunked his army physical. Why? His X-ray eyes read the chart in the next room.

Nearly 80 million went each week to the movies, and the typical admission was 25 cents. Of the 532 movies produced in 1942, none caused as much stir as *The Outlaw*. The Hays Office held up the film's release for five years because of the revealing clothing worn by the female lead, Jane Russell. Meanwhile Miss Russell's cleavage was the talk of the country.

♪ GET YOUR KICKS ♪ ON ROUTE 66

Despite gas rationing, dance bands were still traveling around the country. For example, during the 1941-42 school year the bands of Bunny Berigan, Orrin Tucker, Jimmie Lunceford, Les Brown, and Red

Norvo visited Ann Arbor and played for dancers at the University of Michigan. As on other campuses, students danced beneath patriotic red, white and blue decorations.

As band leaders had feared, they were losing many of their members to the draft. After polling locals of the musicians' union, *Down Beat* announced that 12 percent of members already had been drafted. The regional or "territorial" bands (local groups that didn't travel far from home) seem to have been hit hardest.

In the first few weeks after the attacks on Pearl Harbor, record sales dipped. By May, however, sales were back on track. Columbia discontinued its 35-cent Okehs, and Decca was threatening to stop issuing popular records for 35 cents. In both the U.S. and Europe old disks were being recalled and melted down for recycling and use as war materials.

♪ MUSIC MAKERS ♪

In spite of constant shifts in personnel, Benny Goodman's band continued to head *Down Beat's* list of swing bands; Glenn Miller was still the top sweet band. The Goodman Sextet was again the choice among small groups. (And yes, Lombardo was again elected "King of Corn.") More white fans were admiring Basie and Ellington.

"Swing" and "sweet" did not mean much anymore. In this period, bands such as Tommy Dorsey, Harry James, and Gene Krupa added strings to soften their hard-driving sounds. (Goodman and Ellington declined, insisting that strings dragged the beat.) On the sweet side the trend was in the opposite direction. The Jan Garber and Teddy Powell groups changed over to a swing style, while others, e.g., Kay Kyser, added jazz musicians and arrangers.

Shep Fields, whose opening theme included the sound of a soda straw blowing into a glass of water, formed an interesting but unsuccessful all-reed band, one still admired by many big band buffs. It was inspired by one of Paul Whiteman's groups; his "Sax Soctette" included eight reed players and a rhythm section. Fields' band sounded great, but had two strikes against it: the war and the AFM recording ban came along just as it was getting started.

Many sweet bands were doing just fine without changing. For example, Sammy Kaye announced in January that he had solid bookings all the way through 1942.

Down Beat changed the rules for selecting its All-Star band. Leaders were no longer eligible, taking Ellington, Basie, Goodman, the Dorseys, and others. out of competition.

Of the four blacks elected, only Hodges worked in a black band. Jazz buffs were appalled that Beneke was elected again to a tenor saxophone chair over more talented players such as Coleman Hawkins, Lester Young, Ben Webster, or Bud Freeman. When *Esquire* magazine chose an All-Star band the next year, relying on a panel of experts instead of readers' votes, there were fewer such injustices.

The top five bands on Down Beat's 1941 Swing and Sweet jazz lists.

	SWING	SWEET
1.	Benny Goodman	Glenn Miller
2.	Tommy Dorsey	Tommy Dorsey
3.	Duke Ellington	Jimmy Dorsey
4.	Glenn Miller	Duke Ellington
5.	Count Basie	Benny Goodman

Trumpeters Roy Eldridge and Dizzy Gillespie with Sarah Vaughan (notice the distinctive angled bell of Gillespie's trumpet).

The 1941 winners in Down Beat's All-Star Band

Trumpet:	Roy Eldridge (w/Krupa), Ziggy Elman (w/Tommy Dorsey), and Cootie Williams (w/Goodman)
Trombone:	J.C. Higginbotham (w/Red Allen), Jack Jenney (w/Shaw)
Clarinet:	Irving Fazola (w/Thornhill)
Saxophone:	Johnny Hodges (w/Ellington), Toots Mondello (w/NBC), George Auld (w/Shaw), and Tex Beneke (w/Miller)
Piano:	Jess Stacy (w/Bob Crosby)
Guitar:	Charlie Christian (w/Goodman)
Bass:	Bob Haggart (w/Bob Crosby)
Drums:	Buddy Rich (w/Tommy Dorsey)
Arranger:	Sy Oliver (w/Tommy Dorsey)
Singers:	Helen O'Connell (w/Jimmy Dorsey), Frank Sinatra (w/Tommy Dorsey)

50. Mel Powell & His Orchestra
THE WORLD IS WAITING FOR THE SUNRISE
February 4, 1942
CD 2, Track 20

WIN: Mel Powell's spectacular piano runs and Benny Goodman's exciting clarinet solos highlight this track, a stellar creation. Here again, the jazz-friendly setting of Commodore Records produces a work of art.

Benny Goodman's 19-year-old arranger-pianist, Mel Powell, organized this session at Commodore Records. Powell and five fellow Goodmanites took their boss along to join in the fun. Thus it was that the "Shoeless John Jackson" listed on the label was actually Goodman, who was under contract to Columbia Records.

Rarely had the clarinetist played better, and Powell executed dazzling runs at a breakneck tempo. (His classical training helped him here.) Obviously impressed with this session, Goodman had his own Quartet (including Powell) record the same tune a month later, and they turned out another beauty.

The next year Powell joined the Glenn Miller Army Air Force Band. After the war he composed classical music and taught music theory at Yale and elsewhere, performing jazz occasionally and returning to it in the late 1980s.

This side is not unlike the exciting Goodman sextet sessions, except that there is more piano featured. It certainly deserves to be included in any list of the outstanding small-group recordings ever.

The song's lyrics were written in 1919 by actor Gene Lockhart, who was featured in many Hollywood films. His daughter June starred in the "Lassie" TV series.

51. Red Norvo & His Orchestra

JERSEY BOUNCE

March 5, 1942

CD 2, Track 21

WIN: This version of "Jersey Bounce" reflects the good taste and musicality of the leader. Its tempo is perfect and its solos are original and appropriate.

Encyclopedist Roger Kinkle wrote of Red Norvo: "Important jazz figure as soloist and leader from mid-'20s into '70s. Pioneer on jazz xylophone, late took up vibraphone. Crisp, inventive soloist with impeccable swing and exquisite taste. Leader of advanced big band..."

"Jersey Bounce" was the only instrumental recorded by this band, Norvo's last, a fact regretted by Gunther Schuller and Martin Williams who chose it for their *Smithsonian Collection of Big Band Jazz.* (On the other side of this record, the band backed Mildred Bailey on "Arthur Murray Taught Me Dancing In A Hurry.")

Norvo solos on the wooden xylophone on this record, an instrument no other jazz musician mastered. The next year he would switch permanently to the metal vibraphone, the choice of Lionel Hampton and later, Milt Jackson and Gary Burton.

Norvo gave up the big band business after this. Later he was in on great small-group sessions, first with Benny Goodman, later with Woody Herman's great First Herd, and even later with his own small groups.

Norvo had a long career, reaching stylistically from his days with Paul Whiteman to his trios with modernists Tal Farlow and Charlie Mingus. Quite a stretch, indeed!

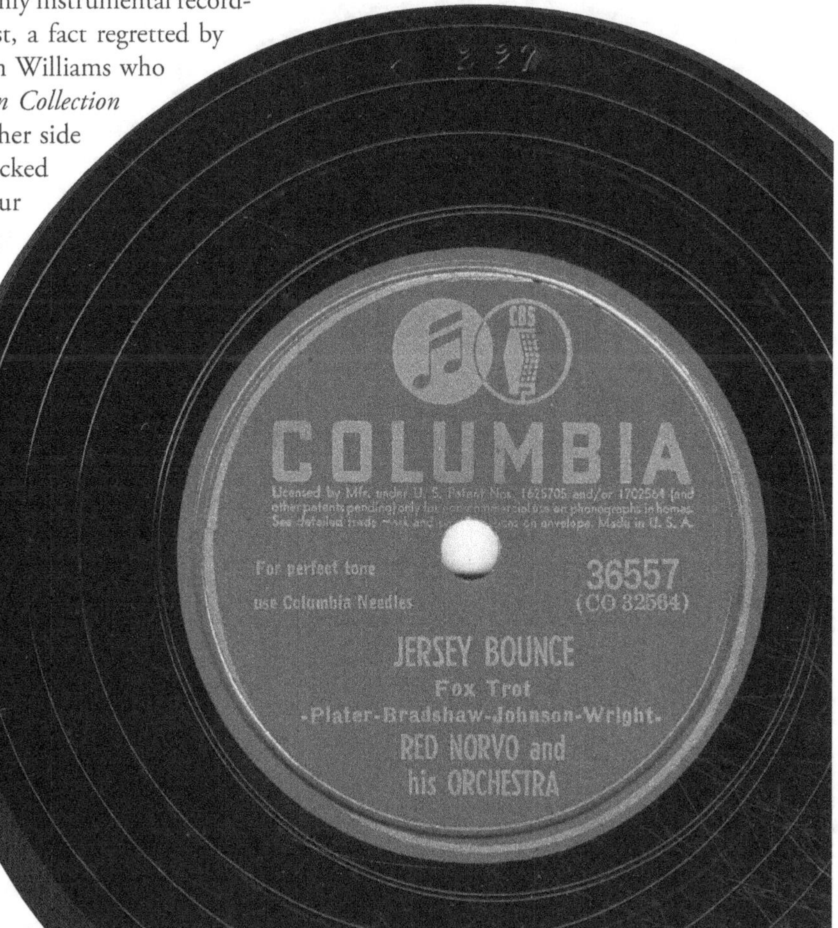

52. Tommy Dorsey & His Orchestra
WELL, GIT IT!
March 9, 1942
CD 2, Track 22

WIN: Sy Oliver's composition and arrangement, with the choice personnel Tommy Dorsey had assembled, elevate this wild, free-swinging creation, one of the finest.

Tommy Dorsey had started his own orchestra in 1935. By 1942 he had pieced together what George Simon in his book, *The Big Bands*, called the best of all the bands – it could play everything so well, from the slowest ballads to the hottest instrumentals. Actually, it didn't do as well in the latter category until Dorsey brought in arranger Sy Oliver from Jimmie Lunceford's band in 1940.

"Well, Git It" begins with the all-out trumpet of Ziggy Elman and ends with Elman and Chuck Peterson in a trumpet duel. Dorsey himself plays some hot trombone and others contribute solos. Driving them is one of the best drummers of all, Buddy Rich.

"Well, Git It" is a prototypical big band swinger. It's loud, fast, has a simple melody, and is played with great precision. It is another chosen for the superb *Smithsonian Collection of Big Band Jazz.*

Tommy Dorsey was the George Steinbrenner of his day. He bought or stole every good singer, arranger, or musician not under contract. When Benny Goodman laid off for a couple of months, Dorsey took Ziggy Elman from him. Artie Shaw quit for a while, so Dorsey grabbed his string section. Harry James wasn't paying Sinatra enough, so in stepped TD. Sy Oliver came from Lunceford, Buddy Rich from Joe Marsala, etc. By 1942, TD had the best band and his recordings of the day show it.

53. Earl Hines & His Orchestra
STORMY MONDAY BLUES
Vocal: Billy Eckstine
March 19, 1942
CD 2, Track 23

WIN:. The fine African-timbre voice of Billy Eckstine and the first-class Earl Hines band combine to make this a big band blues winner.

Billy Eckstine was a blues singer very different from "Big Joe" Turner; he had a deep, smooth sound and a rich African timbre. Although with the Hines band he sang mostly pop tunes, Eckstine shows on this track that he can handle the blues. (In 1940 he had a hit with another blues, "Jelly, Jelly.")

Skeeter Best plays a guitar obbligato behind the singer and trumpeter Shorty McConnell blows a high-note solo. Hines contributes a fine piano introduction. This was the band's last recording session before the recording ban.

During the next year Eckstine took over as leader and encouraged his young bebop-playing sidemen. Because of the recording ban, the Eckstine band of 1943 and 1944 left us little to inherit. Those who heard it insist it was one of the most exciting of all bands. At one time or another its members included Sarah Vaughan, Dizzy Gillespie, Charlie Parker, Fats Navarro, Dexter Gordon, Gene Ammons, and Art Blakey.

Earl 'Fatha' Hines is one of the major figures in jazz. He recorded often with Louis Armstrong in the '20s and had his own band from 1929 to 1942. He joined Armstrong again, but his career sagged until 1960 when a concert showed that he played as well as ever.

54. James P. Johnson, piano solo
SNOWY MORNING BLUES
July 2, 1942
CD 2, Track 24

WIN: James P. Johnson, like his pupil Fats Waller, was both a great composer and a great player. This track shows his feeling for the blues, both in conception and in execution.

"Johnson plays this composition, one of his most beautiful, with great dignity."

This track is from the only recording session during this period by the "Father of the Stride Piano." Although James P. Johnson taught Fats Waller and was much admired by Duke Ellington and Willie "The Lion" Smith, the public never recognized his talents.

This track was made by a small company named for its founder, Moses Asch. He specialized in recording many jazz artists who were overlooked by the larger firms.

Johnson plays this composition, one of his most beautiful, with great dignity. The performance does indeed evoke a "snowy morning." (Johnson claimed he developed his light touch by practicing with a blanket over the keys.) His other compositions included "Charleston," "If I Could Be With You," and "Old-Fashioned Love," in addition to some longer works.

Johnson's compositions are still studied today, including operas he wrote. Prof. James Dapogny has reconstructed some of his early works from fragments of scores and has produced them on stage.

♪ SWING OUT TO VICTORY ♪

Twenty-four records cut in 1942 became million-sellers, twice as many as in 1941 and all the more impressive since recording stopped on August 1. (See "Pre-Ban Flurry" below). Most were Tin Pan Alley songs, novelties, and seasonal songs ("White Christmas" debuted that year). But eight were cut by swing bands; of these, five featured vocals – a trend that would grow.

Harry James had four winners, including an instrumental version of Irving Berlin's "Easter Parade." Helen Forrest sang on "I Had The Craziest Dream" and "I've Heard That Song Before," and John McAfee was the vocalist on James' "Moonlight Becomes You." Glenn Miller had "American Patrol" and "Kalamazoo." Tommy Dorsey scored with "There Are Such Things," with vocals by Frank Sinatra & the Pied Pipers, and Benny Goodman finally got a million-seller with "Why Don't You Do Right?" That memorable vocal was by Peggy Lee (Record 55).

While today two groups don't often record the same tune, back then each of the record companies tried to issue at least one version of every hit. Just one example: Earl Hines recorded "Jersey Bounce" on Bluebird in April 1941. Within the year Goodman and Red Norvo (Record 51) had cut it for Columbia, Jimmy Dorsey for Decca, Les Hite for Hit, and Jan Savitt for Victor.

The war inspired dozens of instrumentals in addition to songs, although few instrumentals climbed high on the charts. Bob Crosby recorded marches of the Field Artillery, the Navy, the Coast Guard, and the Air Corps. Gene Krupa did the same for the Marines. Charlie Barnet suggested a "Victory Walk," and Ray Conniff wrote "V For Victory Hop." Gil Evans modernized "America, I Love You" for Claude Thornhill. Even the songs of World War I were dusted off, including George M. Cohan's "Over There" and Berlin's "This Is The Army." The last was the title song for an all-soldier musical that opened in July at the Broadway Theater, and after 113 performances, it toured and was made into a film. All proceeds went to the Army Emergency Relief Fund.

Duke Ellington warned against rumors in "A Slip of The Lip (Can Sink A Ship)." Fats Waller urged everybody to "Swing Out To Victory," and he and Louis Armstrong promoted recycling in "Cash For Your Trash." Among the best novelties was Johnny Mercer's "GI Jive" ("If you brush the L. I. E. U. T., the MP makes you KP on the QT.").

Americans learned many new words during World War II and Una Mae Carlisle incorporated several into her "Blitzkrieg Baby." "Blitzkrieg" was a German word, known and feared around the world as the description of Hitler's mechanized warfare which had conquered Europe. There were fewer of these tunes in England, perhaps because the besieged citizens needed no musical reminders of the war. The BBC favorite was Geraldo, whose band concentrated on Latin numbers. They waited eagerly for his signature tune, "Hello Again; We're On The Radio Again."

All four US radio networks donated time and costs to produce "This Is War," a weekly hour of patriotic messages broadcast on 550 stations. Regular programs worked in "Buy War Bonds" and other messages. With sponsors lining up for a chance to buy time, the networks could afford to be generous. Revenues of stations more than doubled in the first two years of war.

♪ THE DUKE STEPS OUT ♪

The selection of Duke Ellington to open the new Panther Ballroom at the Hotel Sherman in Chicago on July 17 indicated the growing stature of black bands. At about the same time, fans were dismayed that after a dozen years clarinetist Barney Bigard left the Duke. Another Ellington stalwart, Ben Webster, would depart the next year, but the Duke always seemed to attract outstanding replacements.

In July at the Paramount Theater on New York's Times Square, the audience paid less attention to Benny Goodman than to the skinny kid singer from New Jersey. This was Frank Sinatra's debut as a solo star. Goodman introduced Sinatra, turned to give the downbeat, and then reacted in surprise at the subsequent screaming and shouting – young women expressing their admiration for Sinatra. (Apparently the screaming was originally started by a public relations man, but later it became spontaneous.) Singers were about to overshadow bands, and Sinatra was in the vanguard; Peggy Lee, Dick Haymes, and others were close behind.

Each issue of *Down Beat* and *Metronome* pictured more musicians in uniforms than tuxedos. This paved the way for women to have a chance in the jazz limelight. Guitarist Eddie Durham had organized an all-girl band called the Sweethearts of Rhythm; they played a prime venue – the Savoy Ballroom in Harlem.

When tire and gasoline rationing curtailed the band buses, Cab Calloway and the National Association for the Advancement of Colored People (NAACP) petitioned for an exception, arguing that black bands survived on one-nighters and thus relied heavily on buses. Their request was denied, and while many outfits suspended "for the duration," others toured bases to entertain servicemen.

Frank Sinatra in a 1942 recording session, the first under his own name.

July 15 recording
The Nat "King" Cole, Lester Young, Red Callender (string bass) Trio – "Indiana," "Body and Soul," "I Can't Get Started," and "Tea For Two." This outstanding session was recorded privately by disk jockey Norman Granz and released on the obscure Philo label. Granz later produced the Jazz At The Philharmonic concerts, led Pablo & Verve records, and managed Ella Fitzgerald.

July 25 Your Hit Parade
"Jingle, Jangle, Jingle," a novelty number was the number one tune on "Your Hit Parade," as it was for most of the summer. Sixth on the Saturday night program was "Jersey Bounce."

July 28 recording
Spike Jones and His City Slickers record "Der Fuehrer's Face," an hilarious spoof on the "heil" salutes to Hitler. This first million-seller launched Jones on a career of clever and funny spoofs, satires, and parodies.

55. Benny Goodman & His Orchestra
WHY DON'T YOU DO RIGHT
Vocals: Peggy Lee
July 27, 1942
CD 2, Track 25

WIN: Benny Goodman's clarinet, a brilliant arrangement, and Peggy Lee's inspired vocal all contribute to a superb performance.

Goodman cut this, his first million-selling disc, four days before the ban on recording began. Peggy Lee suggested that Goodman record this song and her powerful vocal had a lot to do with its success. Goodman and the orchestra provided perfect accompaniment on this unconventional blues arranged by Mel Powell. As always, the Goodman band played with both precision and great drive.

Lil Green's earlier version had pleaded for favors; this time we hear a woman demanding her rights. Peggy Lee usually sang pleasant ballads, but this record made her a star. When the big bands faltered, vocalists like Peggy took over popular music.

Benny Goodman had been leading a band now for over seven years. He had been responsible for jazz becoming the popular music of the country (if not the world). He performed on radio shows, at concerts and dances, and made over 400 big band and small group recordings, most of them classics of their kind. But he wouldn't stop now. He experimented with bebop, travelled the world, performed classical music, and never let up. Until the end of his life, he rehearsed every day, worked hard, and remained the consumate professional musician.

The Pre-Ban Flurry

The American Federation of Musicians (AFM) had improved job security and working conditions for its members. Wages, hours, and pensions were better than they had been before. But now AFM President James Caesar Petrillo threatened to ban all recording, claiming that jukeboxes replaced too many live musicians. And rather than patronizing bars and clubs where music was played live, customers were listening at home to records and radio.

Metronome magazine suggested that the AFM and the recording companies agree on an annual blanket fee, patterned after the ASCAP arrangement with radio stations. Negotiations stalled when the AFM demanded royalties for musicians. In those days, only the bandleaders earned royalties.

With future recording threatened by an AFM strike or "Ban" on recording, companies frantically stockpiled records. Some notable just-before-the-Ban recordings:

Glenn Miller: In mid-July, Victor recorded thirteen sides by its hottest property, including fine instrumentals, "Caribbean Clipper," and "Rhapsody In Blue;" lush vocals, "That Old Black Magic," and "Dearly Beloved;" and a clever novelty, "Juke Box Saturday Night." (Miller broke up the band in September to enter the Army Air Corps.)

Harry James: Columbia recorded its meal ticket fifteen times in July and got the usual James mix of tasteful vocals ("I've Heard That Song Before") and instrumentals, both sugary ("Velvet Moon") and bluesy ("Let Me Up").

Tommy Dorsey: In early July Victor recorded one of the best Sy Oliver arrangements, "Mandy, Make Up Your Mind," and the last vocals by Sinatra, Jo Stafford, and the Pied Pipers. (Sinatra's final broadcast with Dorsey in September was recorded off-the-air and not released at the time; it came out later on an LP.)

Jimmy Dorsey: July 14, nine tracks, including the last Bob Eberly-Helen O'Connell duet, "Brazil," and Eberly alone on "Daybreak."

Count Basie: July 24, trumpeter Buck Clayton and tenor saxophonist Don Byas joined his All-American Rhythm Section on eight classic blues sides; July 27, full band with Jimmy Rushing vocals on "Rusty Dusty Blues" and the patriotic "For The Good of Your Country." (Rushing was the model for a tune of the day, "Mr. Five-By-Five.")

Dinah Shore: On July 30, she recorded Cole Porter's "You'd Be So Nice To Come Home To," the only major artist to do so before the Ban. The song became a mega-hit.

The record companies issued some of these records right away and held others to be circulated for as long as the Ban lasted. They dug back in their reject bins and issued sides that they felt weren't good enough to be released before, e.g., Miller's "Blue Rain." They also looked back and found such items as Frank Sinatra's 1939 recording of "All Or Nothing At All" with Harry James. It was re-packaged and re-released and became a million-seller in 1943. The original record was billed as Harry James & His Orchestra. The Ban version became "Frank Sinatra" in large type, with the James credit below it. (James graciously and wisely agreed to the change.)

Many of the jazz labels settled with the union in 1943, as did Decca and Capitol.

By settling early, Capitol got a big jump on Victor and Columbia, e.g., Stan Kenton started recording for Capitol in November, 1943 and very quickly became a top big band, partly because very few others were making new records. On the Dixieland front, Commodore recorded Wild Bill Davison and His Commodores in November, 1943 with some of the finest sides ever made in that genre.

Victor and Columbia didn't settle until late 1944. That doesn't sound like a long holdout until one considers that record releases were big news on a weekly or even daily basis. The country was at war and records were a major source of entertainment. The Ban certainly had a major effect on the music business, particularly when the bands already were having so many problems with travel and the draft.

♪ THE SONG IS ENDED ♪

"All Recording Stops Today" read the headline in *Down Beat* on July 31, 1942. And essentially it did. Now no instrumentalist could enter a recording studio unless he or she was willing to break the strike. The ban did not apply to vocalists since they didn't belong to the musicians' union. A few singers enlisted non-union ukulele players to back them up.

A ten-year-old nasal vocal by Rudy Vallee became a hit. It was the only recorded version of "As Time Goes By." The song was suddenly popular again, thanks to *Casablanca*, a film starring Humphrey Bogart and Ingrid Bergman, which was released in 1943. Not even Dooley Wilson, a veteran pianist who sang the tune in the movie, could record it during the ban since he was a member of the AFM. Vallee had recorded it when it was written in 1931.

Bebop would emerge full-blown at the end of the strike. Actually, some bebop did get recorded during the ban, but the records were on small jazz labels by such groups as Billy Eckstine's band. Unfortunately, these records were of marginal technical quality. Eckstine recalled later how he thought the stylus sometimes cut right through the inferior disks. So it was that the early seminal efforts of Parker, Gillespie, Monk, and Kenny Clarke did not get a proper hearing. (Also, most of the Eckstine sides were vocals by the leader, not instrumentals that would show off the talents of the young beboppers.)

The record companies that did settle with the union in 1943 were faced then with wartime shortages of lacquer and other production materials needed to make records. Also, the materials were allocated on the basis of the companies' pre-war production levels, thus helping the major labels. The majors, Victor and Columbia, kept busy by reissuing jazz from the '20s and '30s. Many fans felt they weren't reissuing enough. (During the ban, one company discovered that its custom division, which pressed records from customers' materials, was producing records of '20s jazz. The customers were using the company's own 78rpms as their pirated source!)

By late 1944, when all parties settled and the ban ended, many artists had not cut a record for two and a half years. That doesn't sound like a long time now, but for some fans it was a lifetime – 30 months without a new record by their favorite band!

At least the servicemen heard the top bands of 1942-44. The AFM allowed its members to record on Army- and Navy-produced *V Discs*, provided none were sold and the master recordings destroyed. Fortunately for buffs, since much fine jazz was recorded, copies of most *V Discs* survived and have been reissued. Most of the *V Discs* were re-issues of earlier records, but many were made at special *V Disc* sessions. Although they were all 78rpm, the *V Discs* were the first unbreakable vinyl records and were all 12".

The AFM ban and the war stopped the recordings. The draft took the players. Miller, Shaw, and Bob Crosby entered the services. The surviving bands faced tighter and tighter travel restrictions. Many of the ballrooms and resorts closed. The singers left the bands to star on their own.

An era had ended, but the tunes the groups had played and the way they played them can still be heard today. Here's one example to consider. In late 2006 pianists Marian McPartland and Bill Charlap were both featured in one concert. First, each of their trios played a set, and then two concert grands were rolled out on the stage. The two stars played four improvised duets on the following tunes: "These Foolish Things," from 1936; "Gone With The Wind," 1937; "Prelude To A Kiss," 1938; and "This Time The Dream's On Me," 1941. The repertoire of tunes from the '30s and early '40s is still the standard for today's musicians.

In 1943, *Metronome* published this judgment: "Some day, when their music has been established for many years as the magnificent thing it is, Americans will look back to Benny Goodman and Duke Ellington, to the Dorseys and Count Basie, Benny Carter and Coleman Hawkins, and all their associates, as the heroes of a Golden Age...(it was) an era as important to American music as the time of Emerson and Thoreau and Whitman and Hawthorne and Melville was to American literature."

Jazz continued as America's popular music until Bill Haley recorded "Rock Around The Clock" in 1952 and rock'n'roll took the center stage. By then television had come along to grab a huge share of the entertainment dollar. But a Golden Age had occurred, and the songs and the instrumentals played in the 1939-42 triennium, and the singers and musicians who played them, are admired around the world for that brief, shining moment.

Harry James & His Orchestra.

Charlie Barnet on tenor saxophone and Benny Carter on alto saxophone.

January recording
Bunny Berigan made his last recordings. Produced on the obscure Elite label, the records were offered as a premium by a tire maker. Berigan's trumpet enhanced many bands, including Benny Goodman's and Tommy Dorsey's. Berigan died in June.

February 9 recording
Pete Brown & His Band, "Mound Bayou." An obscure, but first-class track by an important alto saxophonist who played in a staccato "jump" style. This group also included Dizzy Gillespie on trumpet and clarinetist Jimmy Hamilton, who soon would join Duke Ellington and stay with him for several years.

February 16 Detroit record
Glenn Miller broke the house attendance record at the Michigan Theater in Detroit.

February 20 Gold Record
Glenn Miller received a "Gold Record" for his 1941 million-seller, "Chattanooga Choo-Choo." As a promotional gimmick, RCA-Victor sprayed a record gold and presented it to Miller.

March 1 radio series
The War Department recorded the first "Command Performance" for troops overseas. Cooky Fairchild and his Orchestra accompanied Eddie Cantor, Dinah Shore, and others. Civilians in England and elsewhere often eavesdropped.

March 1 Courier poll
Black weekly in Pittsburgh finds Count Basie the favorite swing band among its readers.

March 7 Your Hit Parade
"Remember Pearl Harbor" became the first real war song to qualify for the weekly "Your Hit Parade" radio show. It was number nine and never went higher.

April recording
Johnny Mercer, "Strip Polka." This tells of the burlesque queen "who stops-and always just in time." Mercer sings his own lyrics with great spirit. The whining saxes, staccato trumpets, and corny introduction parody the sweet bands. Released as one of the first Capitol records just a few days before the recording ban, the disc was a big seller.

May 4 recording

Kay Kyser & His Orchestra, "Pushin' Sand." Although his sweet band was known mostly for its novelties, Kyser had added veteran jazz players and their efforts show here. The Kyser band had almost completed its upgrade to hot music when the AFM recording ban ended the era.

May 16 Your Hit Parade

"Don't Sit Under the Apple Tree" began a four-week reign atop the rankings on radio's "Your Hit Parade." The Andrews Sisters, a close-harmony singing trio, and Glenn Miller had the biggest recordings.

May 18 recording

Tommy Dorsey & His Orchestra, "Just As Though You Were Here" and "Street of Dreams" with vocals by Frank Sinatra & The Pied Pipers. This was the first recording session of Dorsey's 31-piece orchestra, which in addition to the usual brass, reed and rhythm sections, included nine stringed instruments and six singers.

May 26 recording

Lionel Hampton's new big band recorded his theme, "Flying Home." Many tenor saxophonists would imitate Illinois Jacquet's famous improvised solo, with its interpolation from "Martha."

June 11 recording

Bunk Johnson's Original Superior Band, "Yes Lord, I'm Crippled." This was the first recording by a major figure in the New Orleans Revival. Johnson was a top player in New Orleans jazz in the early 1900s. He was brought out of obscurity by some jazz fans. Both his playing and his personality disappointed those who raised funds to buy him a new trumpet and false teeth; he turned out to be a womanizer and insisted on recording current pop tunes. His associate, clarinetist George Lewis, did better – both with music and public relations.

June 12 recording

Paul Whiteman & His Orchestra recorded four sides for the new Capitol label. One had a Johnny Mercer-Jack Teagarden vocal duet, but the prize track was "Trav'lin' Light" with a vocal by "Lady Day" (Billie Holiday recording under a pseudonym, the nickname Lester Young had given her).

Appendix A: Annotated Bibliography

I. JAZZ

Autobiographies

Bechet, Sidney. TREAT IT GENTLE,
Da Capo 1975 (electronic version, 2003).
–One of the giants. Later version has records.

Calloway, Cab. OF MINNIE THE MOOCHER AND ME,
Cromwell 1976.
—Inside look at Harlem & jazz.

Condon, Eddie. WE CALLED IT MUSIC,
Henry Holt 1947.
—Irreverent & humorous look at jazz.

Ellington, Edward Kennedy. MUSIC IS MY MISTRESS,
DaCapo 1976.
–His life in music. Little on personal life.

Freeman, Bud. YOU DON'T LOOK LIKE A MUSICIAN,
Balamp 1974.
–Witty memoir by the fun-loving saxophonist.

Goodman, Benny. THE KINGDOM OF SWING,
Ungar 1939.
–BG's view from the top. Few insights.

Hammond, John, with Irving Townsend. JOHN HAMMOND ON RECORD,
Ridge 1977.
–An impresario's view – from Holiday to Dylan.

Holiday, Billie. LADY SINGS THE BLUES,
Avon 1976.
–Self-pitying, but fascinating.

Mezzrow, Mezz & Bernard Wolfe. REALLY THE BLUES,
Random House 1946.
–Impressions of the seedy side of the jazz life.

Rollini, Arthur. THIRTY YEARS WITH THE BIG BANDS,
University of Illinois 1987.
–Big Band memoir with some negative shots.

Shaw, Artie. THE TROUBLE WITH CINDERELLA,
Farrar Strauss 1956.
–Frank, introspective, and controversial.

Big Bands

Dance, Stanley. THE WORLD OF SWING,
Scribner's 1974.
–Well-written survey of the people of the era.

McCarthy, Albert. BIG BAND JAZZ,
Viking 1960.
–British, several pounds of readable detail.

Rust, Brian. THE DANCE BANDS,
Iam Allen 1972.
–Also British, lots of pictures and esoterica.

Simon, George. THE BIG BANDS,
MacMillan 1967.
–Survey by former Metronome editor.

Walter, Leo. GREAT DANCE BANDS,
Howell-North 1964.
–Far-ranging but sketchy.

Biographies

LOUIS ARMSTRONG

Collier, James Lincoln. LOUIS ARMSTRONG, AN AMERICAN GENIUS,
Oxford University 1983.
–Controversial but insightful look at Satchmo.

Giddins, Gary. SATCHMO,
Doubleday 1988.
–Well-written, great pictures.

Goffin, Robert. HORN OF PLENTY: THE STORY OF LOUIS ARMSTRONG,
Allen, Towne, & Heath 1947.
–Sympathetic treatment by a European writer.

COUNT BASIE

Dance, Stanley. THE WORLD OF COUNT BASIE,
C. Scribner's Sons 1970.
–A top critic's comprehensive assessment.

BENNY CARTER

Berger, Monroe, Edward Berger, & James Patrick. BENNY CARTER, A LIFE IN AMERICAN MUSIC, (2 vols.),
Scarecrow 1982.
–Good biography & discography.

BING CROSBY

Giddens, Gary. BING CROSBY: A POCKETFUL OF DREAMS, THE EARLY YEARS 1903-1940,
Little, Brown 2001.
–A super star's professional and personal life.

BOB CROSBY

Chilton, John. STOMP OFF, LET'S GO!,
Jazz Book Service 1983.
–History of Crosby band plus bios of sidemen.

TOMMY DORSEY

Levinson, Peter J. TOMMY DORSEY, LIVIN' IN A GREAT BIG WAY: A BIOGRAPHY,
Da Capo 2005.
–No-holds-barred bio of the model for Sinatra.

DUKE ELLINGTON

Collier, James Lincoln. DUKE ELLINGTON,
Oxford University 1987.
–Negative tone angered many of Duke's fans.

Dance, Stanley. THE WORLD OF DUKE ELLINGTON,
Scribner's Sons 1970.
–As viewed by a critic and close friend.

Gammond, Peter, ed. DUKE ELLINGTON: HIS LIFE AND HIS MUSIC,
Da Capo 1977.
–A fine collection of tributes from Brits.

Ellington, Mercer. DUKE ELLINGTON IN PERFORMANCE,
Houghton Mifflin 1974.
–Personal memoir by his son and band member.

ELLA FITZGERALD

Colin, Sid. ELLA: THE LIFE AND TIMES OF ELLA FITZGERALD,
London: Elm Tree, 1986.
–Traces career from days with Chick Webb.

BENNY GOODMAN

Collier, James Lincoln. BENNY GOODMAN AND THE SWING ERA,
Oxford University 1989.
–Authoritative, comprehensive, and critical.

JOHN HAMMOND
Prial, Dunstan. THE PRODUCER: JOHN HAMMOND & THE SOUL OF AMERICAN MUSIC,
Farrar Straus Giroux 2006.
–Guide for artists from Goodman to Bob Dylan.

BILLIE HOLIDAY
Chilton, John. BILLIE'S BLUES,
Stein and Day 1976.
–Candid, balanced account of her career.

HARRY JAMES
Levinson, Peter J. TRUMPET BLUES: THE LIFE OF HARRY JAMES,
Oxford University, 1999.
–The intense musical and sex life of the leader.

GLENN MILLER
Simon, George. GLENN MILLER AND HIS ORCHESTRA,
Cromwell 1974.
–Respectful bio by writer who played with GM.

CHARLIE PARKER
Reisner, Robert. BIRD: THE LEGEND OF CHARLIE PARKER,
Da Capo 1975.
–Good review of the brilliant and tragic Bird.

Russell, Ross. BIRD LIVES: THE HIGH LIFE & HARD TIMES OF CHARLIE "YARDBIRD" PARKER,
Da Capo 1996.
–Parker's life as viewed by one who knew him.

DJANGO REINHARDT
Dregni, Michael. DJANGO: THE LIFE AND MUSIC OF A GYPSY LEGEND,
Oxford 2004.
–Review of the guitarist's ups and downs.

NELSON RIDDLE
Levinson, Peter J. SEPTEMBER IN THE RAIN: THE LIFE OF NELSON RIDDLE,
Billboard Books 2001.
–Life, warts and all, of one of best arrangers.

BILLY STRAYHORN
Hajdu, David. LUSH LIFE: A BIOGRAPHY OF BILLY STRAYHORN,
Farrar Straus Giroux 1996.
–The sad but productive life of Duke's alter ego.

FRANK SINATRA
Friedwald, Will, SINATRA! THE SONG IS YOU: A SINGER'S ART,
Scribner 1995.
–Excellent, extensive musical bio, no gossip.

FATS WALLER
Kirkeby, Ed. AIN'T MISBEHAVIN',
Da Capo 1966.
–Good biography by Fats' long-time manager.

Discographies

Allen, Walter. HENDERSONIA,
Walter Allen 1973.
–Specifics of records with a day-by-day Henderson journal.

Connor, D. Russell. BENNY GOODMAN: LISTEN TO HIS LEGACY,
Scarecrow & Institute of Jazz Studies 1988 & WRAPPIN IT UP, Lanham 1996.
–Recordings from all sources.

Cuscuna, Michael & Michel Ruppli. THE BLUE NOTE LABEL: A DISCOGRAPHY, Greenwood 1988.
–Session-by-session detail from 1939 on.

Delaunay, Charles. NEW HOT DISCOGRAPHY, Criterion 1948.
–Good one-volume listing of 1917-47 records.

Flower, John. MOONLIGHT SERENADE, Arlington House 1972.
–Day-by-day of the Glenn Miller civilian band.

Godrich, John & Robert Dixon. BLUES AND GOSPEL RECORDS 1902-1942, Storyville 1969.
–Essential reference work.

Jepsen, Jorgen. JAZZ RECORDS 1942-'60s: A DISCOGRAPHY (11 vols.), Holte, Denmark: K. E. Knudsen 1965.
–Hand-typed, hard-to-read but invaluable.

Laubich, Arnold & Ray Spencer. ART TATUM, A GUIDE TO HIS MUSIC, Scarecrow 1982.
–Complete listing of the pianist's records.

Massagli, Luciano & Librorio Pusateri & Giovanni Volonte. DUKE ELLINGTON'S STORY ON RECORDS 1925-1974, Milan 1966-1983.
–Complete, but very hard to find.

Millar, Jack. BORN TO SING: A DISCOGRAPHY OF BILLIE HOLIDAY, Jazzmedia 1979.
–Helpful in sorting out the Holiday LPs.

Rust, Brian. THE AMERICAN DANCE BAND DISCOGRAPHY 1917-1942 (2 vols.), Arlington House 1972.

THE AMERICAN RECORD LABEL BOOK, Arlington House 1978.

JAZZ RECORDS 1897-1942 (2 vols.), Storyville 1982.
–Indispensable, by "Prince of Discographers."

Sears, Richard. V DISCS: A HISTORY AND DISCOGRAPHY, Greenwood 1980.
–Incredible detail about everything on V Discs.

Sheridan, Chris. COUNT BASIE: A BIO-DISCOGRAPHY, Greenwood 1988.
–Great detail on broadcasts, concerts, venues.

Encyclopediae

Case, Brian & Stan Britt. THE ILLUSTRATED ENCYCLOPEDIA OF JAZZ, Harmony 1978.
–Handsome, clear, and concise.

Chilton, John. WHO'S WHO OF JAZZ, Bloomsbury 1970.
–Brief biographical sketches of nearly everyone.

Feather, Leonard. THE ENCYLOPEDIA OF JAZZ, De Capo 1984.
–Bios and articles by a top authority.

Kernfeld, Barry (ed.) THE NEW GROVE DICTIONARY OF JAZZ (2 vols.), Macmillan 2002.
–Particularly strong on technical details.

Kinkle, Roger. THE COMPLETE ENCYCLOPEDIA OF POPULAR MUSIC AND JAZZ, 1900-1950 (4 vols.),
Arlington House 1974.
–Exhaustive, expensive, and excellent.

Histories

Blesh, Rudi. SHINING TRUMPETS,
Da Capo 1975.
–Early work by a pioneer jazz writer.

Collier, James Lincoln. THE MAKING OF JAZZ,
Dell 1978.
–Most comprehensive one-volume history.

Erenberg, Lewis A. SWINGIN' THE DREAM,
University of Chicago 1998.
–Excellent academic study of swing and culture.

Feather, Leonard. FROM SATCHMO TO MILES,
Da Capo 1984.
–History as seen by a critic, writer, and musician.

Friedwald, Will. JAZZ SINGING: AMERICA'S GREAT VOICES FROM BESSIE SMITH TO BEBOP AND BEYOND,
Da Capo 1996.
–Good writer's survey of vocal jazz.

Gitler, Ira. JAZZ MASTERS OF THE FORTIES,
MacMillan 1983.
–Part of MacMillan's admirable series.

Hasse, John Edward (ed.). JAZZ: THE FIRST CENTURY,
Morrow 2000.
–Excellent one-volume. Pics and sidebars.

Russell, Ross. JAZZ STYLE IN KANSAS CITY & THE SOUTHWEST,
University of California 1971.
–Fine survey of the roots of many jazzmen.

Schuller, Gunther. THE SWING ERA,
Oxford University 1989.
–The second volume of his definitive history.

Sanjek, Russell. AMERICAN POPULAR MUSIC AND ITS BUSINESS: THE FIRST FOUR HUNDRED YEARS (3 vols.),
Oxford University1988.
–Vol 3 discusses recent production & profits.

Stearns, Marshall. THE STORY OF JAZZ,
Oxford University 1971.
–Survey by one of the great jazz scholars.

Ward, Geoffrey C. & Ken Burns. JAZZ: A HISTORY OF AMERICA'S MUSIC,
Knopf 2000.
–More comprehensive than the fine PBS series.

Liner Notes

Although album notes normally don't qualify for a bibliography, at least two sets must be included in any survey of the 1939-42 period. They are the books which accompany the Smithsonian's "Classic Jazz" and "Big Band Jazz" collections. Both include perceptive comments about the artists and music on each of the tracks as well as a narrative on the place of the music in American culture. Martin Williams wrote the notes for both, joined in the latter by Gunther Schuller.

Magazine Article Collections

New Yorker
Balliett, Whitney.
AMERICAN MUSICIANS,
Oxford University 1986.

AMERICAN SINGERS,
Oxford University 1988.

DINOSAURS IN THE MORNING,
Scholarly 1962.

NIGHT CREATURES,
Oxford University 1981.

THE SOUND OF SURPRISE,
Da Capo 1978.

SUCH SWEET THUNDER,
Bobbs-Merrill 1966.
–New Yorker articles by a stylish jazz writer.

The Jazz Record
Hodes, Art & Chadwick, Hansen.
SELECTIONS FROM THE GUTTER,
University of California 1977.
–Cullings from the 1940s The Jazz Record.

Metronome
Simon, George. SIMON SAYS,
Arlington House 1971.
–Some of Simon's Metronome articles, 1935-1955.

Miscellaneous

Condon, Eddie & Richard Gehman (eds.)
A TREASURY OF JAZZ,
Dial 1955.
–Excellent collection on many topics.

Crow, Bill. JAZZ ANECDOTES,
Oxford University 1990.
–Hilarious stories with informed comments.

Feather, Leonard. LAUGHTER FROM THE HIP,
Horizon 1963.
–Jazz-oriented laughs.

Gleason, Ralph. CELEBRATING THE DUKE AND LOUIS, ETC.,
Delta 1975.
–Informal, loving tributes.

Gottlieb, Robert (ed.). READING JAZZ,
Pantheon 1996.
–Amazing compilation of reporting, reviews, etc.

Gottlieb, Robert & Robert Kimball (eds.)
READING LYRICS,
Pantheon 2000.
–The words to over 1,000 of the best songs.

Green, Benny. THE RELUCTANT ART,
Horizon 1963.
–Informed essays on Parker, Goodman, etc.

Gridley, Mark. JAZZ STYLES: HISTORY AND ANALYSIS,
Prentice-Hall 1978.
–Textbook-like but not overly technical.

Harrison, Max. A JAZZ RETROSPECT,
Crescendo 1976.
–Perceptive remarks by a cantankerous Brit.

Lees, Gene. ARRANGING THE SCORE: PORTRAITS OF THE GREAT ARRANGERS,
Cassell 2000.
–Prolific writer's pertinent look at arrangers.

Lyons, Len. THE GREAT JAZZ PIANISTS,
Quill 1983.
–Good survey of the keyboard kings.

Lyttelton, Humphrey. THE BEST OF JAZZ (2 vols.),
Taplinger 1978 and 1981.
–Brit musician writes with knowledge and skill.

Morganstern, Dan. LIVING WITH JAZZ: A READER,
Oxford University 2004.
–A big book by one of the best jazz writers.

Murrells, Joseph. MILLION SELLING RECORDS,
Arco 1985.
–Good details about the gold records.

Shaw, Arnold. THE STREET THAT NEVER SLEPT,
Coward, McCann, & Geohegan 1971.
–The story of 52nd Street during its jazz days.

Tucker, Mark (ed.). THE DUKE ELLINGTON READER,
Oxford University 1993.
–Impressive compilation. A must for any library.

Ulanov, Barry. HANDBOOK OF JAZZ,
Viking 1960.
–Scholarly, opinionated, thoughtful.

Williams, Martin.
THE JAZZ TRADITION (Rev.)
Oxford University 1983.

JAZZ IN ITS TIME,
Oxford University 1989.
–Beautifully-written essays on many greats.

Zwerin, Mike. LA TRISTESSE DE SAINT LOUIS,
Beach Tree 1985.
–Nazi Europe; much on Django Reinhardt.

Mostly Pictures

Baron, Stanley, intro. BENNY: KING OF SWING,
William Morrow 1979.
–Pictures and biography.

Condon, Eddie & Hank O'Neal. EDDIE CONDON'S SCRAPBOOK OF JAZZ,
Galahad 1973.
–Photos, record labels, and memorabilia.

Driggs, Frank & Harris Lewine. BLACK BEAUTY, WHITE HEAT, William Morrow 1982.
–Good pics, captions, and record labels.

Fox, Charles. THE JAZZ SCENE, Hamlyn 1972.
–Color photos plus intelligent comments.

Gottlieb, William. THE GOLDEN AGE OF JAZZ, Simon & Schuster 1979.
–Hundreds of pictures with savvy commentary.

Morganstern, Dan. JAZZ PEOPLE, Prentice-Hall 1976.
–Text by veteran observer. Good pictures.

Schiedt, Duncan. JAZZ IN BLACK AND WHITE: THE PHOTOGRAPHS OF DUNCAN SCHIEDT, Indiana University 2004.
–Great pics by a master photographer.

Record Reviews

Lyons, Len. THE 101 BEST JAZZ ALBUMS, William Morrow 1980.
–Fifteen from swing era. Album cover photos.

McCarthy, Albert, et al. JAZZ ON RECORD, Oak 1963.
–Critical reviews of thousands of records.

Ratliff, Ben. NEW YORK TIMES ESSENTIAL LIBRARY: A CRITIC'S GUIDE TO THE 100 MOST IMPORTANT JAZZ RECORDINGS, Henry Holt 2002.
–Good advice for the record buyer.

Smith, Charles Edward et al. THE JAZZ RECORD BOOK, Smith & Durrell 1942.
–Perceptive comments; long out-of-print.

II. NATIONAL AND WORLD EVENTS

Much of the historical material was drawn from the *New York Times, Variety, Metronome* and *Down Beat*. Books which were especially useful included the following:

Barnouw, Erik. THE GOLDEN WEB, Oxford University 1968.
–Relevant volume in a masterful history of radio.

Bernstein, Irving. TURBULENT YEARS: A HISTORY OF THE AMERICAN WORKER 1933-1941, Houghton Mifflin 1962.
–Illuminates economic conditions.

Blum, John H. V WAS FOR VICTORY, Harcourt Brace 1976.
–Breezy view of war on the home front.

Bureau of the Census. HISTORICAL STATISTICS OF THE UNITED STATES, COLONIAL TIMES TO 1957, Government Printing Office 1960.

Bureau of the Census. VITAL STATISTICS OF THE UNITED STATES, 1941, Government Printing Office 1944.

Buxton, Frank and Bill Owen, THE BIG BROADCAST, 1920-1950, Viking Press 1972.
–Definitive comments on network radio shows.

Cantril, Hadley, PUBLIC OPINION 1935-1946, Princeton University 1951.
–Summarizes opinion polls.

CHRONICLE OF THE 20TH CENTURY, Chronicle Publications 1987.
–Useful month-by-month listing.

Clifford, Dennis, THE GOLDEN AGE OF RADIO, B.T. Batsford 1985.
–British programs.

Cole, Wayne S. CHARLES A. LINDBERGH AND THE BATTLE AGAINST AMERICAN INTERVENTION IN WORLD WAR II, Harcourt Brace Jovanich 1974.
–Isolationist views examined.

Furnas, J. C. HOW AMERICA LIVES, Holt 1941.
–Describes daily life in this period.

Gregory, Ross. AMERICA 1941, Free Press 1989.
–Scholarly treatment of the period.

Guzman, James P, (ed.). NEGRO YEARBOOK: A REVIEW OF EVENTS AFFECTING NEGRO LIFE, 1941-1946. Tuskegee Institute 1947.

Hackett, Alice P. 60 YEARS OF BEST SELLERS 1895-1955, Bowker 1956.
–What the public really read.

Hart, James D. THE POPULAR BOOK, Oxford University 1950.
–Compiles useful statistics on readership.

Keegan, John. THE SECOND WORLD WAR, Viking 1989.
–Military history at its finest.

Kennett, Lee. FOR THE DURATION, Scribner's 1985.
–First six months of World War II.

Ketchum, Richard M. THE BORROWED YEARS, 1938-1941, Random House 1989.
–Detailed but readable.

Lingeman, Richard. DON'T YOU KNOW THERE'S A WAR ON?, Putnam's Sons 1970.
–Best of the popular histories of the home front.

MacDonald, J. Fred. DON'T TOUCH THAT DIAL! RADIO PROGRAMMING IN AMERICAN LIFE, 1920-1960, Nelson-Hall 1979.
–Lots of anecdotes woven into chronology.

Myrdal, Gunnar. AN AMERICAN DILEMMA (2 vols.), Harper 1944.
–Monumental racial survey by a great scholar.

Perett, Geoffrey. DAYS OF SORROW, YEARS OF TRIUMPH, Holt 1972.
–Careful historian surveys America.

Polenberg, Richard. ONE NATION DIVISIBLE: CLASS, RACE AND ETHNICITY IN THE UNITED STATES SINCE 1938, Viking 1988.
–Details differences by race.

Pommeranz, Alan, REPEAL OF THE BLUES, Citadel Press 1988.
–Blacks in the arts. Chapter on John Hammond.

Time Inc. TIME CAPSULES, 1939, 1940, 1941, 1942.
–Concise and useful.

Trager, James. THE PEOPLE'S CHRONOLOGY,
Holt, Reinhart, & Winston 1979.
–Parallel activities in news, science, arts, etc.

Appendix B: Recommended Recordings From Mid 1939 - Mid 1942

Arranged in four tiers of priority

The authors chose this list of over 1,000 tracks from many sources, including the standard discographies and bibliographies. They consulted with many collectors and broadcasters; Michael Jewett, Hans Schmidt, and Arthur Hilgart were especially helpful. The major anthologies of the period were consulted, e.g., the Smithsonian Collections, Time-Life Giants of Jazz, RCA'S Vintage series, etc. But in the end, this, like any other list, reflects the biases of the authors, who take full responsibility for errors of omission or commission.

1. First Tier - *QUINTESSENTIAL*

LOUIS ARMSTRONG & SIDNEY BECHET
Louis Armstrong & His Orchestra
(see also Tier 2)

PERDIDO STREET BLUES	05/27/40
219 BLUES, *vo Louis Armstrong*	05/27/40
COAL CART BLUES, *vo LA*	05/27/40
DOWN IN HONKY TONK TOWN	05/27/40

COUNT BASIE
& His Orchestra, Instrumentals

CLAP HANDS, HERE COMES CHARLIE	08/04/39
SONG OF THE ISLANDS	08/04/39
RIFF INTERLUDE	11/06/39
VOLCANO	11/06/39
I NEVER KNEW	03/19/40
TICKLE TOE	03/19/40
LOUISIANA	03/19/40
EASY DOES IT	03/20/40
LET ME SEE	03/20/40
BLOW TOP	03/31/40
SUPER CHIEF	03/31/40
MOTEN SWING	08/08/40
FIVE O'CLOCK WHISTLE	11/19/40
BROADWAY	11/19/40
JUMP THE BLUES AWAY	01/28/41
TUESDAY AT TEN	01/28/41
9:20 SPECIAL	04/10/41
DOWN, DOWN, DOWN	05/21/41
BASIE BOOGIE	07/02/41
FIESTA IN BLUE	09/24/41
PLATTERBRAINS	11/03/41
ONE O'CLOCK JUMP	01/21/42
BASIE BLUES	04/03/42

& His Orchestra, Vocals

EVENIN' *vo Jimmy Rushing*	08/08/40
I WANT A LITTLE GIRL, *vo JR*	08/08/40
GOIN' TO CHICAGO, *vo JR*	04/10/41
KING JOE, *vo Paul Robeson*	10/01/41
HARVARD BLUES, *vo JR*	11/17/41
I'M GONNA MOVE TO THE OUTSKIRTS OF TOWN, *vo JR*	04/03/42

& His Kansas City Seven

LESTER LEAPS IN	09/05/39
DICKIE'S DREAM	09/05/39

& His All-American Rhythm Section

ROYAL GARDEN BLUES	07/24/42
BUGLE BLUES	07/24/42
SUGAR BLUES	07/24/42
WAY BACK BLUES	07/24/42
ST. LOUIS BLUES	07/24/42

SIDNEY BECHET
& His Blue Note Quartet

SUMMERTIME	08/06/39
LONESOME BLUES	03/27/40
DEAR OLD SOUTHLAND	03/27/40
BECHET'S STEADY RIDER	03/27/40

& His New Orleans Feetwarmers

INDIAN SUMMER	02/05/40
SHAKE IT AND BREAK IT	06/04/40
OLD MAN BLUES	06/04/40
WILD MAN BLUES	06/04/40
NOBODY KNOWS THE WAY I FEEL DIS MORNIN'	06/04/40
BLUES IN THIRDS	09/06/40
SAVE IT, PRETTY MAMA	09/06/40
STOMPY JONES	09/06/40
EGYPTIAN FANTASY	01/08/41
SLIPPIN' AND SLIDIN'	01/08/41
AIN'T GONNA GIVE NOBODY NONE OF MY JELLY ROLL	04/28/41
TEXAS MOANER	09/13/41
STRANGE FRUIT	09/13/41
BLUES IN THE AIR	10/14/41
THE MOOCHE	10/14/41
MOOD INDIGO	10/24/41
WHAT IS THIS THING CALLED LOVE	10/24/41

& His One Man Band

THE SHEIK OF ARABY	04/18/41

BECHET-SPANIER BIG FOUR

FOUR OR FIVE TIMES	03/28/40
SWEET LORRAINE	03/28/40
LAZY RIVER	03/28/40
CHINA BOY	03/28/40
IF I COULD BE WITH YOU	04/06/40
THAT'S A PLENTY	04/06/40
SQUEEZE ME	04/06/40
SWEET SUE	04/06/40

BARNEY BIGARD

(see Duke Ellington)

CHOCOLATE DANDIES

SMACK	05/25/40
I SURRENDER DEAR	05/25/40
I CAN'T BELIEVE THAT YOU'RE IN LOVE WITH ME	05/25/40

CHARLIE CHRISTIAN

(Men of Minton's)

STOMPIN' AT THE SAVOY	1941
CHARLIE'S CHOICE	1941
UP ON TEDDIE'S HILL	1941

NAT "KING" COLE, LESTER YOUNG, RED CALLENDER TRIO

INDIANA	07/15/42
I CAN'T GET STARTED	07/15/42
BODY AND SOUL	07/15/42

DUKE ELLINGTON

Piano Solo

DEAR OLD SOUTHLAND	05/14/41

Duets with Jimmy Blanton

BLUES	11/22/39
PLUCKED AGAIN	11/22/39
PITTER PANTHER PATTER	10/01/40
MR. J. B. BLUES	10/01/40

& His Famous Orchestra, Instrumentals

THE SERGEANT WAS SHY	08/28/39
GRIEVIN'	10/14/39
COUNTRY GAL	10/16/39
KO KO	03/06/40
JACK THE BEAR	03/06/40
CONGA BRAVA	03/15/40
CONCERTO FOR COOTIE (DO NOTHIN' 'TIL YOU HEAR FROM ME)	03/15/40
COTTONTAIL	05/04/40
NEVER NO LAMENT (DON'T GET AROUND MUCH ANY MORE)	05/04/40
DUSK	05/28/40
BOJANGLES	05/28/40
SEPIA PANORAMA	07/14/40
HARLEM AIR SHAFT	07/22/40
ALL TOO SOON	07/22/40
RUMPUS IN RICHMOND	07/22/40
IN A MELLOTONE	09/05/40
WARM VALLEY	10/01/40
FLAMING SWORD	10/17/40
ACROSS THE TRACK BLUES	10/28/40
TAKE THE "A" TRAIN	02/15/41
BLUE SERGE	02/15/41
JOHN HARDY'S WIFE	02/15/41
JUST A-SITTIN' AND A-ROCKIN'	06/05/41
CHELSEA BRIDGE	09/26/41
PERDIDO	01/21/42
C JAM BLUES	01/21/42
MOON MIST	01/21/42
MAIN STEM	01/21/42

& His Famous Orchestra, Vocals

SOLITUDE, *vo Ivy Anderson*	02/14/40
STORMY WEATHER, *vo IA*	02/14/40
MOOD INDIGO, *vo IA*	02/14/40
FLAMINGO, *vo Herb Jeffries*	12/28/40
I GOT IT BAD, *vo IA*	06/26/41
JUMP FOR JOY, *vo HJ*	07/02/41
JUMP FOR JOY, *vo IA*	07/02/41
I DON'T KNOW WHAT KIND OF BLUES I GOT, *vo HJ*	12/02/41
I DON'T MIND, *vo IA*	02/06/42

(The five sets of recordings listed below were all sub-groups of the Ellington Orchestra, except for the last four tracks by Rex Stewart and the last five by Cootie Williams, which were recorded under different auspices.)

Barney Bigard's Orchestra

EARLY MORNIN'	10/16/39
MINUET IN BLUE	11/22/39
LOST IN TWO FLATS	11/22/39
HONEY HUSH	11/22/39
PELICAN DRAG	02/14/40
TAPIOCA	02/14/40
MARDI GRAS MADNESS	02/14/40
WATCH THE BIRDIE	02/14/40
LAMENT FOR JAVANETTE	11/11/40
CHARLIE THE CHULO	11/11/40
READY EDDY	11/11/40
C JAM BLUES	09/29/41

Johnny Hodges & His Orchestra

THE RABBIT'S JUMP	09/01/39
DREAM BLUES	09/01/39
SKUNK HOLLOW BLUES	10/14/39
DAY DREAM	11/02/40
GOOD QUEEN BESS	11/02/40
THAT'S THE BLUES, OLD MAN	11/02/40
JUNIOR HOP	11/02/40
PASSION FLOWER	07/03/41
THINGS AIN'T WHAT THEY USED TO BE	07/03/41
GOIN' OUT THE BACK WAY	07/03/41
SQUATTY ROO	07/03/41

Rex Stewart's Orchestra

WITHOUT A SONG	11/02/40
MY SUNDAY GAL	11/02/40
MOBILE BAY BLUES	11/02/40
LINGER AWHILE	11/02/40
SOME SATURDAY	07/03/41
SUBTLE SLOUGH	07/03/41
MENELINK	07/03/41
SUBTLE SLOUGH	07/03/41
POOR BUBBER	07/03/41

Rex Stewart's Big Seven

CHERRY	07/23/40
SOLID ROCK	07/23/40
BUGLE CALL RAG	07/23/40
DIGA DIGA DOO	07/23/40

Cootie Williams & His Rug Cutters

BLACK BUTTERFLY	02/15/40
DRY LONG SO, *vo Cootie Williams*	02/15/40
TOASTED PICKLES	02/15/40
GIVE IT UP	02/15/40
WEST END BLUES	05/07/41
AIN'T MISBEHAVIN'	05/07/41
BLUES IN MY CONDITION	05/07/41
G-MEN	05/07/41
FLY RIGHT (EPISTROPHY)	04/01/42

BUD FREEMAN

& His Summa Cum Laude Orchestra

I FOUND A NEW BABY	07/19/39
CHINA BOY	07/19/39
THE EEL	07/19/39
THE SAIL FISH	09/18/39
SUNDAY	09/18/39
SATANIC BLUES	09/18/39
I NEED SOME PETTIN'	03/25/40
BIG BOY	03/25/40
TIA JUANA	04/04/40
COPENHAGEN	04/04/40

& His Famous Chicagoans

JACK HITS THE ROAD, *vo Jack Teagarden*	07/23/40
47TH AND STATE	07/23/40
MUSKRAT RAMBLE	07/23/40
SHIM-ME-SHA-WABBLE	07/23/40
AT THE JAZZ BAND BALL	07/23/40
PRINCE OF WAILS	07/23/40

BENNY GOODMAN

& His Orchestra, Instrumentals

JUMPIN' AT THE WOODSIDE	08/10/39
STEALIN' APPLES	08/16/39
LET'S DANCE	10/24/39
HONEYSUCKLE ROSE	11/22/39

COCOANUT GROVE	04/10/40
HOUR OF PARTING	04/16/40
BENNY RIDES AGAIN	11/13/40
SUPERMAN	12/18/40
SCARECROW	02/19/41
SOLO FLIGHT	03/04/41
POUND RIDGE	08/01/41
THE EARL	09/25/41
CLARINET ALA KING	10/23/41
JERSEY BOUNCE	01/23/42
STRING OF PEARLS	02/05/42
SIX FLATS UNFURNISHED	07/27/42
MISSION TO MOSCOW	07/30/42

& His Orchestra, Vocals

DARN THAT DREAM, *vo Mildred Bailey*	11/22/39
HOW HIGH THE MOON, *vo Helen Forrest*	02/07/40
THE MAN I LOVE, *vo HF*	11/13/40
PERFIDIA, *vo HF*	01/28/41
HOW DEEP IS THE OCEAN, *vo Peggy Lee*	09/25/41
SOMEBODY ELSE IS TAKING MY PLACE, *vo PL*	11/13/41
THAT DID IT MARIE, *vo PL*	11/13/41
ON THE SUNNY SIDE OF THE STREET, *vo PL*	12/24/41
THE WAY YOU LOOK TONIGHT, *vo PL*	03/10/42
I'VE GOT A GAL IN KALAMAZOO, *vo Dick Haymes*	06/17/42
IDAHO, *vo DH*	06/17/42
WHY DON'T YOU DO RIGHT, *vo PL*	07/27/42

& His Small Groups

FLYING HOME, *Sextet*	10/02/39
ROSE ROOM, *Sextet*	10/02/39
STAR DUST, *Sextet*	10/02/39
MEMORIES OF YOU, *Sextet*	11/22/39
SEVEN COME ELEVEN, *Sextet*	11/22/39
AC-DC CURRENT, *Sextet*	12/20/39
I'M CONFESSIN', *Sextet*	12/20/39
SHIVERS, *Sextet*	12/20/39
TILL TOM SPECIAL, *Sextet*	02/07/40
GONE WITH WHAT WIND, *Sextet*	02/07/40
I NEVER KNEW, *Septet*	10/28/40
LESTER'S DREAM, *Septet*	10/28/40
CHARLIE'S DREAM, *Septet*	10/28/40
WHOLLY CATS, *Septet*	10/28/40
WHOLLY CATS, *Sextet*	11/07/40

ROYAL GARDEN BLUES, *Sextet*	11/07/40
AS LONG AS I LIVE, *Sextet*	11/07/40
I CAN'T GIVE YOU ANYTHING BUT LOVE, *Sextet*	12/19/40
I FOUND A NEW BABY, *Sextet*	01/15/41
GONE WITH WHAT DRAFT, *Sextet*	01/15/41
BREAKFAST FEUD, *Sextet*	01/15/41
ON THE ALAMO, *Sextet*	01/15/41
GOOD ENOUGH TO KEEP (AIR MAIL SPECIAL), *Sextet*	03/13/41
LIMEHOUSE BLUES, *Sextet*	10/28/41
WANG WANG BLUES, *Quartet*	03/10/42
THE WORLD IS WAITING FOR THE SUNRISE, *Quartet*	03/10/42

The Philharmonic-Symphony Society of New York

DEBUSSY'S FIRST RHAPSODY FOR CLARINET	12/16/40

LIONEL HAMPTON

& His Orchestra, Instrumentals

WHEN LIGHTS ARE LOW	09/11/39
HOT MALLETS	09/11/39
EARLY SESSION HOP	09/11/39
ONE SWEET LETTER FROM YOU	09/11/39
HAVEN'T NAMED IT YET	10/12/39
THE MUNSON STREET BREAKDOWN	10/30/39
I'VE FOUND A NEW BABY	10/30/39
DINAH	12/21/39
TILL TOM SPECIAL	02/26/40
FLYING HOME	02/26/40
CENTRAL AVENUE BREAKDOWN	05/17/40
JACK THE BELLBOY	05/17/40
ALTITUDE	12/19/40
FIDDLE-DEE-DEE	12/19/40
CHASIN' WITH CHASE	04/08/41
ROYAL FAMILY	03/02/42
BLUES IN THE NEWS	03/02/42
FLYING HOME	05/26/42

& His Orchestra, Vocals

ONE SWEET LETTER FROM YOU, *vo LH*	09/11/39
I'M ON MY WAY FROM YOU, *vo LH*	10/12/39
I'D BE LOST WITHOUT YOU, *vo Helen Forrest*	05/10/40
JIVIN' WITH JARVIS, *vo King Cole Trio*	07/17/40

COLEMAN HAWKINS

(see also Tier 2)

& His Orchestra

BODY AND SOUL	10/11/39

EARL HINES

(see also Tier 2)

Piano Solos

THE FATHER'S GETAWAY	07/29/39
REMINISCING AT BLUE NOTE	07/29/39
ROSETTA	10/21/39
BODY AND SOUL *(Storytone piano)*	02/26/40
CHILD OF A DISORDERED BRAIN	02/26/40
ON THE SUNNY SIDE OF THE STREET	04/03/41
MY MELANCHOLY BABY	04/03/41

JOHNNY HODGES

(see Duke Ellington)

BILLIE HOLIDAY

& Her Orchestra

SOME OTHER SPRING	07/05/39
THEM THERE EYES	07/05/39
SWING, BROTHER, SWING	07/05/39
NIGHT AND DAY	12/13/39
THE MAN I LOVE	12/13/39
BODY AND SOUL	02/29/40
LAUGHING AT LIFE	06/07/40
I'M ALL FOR YOU	09/12/40
I HEAR MUSIC	09/12/40
ST. LOUIS BLUES	10/15/40
LET'S DO IT	03/21/41
GEORGIA ON MY MIND	03/21/41
ALL OF ME	03/21/41
GOD BLESS THE CHILD	05/09/41
SOLITUDE	05/09/41
JIM	08/07/41
I COVER THE WATERFRONT	08/07/41
LOVE ME OR LEAVE ME	08/07/41
GLOOMY SUNDAY	08/07/41
MANDY IS TWO	02/10/42

With Paul Whiteman & His Orchestra

TRAV'LIN' LIGHT	06/12/42

JAM SESSION AT COMMODORE

A GOOD MAN IS HARD TO FIND, *Parts 1-4* — 03/23/40

KANSAS CITY SIX

GOOD MORNING BLUES — 12/24/39
'WAY DOWN YONDER IN NEW ORLEANS — 12/24/39

METRONOME ALL STAR GROUPS

All Star Band

KING PORTER STOMP — 02/07/40
BUGLE CALL RAG — 01/16/41
ONE O'CLOCK JUMP — 01/16/41
ROYAL FLUSH — 12/13/41
DEAR OLD SOUTHLAND — 12/13/41

All Star Nine

ALL STAR STRUT — 02/07/40

Leaders

I GOT RHYTHM — 01/16/42

JELLY ROLL MORTON

& His New Orleans Jazzmen

OH, DIDN'T HE RAMBLE — 09/14/39
HIGH SOCIETY — 09/14/39
I THOUGHT I HEARD BUDDY BOLDEN SAY, *vo Jelly Roll Morton* — 09/14/39
WININ' BOY BLUES, *vo JRM* — 09/14/39

& His Seven

SWEET SUBSTITUTE, *vo JRM* — 01/04/40
PANAMA — 01/04/40
GOOD OLD NEW YORK, *vo JRM* — 01/01/40
SWINGING THE ELKS — 01/30/40

Piano Solos

CLIMAX RAG — 09/28/39
DON'T YOU LEAVE ME HERE, *vo JRM* — 09/28/39
WEST END BLUES — 09/28/39
BALLIN' THE JACK, *vo JRM* — 09/28/39
KING PORTER STOMP — 12/14/39
MAMIE'S BLUES, *vo JRM* — 12/16/39
MICHIGAN WATER BLUES, *vo JRM* — 12/18/39

MUGGSY SPANIER

(see also Tier 2)

& His Ragtime Band

BIG BUTTER & EGG MAN, *vo George Brunies*	07/07/39
SOMEDAY, SWEETHEART	07/07/39
ECCENTRIC	07/07/39
THAT DA DA STRAIN	07/07/39
AT THE JAZZ BAND BALL	11/10/39
I WISH I COULD SHIMMY LIKE MY SISTER KATE, *vo GB*	11/10/39
DIPPER MOUTH BLUES	11/10/39
LIVERY STABLE BLUES	11/10/39
RIVERBOAT SHUFFLE	11/22/39
RELAXIN' AT THE TOURO	11/22/39
AT SUNDOWN	11/22/39
BLUIN' THE BLUES	11/22/39
LONESOME ROAD	12/12/39
DINAH, *vo GB*	12/12/39
BLACK AND BLUE	12/12/39
MANDY, MAKE UP YOUR MIND	12/12/39

REX STEWART

(see Duke Ellington)

ART TATUM

Piano Solos

ELEGIE	02/22/40
HUMORESQUE	02/22/40
SWEET LORRAINE	02/22/40
GET HAPPY	02/22/40
LULLABY OF THE LEAVES	02/22/40
TIGER RAG	02/22/40
EMALINE	02/22/40
MOON GLOW	02/22/40
COCKTAILS FOR TWO	02/22/40
ST. LOUIS BLUES	07/26/40
BEGIN THE BEGUINE	07/26/40
ROSETTA	07/26/40
INDIANA	07/26/40
MIGHTY LAK A ROSE	07/27/41
TOLEDO BLUES	07/27/41
BODY AND SOUL	07/27/41
THERE'LL BE SOME CHANGES MADE	07/27/41
LADY BE GOOD	09/16/41
SWEET GEORGIA BROWN	09/16/41

& His Band

WEE BABY BLUES, *vo Big Joe Turner*	01/21/41
STOMPIN' AT THE SAVOY	01/21/41
LAST GOODBYE BLUES, *vo BJT*	01/21/41
BATTERY BOUNCE	01/21/41
LUCILLE	06/13/41
ROCK ME, MAMA, *vo BJT*	06/13/41
CORRINE CORRINA, *vo BJT*	06/13/41
LONESOME GRAVEYARD, *vo BJT*	06/13/41

THOMAS "FATS" WALLER

& His Rhythm, Vocals by Fats Waller

SQUEEZE ME	08/10/39
SUITCASE SUZIE	11/03/39
YOUR FEETS TOO BIG	11/03/39
I CAN'T GIVE YOU ANYTHING BUT LOVE *with Una Mae Carlisle*	11/03/39
AT TWILIGHT	01/12/40
ORIGINAL E FLAT BLUES	07/16/40
I'LL NEVER SMILE AGAIN	07/16/40
DRY BONES	07/16/40
SHORTNIN' BREAD	01/02/41
BUCK JUMPIN'	10/01/41
YOUR SOCKS DON'T MATCH	12/26/41
BY THE LIGHT OF THE SILVERY MOON, *with The Delta Rhythm Boys*	07/13/42

Electric Organ solos

HAND ME DOWN MY WALKING CANE	11/20/39
PANTIN' IN THE PANTHER ROOM	01/02/41
CLARINET MARMALADE	10/01/41
JITTERBUG WALTZ	03/16/42

Piano solos

GEORGIA ON MY MIND	05/13/41
ROCKIN' CHAIR	05/13/41
CAROLINA SHOUT	05/13/41
HONEYSUCKLE ROSE	05/13/41
RING DEM BELLS	05/13/41

COOTIE WILLIAMS

(see Duke Ellington)

TEDDY WILSON

& His Orchestra, Instrumentals

EARLY SESSION HOP	07/26/39
LADY OF MYSTERY	07/26/39
JUMPIN' ON THE BLACKS AND WHITES	09/12/39
HALLELUJAH	09/12/39
SWEET LORRAINE	12/11/39
LIZA	12/11/39
IN THE MOOD	01/18/40
COCOANUT GROVE	01/18/40
71	01/18/40
I NEVER KNEW	12/09/40
OH, LADY BE GOOD	12/09/40

& His Orchestra, Vocals

SOME OTHER SPRING, *vo Jean Eldridge*	09/12/39
WHAM, *vo J. C. Heard & Chorus*	12/11/39
CRYING MY SOUL OUT FOR YOU, *vo JE*	01/18/40
OUT OF NOWHERE, *vo Lena Horne*	09/16/41

Piano Solos

SMOKE GETS IN YOUR EYES	04/07/41
ROSETTA	04/07/41
I KNOW THAT YOU KNOW	04/11/41
THEM THERE EYES	04/11/41
CHINA BOY	04/11/41
BODY AND SOUL	04/11/41
THESE FOOLISH THINGS	01/21/42

2. Second Tier – *VERY GOOD*

HENRY "RED" ALLEN
& His Orchestra

DOWN IN JUNGLE TOWN	05/28/40
CANAL STREET BLUES	05/28/40
K. K. BOOGIE	04/17/41
OL' MAN RIVER, vo Henry Allen	04/17/41
A SHERIDAN "SQUARE"	07/22/41
INDIANA	07/22/41

ALBERT AMMONS
(also with Pete Johnson & Meade Lux Lewis)
Piano Solos

SUITCASE BLUES	1942
BASS GOIN' CRAZY	1942

LOUIS ARMSTRONG
(see also Tier 1)
with The Mills Brothers

W.P.A.	04/10/40
BOOG IT	04/10/40
CHERRY	04/10/40
MARIE	04/10/40

& His Orchestra

LEAP FROG	11/16/41
AMONG MY SOUVENIRS, *vo LA*	04/17/42

BUSTER BAILEY
& His Sextet, Instrumentals

SHOULD I	05/40
THE BLUE ROOM	05/40
APRIL IN PARIS	05/40
AM I BLUE	05/40
PINETOP'S BOOGIE WOOGIE	06/40
ECCENTRIC RAG	06/40

& His Sextet, Vocals

SEEMS LIKE A MONTH OF SUNDAYS, *vo Judy Ellington*	06/40
FABLE OF A ROSE, *vo JE*	06/40

MIDLRED BAILEY

Accompanied by various groups

NOBODY KNOW THE TROUBLE I'VE SEEN	11/30/39
ALL THE THINGS YOU ARE	11/30/39
HOLD ON	11/30/39
FOOLS RUSH IN	04/02/40
I'M NOBODY'S BABY	04/02/40
ROCKIN' CHAIR	03/14/41
SOMETIMES I'M HAPPY	03/14/41
LOVER COME BACK TO ME	06/13/41
IT'S SO PEACEFUL IN THE COUNTRY *with The Delta Rhythm Boys*	06/24/41
MORE THAN YOU KNOW	02/12/42

CHARLIE BARNET

& His Orchestra, Instrumentals

CHEROKEE	07/17/39
THE DUKE'S IDEA	09/10/39
THE COUNT'S IDEA	09/10/39
THE WRONG IDEA	10/09/39
THE RIGHT IDEA	10/09/39
CLAP HANDS, HERE COMES CHARLIE	12/11/39
POMPTON TURNPIKE	07/19/40
THE SERGEANT WAS SHY	07/19/40
WINGS OVER MANHATTAN, 1 & 2	09/17/40
REDSKIN RHUMBA	10/14/40
BLUE JUICE	01/07/41
CHARLESTON ALLEY	01/07/41
BIRMINGHAM BREAKDOWN	01/23/41
MURDER AT PEYTON HALL	08/14/41
MOTHER FUZZY	09/11/41
SMILES	09/11/41
SHADY LADY	09/11/41
WASHINGTON WHIRLIGIG	07/17/42

& His Orchestra, Vocals

GOOD-FOR-NOTHIN' JOE, *vo Lena Horne*	01/07/41
YOU'RE MY THRILL, *vo LH*	01/07/41
I LIKE TO RIFF, *vo Peanuts Holland*	04/30/42

LEON "CHU" BERRY

& His Jazz Ensemble

BLOWING UP A BREEZE	08/28/41
SUNNY SIDE OF THE STREET	08/28/41
MONDAY AT MINTONS	08/28/41
GEE BABY, AIN'T I GOOD TO YOU, *vo Hot Lips Page*	08/28/41

CAB CALLOWAY

& His Orchestra, Instrumentals

TRYLON SWING	07/17/39
CRESCENDO IN DRUMS	07/17/39
PLUCKIN' THE BASS	08/30/39
PICKIN' THE CABBAGE	03/08/40
PARADIDDLE	03/08/40
GHOST OF A CHANCE	06/27/40
LONESOME NIGHTS	08/28/40
WILLOW WEEP FOR ME	01/16/41
JONAH JOINS THE CAB	03/05/41

& His Orchestra, Vocals

THE JUMPIN' JIVE, *vo Cab Calloway*	07/17/39
GEECHIE JOE, *vo CC*	03/05/41
MY GAL, *vo CC*	07/03/41
ST. JAMES INFIRMARY, *vo CC*	07/03/41
I'LL BE AROUND, *vo CC*	02/02/42

BENNY CARTER

& His Orchestra

RIFF ROMP	08/31/39
SHUFFLEBUG SHUFFLE	11/01/39
MORE THAN YOU KNOW, *vo Roy Felton*	11/01/39
SLEEP	01/30/40
FISH FRY	01/30/40
SLOW FREIGHT	01/30/40
NIGHT HOP	05/20/40
POM POM	05/20/40
OKAY FOR BABY	05/20/40
ALL OF ME	11/19/40
COCKTAILS FOR TWO	11/19/40
TAKIN' MY TIME	11/19/40
MY FAVORITE BLUES	04/01/41
WHAT A DIFFERENCE A DAY MADE	04/01/41
SUNDAY	10/16/41
ILL WIND	10/16/41
BACK BAY BOOGIE	10/16/41

NAT "KING" COLE

The King Cole Trio, Instrumentals

HONEYSUCKLE ROSE	12/06/40
EARLY MORNING BLUES	03/14/41

The King Cole Trio, Vocals

SWEET LORRAINE, *vo NKC*	12/06/40
GONE WITH THE DRAFT, *vo NKC*	12/06/40
SCOTCHIN' WITH THE SODA, *vo Trio*	03/14/41
THIS WILL MAKE YOU LAUGH, *vo NKC*	07/16/41
THAT AIN'T RIGHT, *vo NKC*	10/22/41
HIT THAT JIVE JACK, *vo Trio*	10/22/41

EDDIE CONDON

& His Chicagoans

THERE'LL BE SOME CHANGES MADE	08/11/39
NOBODY'S SWEETHEART	08/11/39
FRIARS POINT SHUFFLE	08/11/39
SOMEDAY SWEETHEART	08/11/39

& His Band

STRUT MISS LIZZIE	11/30/39
IT'S RIGHT HERE FOR YOU	11/30/39
BALLIN' THE JACK	11/30/39
GEORGIA GRIND	11/11/40
OH, SISTER, AIN'T THAT HOT	11/11/40
DANCING FOOL	11/11/40
PRETTY DOLL	11/11/40
DON'T LEAVE ME DADDY	01/21/42
FIDGETY FEET	01/21/42
MAMMY O'MINE	01/21/42
LONESOME TAG BLUES	01/21/42
TORTILLA IN B FLAT	01/21/42
MORE TORTILLA IN B FLAT	01/21/42

IDA COX

& Her All-Star Band

DEEP SEA BLUES	10/31/39
ONE HOUR MAMA	10/31/39
FOUR DAY CREEP	10/31/39
PINK SLIP BLUES	10/31/39
HARD TIMES BLUES	10/31/39
TAKE HIM OFF MY MIND	10/31/39

& Her All-Star Orchestra

LAST MILE BLUES	12/20/40
I AIN'T GONNA LET NOBODY BREAK MY HEART	12/20/40
I CAN'T QUIT THAT MAN	12/20/40
YOU GOT TO SWING AND SWAY	12/20/40

BOB CROSBY

& His Orchestra

BOOGIE WOOGIE MAXIXE	08/29/39
THE WORLD IS WAITING FOR THE SUNRISE	08/29/39
HIGH SOCIETY	10/02/39
AIR MAIL STOMP	10/02/39
FOR DANCERS ONLY	10/23/39
RUN, RABBIT, RUN *vo Marion Mann*	02/19/40
SYMPATHY	04/03/40
VULTEE SPECIAL	01/20/42
BRASS BOOGIE, *Parts 1 & 2*	01/20/42
SUGAR FOOT STOMP	01/27/42
KING PORTER STOMP	01/27/42
MILENBERG JOYS	01/27/42
BLACK ZEPHYR	02/17/42
BLACK SURREAL	02/17/42
EC-STACY	02/17/42

& His Bob Cats

'TIL WE MEET AGAIN	09/18/39
WASHINGTON AND LEE SWING	09/25/39
PERUNA	09/25/39
SPAIN	02/06/40
ALL BY MYSELF, *vo Marion Mann*	02/06/40
JAZZ ME BLUES	02/06/40
SWEETHEARTS ON PARADE	01/29/42
IT'S A LONG WAY TO TIPPERARY	01/29/42

TOMMY DORSEY

& His Orchestra, Instrumentals

ANOTHER ONE OF THEM THINGS	08/29/40
SWING HIGH	10/16/40
SWANEE RIVER	10/16/40
DEEP RIVER	02/17/41
SWING LOW, SWEET CHARIOT	02/17/41
LOOSE LID SPECIAL	07/15/41
WELL, GIT IT	03/13/42
MANDY, MAKE UP YOUR MIND	06/17/42
BLUE BLAZES	07/02/42

& His Orchestra, Vocals

I'LL NEVER SMILE AGAIN, *vo Frank Sinatra, Jo Stafford, & The Pied Pipers*	05/23/40
THE ONE I LOVE, *vo FS & PP*	06/27/40
STAR DUST, vo FS & PP	11/11/40
OH, LOOK AT ME NOW, *vo FS, Connie Haines, & PP*	01/06/41
FOR YOU, *vo Jo Stafford*	01/20/41
WHATCHA KNOW JOE, *vo PP*	02/07/41
EVERYTHING HAPPENS TO ME, *vo FS*	02/07/41
YES, INDEED, *vo Sy Oliver & Jo Stafford*	02/07/41
BLUE SKIES, *vo FS & Chorus*	05/28/41
SWINGIN' ON NOTHIN', *vo SO & JS*	07/15/41
THERE ARE SUCH THINGS, *vo FS & PP*	07/01/42
DAYBREAK, *vo FS*	07/01/42
MANHATTAN SERENADE, *vo JS*	07/02/42

& His Sentimentalists

EAST OF THE SUN, vo FS	04/23/40

ELLA FITZGERALD

& Her Orchestra

AFTER I SAY I'M SORRY	10/12/39
BABY, WHAT ELSE CAN I DO	10/12/39
BABY WON'T YOU PLEASE COME HOME	02/15/40
CABIN IN THE SKY	11/08/40
I'M THE LONESOMEST GAL IN TOWN	11/08/40
THE ONE I LOVE	01/08/41
JIM	10/06/41
THIS LOVE OF MINE	10/06/41
I GOT IT BAD	07/31/41

EDMOND HALL

Celeste Quartet

EDMOND HALL BLUES	02/05/41
CELESTIAL EXPRESS	02/05/41
JAMMING IN FOUR	02/05/41
PROFOUNDLY BLUE	02/05/41

HORACE HENDERSON

& His Orchestra, Fletcher Henderson conducting

SHUFFLIN' JOE	02/27/40
OH BOY, I'M IN THE GROOVE, *vo Viola Jefferson*	02/27/40
KITTY ON TOAST	02/27/40
I GOT RHYTHM, *vo VJ*	02/27/40

& His Orchestra

SULTAN SERENADE	07/12/40
WHEN DREAMS COME TRUE	08/13/40
I STILL HAVE MY DREAMS	08/13/40
TURKEY SPECIAL	08/13/40
FLINGING A WING DING	08/13/40
COQUETTE	08/13/40
SMOOTH SAILING	10/23/40
AIN'T MISBEHAVIN'	10/23/40
I'LL ALWAYS BE IN LOVE WITH YOU, *vo Harold Johnson*	10/23/40

WOODY HERMAN

& His Orchestra, Instrumentals

BLUES ON PARADE	12/13/39
PICK-A-RIB	01/05/40
HERMAN AT THE SHERMAN	04/10/40
GOLDEN WEDDING	11/09/40
BLUE FLAME	02/13/41
FUR TRAPPERS BALL	02/13/41
BISHOP'S BLUES	08/21/41
WOODSHEDDIN' WITH WOODY	08/21/41
THREE WAYS TO SMOKE A PIPE	09/05/41
TEN DAY FURLOUGH	09/05/41
HOT CHESTNUTS	09/10/41
DOWN UNDER	07/14/42

& His Orchestra, Vocals

JUMPIN' BLUES, *vo Woody Herman*	07/18/39
FINE AND DANDY, *vo WH*	09/11/39
I'LL REMEMBER APRIL, *vo WH*	08/28/41
BLUES IN THE NIGHT, *vo WH*	09/10/41
AMEN, *vo WH*	04/02/42

& His Woodchoppers

SOUTH	02/13/41
FAN IT, *vo WH*	02/13/41

EARL HINES

(see also Tier 1)

& His Orchestra, Instrumentals

G. T. STOMP	07/12/39
RIDIN' AND JIVIN'	07/12/39
GRAND TERRACE SHUFFLE	07/12/39

FATHER STEPS IN	07/12/39
RIFF MEDLEY	10/06/39
XYZ	10/06/39
'GATOR SWING	10/06/39
BOOGIE WOOGIE ON ST. LOUIS BLUES	02/13/40
DEEP FOREST	02/13/40
NUMBER 19	02/13/40
TANTALIZING A CUBAN	06/19/40
JERSEY BOUNCE	04/03/41
WINDY CITY JIVE	08/20/41
SWINGIN' ON C	08/20/41
YELLOW FIRE	08/20/41
THE FATHER JUMPS	10/28/41
THE EARL	11/17/41
SECOND BALCONY JUMP	03/19/42

& His Orchestra, Vocals

PIANO MAN, *vo Walter Fuller*	07/12/39
JELLY, JELLY, *vo Billy Eckstine*	12/02/40
SKYLARK, *vo BE*	03/19/42
STORMY MONDAY BLUES, *vo BE*	03/19/42

JAMES P. JOHNSON

Piano Solos

BOOGIE WOOGIE STRIDE	07/02/42
IMPRESSIONS	07/02/42
SNOWY MORNING BLUES	07/02/42

PETE JOHNSON

(also with Meade Lux Lewis)

Piano Solos

BOOGIE WOOGIE	10/13/39
BLUES ON THE DOWN BEAT	08/23/40
KAYCEE ON MY MIND	08/23/40
BASEMENT BOOGIE	05/08/41
DEATH RAY BOOGIE	05/08/41
JUST FOR YOU	05/08/41
PETE'S MIXTURE	05/08/41

& His Band

627 STOMP	11/11/40

Duets with Albert Ammons

CUTTIN' THE BOOGIE	05/07/41
WALKIN' THE BOOGIE	06/17/41
SIXTH AVENUE EXPRESS	06/17/41

JOHN KIRBY
& His Orchestra

FRONT AND CENTER	07/28/39
ROYAL GARDEN BLUES	07/28/39
OPUS 5	07/28/39
BLUE SKIES	08/10/39
I MAY BE WRONG	08/10/39
NOCTURNE	10/12/39
DVORAK'S HUMORESQUE	10/12/39
SCHUBERT'S SERENADE	10/12/39
JUMPIN' IN THE PUMP ROOM	04/22/40
BLUES PETITE	05/27/40
AUDIOLOGY	07/09/40
CAN'T WE BE FRIENDS	07/09/40
COQUETTE	07/09/40
ZOOMING AT THE ZOMBIE	07/09/40
BEETHOVEN RIFFS ON	01/15/41
DOUBLE TALK	01/15/41
IT'S ONLY A PAPER MOON	07/25/41
TWEED ME	10/07/41
ST. LOUIS BLUES	02/11/42

ANDY KIRK
& His Orchestra, Instrumentals

BIG JIM BLUES	11/15/39
LITTLE MISS	07/08/40
THE COUNT	11/07/40
TWELFTH STREET RAG	11/07/40
RING DEM BELLS	01/03/41
BOOGIE WOOGIE COCKTAIL	07/14/42
MC GHEE SPECIAL	07/14/42

& His Orchestra, Vocals

WHAM, *vo June Richmond*	01/02/40
FINE AND MELLOW, *vo JR*	06/25/40
47TH STREET JIVE, *vo JR*	07/17/41
UNLUCKY BLUES, *vo JR*	07/29/42

GENE KRUPA
& His Orchestra, Instrumentals

SYMPHONY IN RIFFS	09/20/39
BLUE RHYTHM FANTASY, 1 & 2	01/02/40
MANHATTAN TRANSFER	02/19/40
TUXEDO JUNCTION	03/08/40

SWEET GEORGIA BROWN	10/24/40
AFTER YOU'VE GONE	06/05/41
TUNIN' UP	07/02/41
THAT DRUMMERS BAND	07/13/42

& His Orchestra, Vocals

DRUMMIN' MAN, *vo Irene Daye*	11/02/39
DEEP IN THE BLUES, *vo ID*	11/28/40
DRUM BOOGIE, *vo ID & Chorus*	01/17/41
GEORGIA ON MY MIND, *vo Anita O'Day*	03/12/41
FOOL AM I, *vo AO'D*	03/12/41
LET ME OFF UPTOWN, *vo AO'D & Roy Elridge*	05/08/41
ROCKIN' CHAIR, *vo RE*	07/02/41
THE WALLS KEEP TALKING, *vo AO'D & RE*	08/28/41
SKYLARK, *vo AO'D*	11/25/41
THAT'S WHAT YOU THINK, *vo AO'D*	02/26/42
KNOCK ME A KISS, *vo RE*	04/02/42
MASSACHUSETTS, *vo AO'D*	07/13/42
MURDER, HE SAYS, *vo AO'D*	07/13/42

LEADBELLY (HUDDIE LEDBETTER)

Vocal, accompanied by own guitar

ROCK ISLAND LINE	06/14/40
ALBERTA	06/15/40
YOU CAN'T LOSE-A ME CHOLLY	06/17/40

MEADE LUX LEWIS

Trio with Albert Ammons & Pete Johnson

BOOGIE WOOGIE PRAYER	9or10/39

Piano solos

WHISTLING BLUES	9or10/39
THE BLUES, *Parts 1-4*	11/06/39
HONKY TONK TRAIN BLUES	10/04/40
BASS ON TOP	10/04/40
SIX WHEEL CHASER	10/04/40
TELL YOUR STORY, No. 2	10/04/40
RISING TIDE BLUES	04/09/41
SCHOOL OF RHYTHM	04/09/41
YANCEY SPECIAL	04/09/41

Harpsichord solos

NINETEEN WAYS OF PLAYING A CHORUS	04/09/41
SELF PORTRAIT	04/09/41

JIMMIE LUNCEFORD

& His Orchestra, Instrumentals

BELGIUM STOMP	09/14/39
LIZA	09/14/39
I'M ALONE WITH YOU	12/14/39
UPTOWN BLUES	12/14/39
LUNCEFORD BLUES	12/14/39
WHAT'S YOUR STORY, MORNING GLORY	02/28/40
CHOPIN PRELUDE NO. 7	05/09/40
MONOTONY IN FOUR FLATS	05/09/40
PAVANNE	06/19/40
OKAY FOR BABY	12/23/40
FLIGHT OF THE JITTERBUG	12/23/40
BATTLE AXE	03/26/41
CHOCOLATE	04/22/41
HI SPOOK	08/26/41
YARD DOG MAZURKA	08/26/41
STRICTLY INSTRUMENTAL	06/26/42

& His Orchestra, Vocals

DINAH, 1 & 2, vo Joe Thomas	02/28/40
I AIN'T GONNA STUDY WAR NO MORE, vo Dandridge Sisters	06/19/40
BLUES IN THE NIGHT, 1 & 2, vo Willie Smith	12/22/41
KNOCK ME A KISS, vo WS	06/26/42

JAY MC SHANN

Combo

COQUETTE	12/02/40
MOTEN STOMP	12/02/40
VINE STREET BOOGIE	04/30/41

Quartet

CONFESSIN' THE BLUES, *vo Walter Brown*	04/30/41
HOLD'EN HOOTIE	04/30/41
HOOTIE'S IGNORANT OIL, *vo WB*	11/18/41

& His Orchestra, Instrumentals

SWINGMATISM	04/30/41
DEXTER BLUES	04/30/41

& His Orchestra, Vocals

HOOTIE BLUES, *vo Walter Brown*	04/30/41
RED RIVER BLUES, *vo WB*	11/18/41
LONELY BOY BLUES, *vo WB*	07/02/42

GET ME ON YOUR MIND, *vo Al Hibbler*	07/02/42
THE JUMPING BLUES, *vo WB*	07/02/42
SEPIAN BOUNCE, *vo AH*	07/02/42

RED NORVO
& His Orchestra

JERSEY BOUNCE	03/05/42
ARTHUR MURRAY TAUGHT ME DANCING IN A HURRY, *vo Mildred Bailey*	03/05/42

MEL POWELL
& His Orchestra

WHEN DID YOU LEAVE HEAVEN	02/04/42
THE WORLD IS WAITING FOR THE SUNRISE	02/04/42
BLUE SKIES	02/04/42
MOOD AT TWILIGHT	02/04/42

QUINTETTE OF THE HOT CLUB OF FRANCE

UNDECIDED	08/25/39
H. C. Q. STRUT	08/25/39
THE MAN I LOVE	08/25/39
NUAGES	12/13/40
SWEET SUE	12/13/40

Stephane Grappelly & His Musicians

AFTER YOU'VE GONE	07/30/40
STEPHANE'S TUNE	07/30/40
STEPHANE'S BLUES	02/28/41

Django's Music

LIMEHOUSE BLUES	03/22/40
DAPHNE	03/22/40

ARTIE SHAW
& His Orchestra, Instrumentals

OH, LADY BE GOOD	08/27/39
I SURRENDER DEAR	08/27/39
FRENESI	03/03/40
TEMPTATION	09/07/40
CHANTEZ-LES BAS	09/07/40
STAR DUST	10/07/40
BLUES, *Parts 1 & 2*	12/04/40
DANCING IN THE DARK	01/23/41
MOON GLOW	01/23/41

IF I HAD YOU	03/20/41
GEORGIA ON MY MIND	03/20/41
IT HAD TO BE YOU	03/20/41
CONFESSIN'	06/26/41
ROCKIN' CHAIR	09/02/41
TWO IN ONE BLUES	01/21/42

& His Orchestra, Vocals

DAY IN, DAY OUT, *vo Helen Forrest*	08/27/39
ALL IN FUN, *vo HF*	10/26/39
ALL THE THINGS YOU ARE, *vo HF*	10/26/39
GLOOMY SUNDAY, *vo Pauline Byrne*	03/03/40
LOVE ME A LITTLE LITTLE, *vo Lena Horne*	06/26/41
ST. JAMES INFIRMARY, *vo Hot Lips Page*	11/12/41
SOMETIMES I FEEL LIKE A MOTHERLESS CHILD, *vo HLP*	01/21/42

& His Gramercy Five

SPECIAL DELIVERY STOMP	09/03/40
SUMMIT RIDGE DRIVE	09/03/40
KEEPIN' MYSELF FOR YOU	09/03/40
CROSS YOUR HEART	09/03/40
DR.LIVINGSTONE, I PRESUME	12/05/40
WHEN THE QUAIL COME BACK TO SAN QUENTIN	12/05/40
MY BLUE HEAVEN	12/05/40
SMOKE GETS IN YOUR EYES	12/05/40

ZUTTY SINGLETON

& His Orchestra

KING PORTER STOMP	05/28/40
SHIM-ME-SHA-WABBLE	05/28/40

MUGGSY SPANIER

(see also Tier 1)

& His Orchestra

LITTLE DAVID, PLAY ON YOUR HARP	01/02/42
CAN'T WE BE FRIENDS	01/02/42
CHICAGO	01/02/42
HESITATING BLUES	01/02/42
AMERICAN PATROL	06/01/42
TWO O'CLOCK JUMP	06/01/42
MORE THAN YOU KNOW, *vo Dottie Reid*	06/01/42

JOE SULLIVAN
& His Café Society Orchestra, Instrumentals

SOLITUDE	02/09/40
OH, LADY BE GOOD	02/09/40
POM POM	04/29/40
COQUETTE	04/29/40

& His Café Society Orchestra, Vocals

LOW DOWN DIRTY SHAME, *vo Big Joe Turner*	02/09/40
I CAN'T GIVE YOU ANYTHING BUT LOVE, *vo BJT*	02/09/40
I COVER THE WATERFRONT, *vo Helen Ward*	04/29/40
I'VE GOT A CRUSH ON YOU, *vo HW*	04/29/40

Piano Solos

ANDY'S BLUES	03/25/41
DEL MAR RAG	03/25/41
FOREVERMORE	03/28/41
SUMMERTIME	03/28/41

JACK TEAGARDEN
& His Orchestra, Instrumentals

BLUES TO THE DOLE	07/19/39
PEG O' MY HEART	08/25/39
WOLVERINE BLUES	10/06/39
SOMEWHERE A VOICE IS CALLING	11/01/39
SWINGIN' ON THE TEAGARDEN GATE	11/01/39
CHICKS IS WONDERFUL	01/31/41

& His Orchestra, Vocals

PUTTIN' AND TAKIN', *vo JT*	07/19/39
I SWUNG THE ELECTION, *vo JT*	07/19/39
MUDDY RIVER BLUES, *vo JT*	10/06/39
BEALE STREET BLUES, *vo JT*	11/01/39
BLUES TO THE LONELY, *vo JT*	01/31/41
ST. JAMES INFIRMARY, *vo JT*	05/26/41
BLACK AND BLUE, *vo JT*	05/26/41
NOBODY KNOWS THE TROUBLE I'VE SEEN, *vo JT*	07/07/41

Big Eight

ST. JAMES INFIRMARY, *vo JT*	12/15/40
THE WORLD IS WAITING FOR THE SUNRISE	12/15/40
THE BIG EIGHT BLUES	12/15/40
SHINE	12/15/40

CLAUDE THORNHILL

& His Orchestra, Instrumentals

O SOLO MIO	03/10/41
HUNGARIAN DANCE NO. 5	03/10/41
TRAUMEREI	03/10/41
SLEEPY SERENADE	04/16/41
PORTRAIT OF A GUINEA FARM	04/16/41
SNOWFALL	05/21/41
WHERE OR WHEN	05/21/41
AUTUMN NOCTURNE	10/06/41
NIGHT AND DAY	02/06/42
GRIEG'S PIANO CONCERTO	02/23/42
BUSTER'S LAST STAND	06/19/42

& His Orchestra, Vocals

THERE'S A SMALL HOTEL, *vo Snowflakes*	07/25/42
MOONLIGHT BAY, *vo S*	07/25/42

THREE DEUCES

(Pee Wee Russell, Joe Sullivan, Zutty Singleton)

JIG WALK	03/25/41
DEUCES WILD	03/25/41
THE LAST TIME I SAW CHICAGO	03/25/41
ABOUT FACE	03/25/41

BIG JOE TURNER

& His Fly Cats

PINEY BROWN BLUES	11/11/40

Vocals

DOGGIN' THE DOG	11/26/40
CARELESS LOVE	11/26/40
JUMPIN' DOWN BLUES	11/26/40
RAINY DAY BLUES	11/26/40

THE VARSITY SEVEN

Instrumentals

SCRATCH MY BACK	12/14/39
A PRETTY GIRL IS LIKE A MELODY	01/15/40
POM POM	01/15/40

Vocals

IT'S TIGHT LIKE THAT, *vo Jeanne Burns*	12/14/39
EASY RIDER, *vo JB & Ulysses Livingston*	12/14/39

SAVE IT, PRETTY MAMA, *vo Jeanne Burns*	12/14/39
HOW LONG, HOW LONG BLUES, *vo Big Joe Turner*	01/15/40
SHAKE IT AND BREAK IT, *vo BJT*	01/15/40

LEE WILEY

Vocals, accompanied by various groups

SWEET AND LOWDOWN	11/13/39
SAM AND DELILAH	11/13/39
MY ONE AND ONLY	11/13/39
S'WONDERFUL	11/13/39
I'VE GOT A CRUSH ON YOU	11/15/39
SOMEONE TO WATCH OVER ME	11/15/39
HOW LONG HAS THIS BEEN GOING ON?	11/15/39
BUT NOT FOR ME	11/15/39
BABY'S AWAKE NOW	02/40
A LITTLE BIRDIE TOLD ME SO	02/40
I'VE GOT FIVE DOLLARS	02/40
YOU TOOK ADVANTAGE OF ME	02/40
A SHIP WITHOUT A SAIL	02/40
AS THOUGH YOU WERE THERE	02/40
GLAD TO BE UNHAPPY	02/40
HERE IN MY ARMS	02/40
LET'S FLY AWAY	04/10/40
LET'S DO IT	04/10/40
HOT HOUSE ROSE	04/10/40
FIND ME A PRIMITIVE MAN	04/10/40
EASY TO LOVE	04/15/40
YOU DO SOMETHING TO ME	04/15/40
LOOKING AT YOU	04/15/40
WHY SHOULDN'T I	04/15/40
DOWN TO STEAMBOAT TENNESSEE	07/10/40
SUGAR	07/10/40

JIMMY YANCEY

Piano Solos & Vocals

YANCEY STOMP	10/25/39
STATE STREET SPECIAL	10/25/39
TELL'EM ABOUT ME	10/25/39
SLOW AND EASY BLUES	10/25/39
THE MELLOW BLUES	10/25/39
BEAR TRAP BLUES	02/23/40
CRYIN' IN MY SLEEP, vo JY	09/06/40
DEATH LETTER BLUES, vo JY	09/06/40
35TH AND DEARBORN	09/06/40

3. Third Tier – *GOOD*

BUNNY BERIGAN
& His Orchestra

AIN'T SHE SWEET	11/28/39

PETE BROWN
& His Band

MOUND BAYOU	02/09/42

TEDDY BUNN
Guitar Solos

KING PORTER STOMP	12/05/39
GUITAR IN HIGH	12/05/39

JOE BUSHKIN
Piano Solos

I CAN'T GET STARTED	05/17/40
IN A LITTLE SPANISH TOWN	05/17/40

WILD BILL DAVISON
Collector's Item Cats

I SURRENDER DEAR	02/12/40

ROY ELDRIDGE
& His Orchestra

HIGH SOCIETY	12/39

SLIM GAILLARD
& His Flat Foot Floogie Boys

CHICKEN RHYTHM	09/15/39
RA-DA-DA-DA	04/04/42
GROOVE JUICE SPECIAL	04/04/42

LIL GREEN
Vocals

ROMANCE IN THE DARK	05/09/40
WHY DON'T YOU DO RIGHT	04/23/41

BOBBY HACKETT
& His Orchestra

BUGLE CALL RAG	07/17/39
JA DA	07/17/39
DARDANELLA	07/17/39
AFTER I SAY I'M SORRY, *vo Tempo Twisters*	01/25/40
CLARINET MARMALADE	01/25/40
SINGIN' THE BLUES	02/01/40

COLEMAN HAWKINS

(see also Tier 1)

& His Orchestra

MEET DR. FOO	10/11/39
FINE DINNER	10/11/39
WHEN DAY IS DONE	01/03/40
THE SHEIK OF ARABY	01/03/40
MY BLUE HEAVEN	01/03/40
DEDICATION	05/25/40
PASSIN' IT AROUND	08/09/40
ROCKY COMFORT	08/09/40

ERSKINE HAWKINS

& His Orchestra

HOT PLATTER	07/18/39
GIN MILL SPECIAL	07/18/39
TUXEDO JUNCTION	07/18/39
UPTOWN SHUFFLE	10/02/39
MIDNIGHT STROLL	04/26/40
SWEET GEORGIA BROWN	06/10/40
AFTER HOURS	06/10/40
NORFOLK FERRY	11/06/40
NONA	11/06/40
RIFFTIME	11/20/40
HEY DOC	08/08/41
DON'T CRY BABY, *vo Jimmy Mitchelle*	05/27/42
BEAR MASH BLUES	06/29/42

FLETCHER HENDERSON

& His Orchestra

LET'S GO HOME	04/24/41
A PIXIE FROM DIXIE	04/24/41

ART HODES

Piano Solos

SOUTH SIDE SHUFFLE	08/10/39
A SELECTION FROM THE GUTTER	01/40
SNOWY MORNING BLUES	07/17/42
ART'S BOOGIE	07/17/42
ST. LOUIS BLUES	07/17/42

Blue Three

I'VE FOUND A NEW BABY	05/40

Chicago Rhythm Kings

THERE'LL BE SOME CHANGES MADE	08/17/40

Columbia Quintet

103RD STREET BOOGIE	12/40
ROYAL GARDEN BLUES	12/40
AT THE JAZZ BAND BALL	12/40
FAREWELL BLUES	12/40

& His Orchestra

GEORGIA CAKE WALK	03/17/42
LIBERTY INN DRAG	03/17/42
INDIANA	03/17/42
GET HAPPY	03/17/42

ALBERTA HUNTER

Vocals, accompanied by various groups

DOWNHEARTED BLUES	08/15/39
FINE AND MELLOW	08/15/39
THE LOVE I HAVE FOR YOU	06/03/40
THE CASTLE'S ROCKIN'	06/03/40

HARRY JAMES

& His Orchestra, Instrumentals

FEET DRAGGIN' BLUES	09/17/39
SLEEPY-TIME GAL	10/13/39
FLASH	11/08/39
NIGHT SPECIAL	11/30/39
BACK BEAT BOOGIE	11/30/39
TUXEDO JUNCTION	02/12/40
HODGE PODGE	03/18/40
SHEIK OF ARABY	04/18/40
SUPER CHIEF	05/04/40
TEMPO DE LUXE	08/12/40
SWANEE RIVER	08/12/40
EXACTLY LIKE YOU	08/12/40
MUSIC MAKERS	01/08/41
DUKE'S MIXTURE	03/26/41
JEFFRIE'S BLUES	04/28/41
SHARP AS A TACK	04/28/41
RECORD SESSION	06/30/41
NOBODY KNOWS THE TROUBLE I'VE SEEN	10/06/41
THE MOLE	12/30/41
STRICTLY INSTRUMENTAL	12/30/41

THE CLIPPER	01/29/42
CRAZY RHYTHM	02/24/42
LET ME UP	06/05/42
PRINCE CHARMING	07/22/42
JUMP TOWN	07/22/42

& His Orchestra, Vocals

HERE COMES THE NIGHT, *vo Frank Sinatra*	08/31/39
ALL OR NOTHING AT ALL, *vo FS*	08/31/39
I'LL GET BY, *vo Dick Haymes*	04/07/41
YOU DON'T KNOW WHAT LOVE IS, *vo DH*	10/29/41
I HAD THE CRAZIEST DREAM, *vo Helen Forrest*	07/22/42
I'VE HEARD THAT SONG BEFORE, *Vo HF*	07/31/42

BUDDY JOHNSON
& His Band

JAMMIN' IN GEORGIA, *vo Mack Sisters*	11/16/39
REESE'S IDEA	11/16/39
SOUTHERN ECHOES	10/25/40
IN THERE	04/09/41
TROYON SWING	05/01/41
SOUTHERN EXPOSURE	05/01/41

LOUIS JORDAN
& His Tympani Five

JAKE, WHAT A SNAKE	11/14/39
HONEYSUCKLE ROSE, *vo Louis Jordan*	11/14/39
'FORE DAY BLUES, *vo LJ*	11/14/39
JUNE 10TH JAMBOREE, *vo LJ*	01/25/40
YOU RUN YOUR MOUTH AND I'LL RUN MY BUSINESS, *vo LJ*	01/25/40
MAMA MAMA (RUSTY DUSTY) BLUES, *vo LJ*	11/15/41
KNOCK ME A KISS, *vo LJ*	11/15/41
I'M GONNA MOVE TO THE OUTSKIRTS OF TOWN, *vo LJ*	11/22/41
WHAT'S THE USE OF GETTING SOBER, *vo LJ*	07/21/42
FIVE GUYS NAMED MOE, *vo LJ*	07/21/42

STAN KENTON
& His Orchestra

THE NANGO	09/11/41
ADIOS	09/11/41
REED RAPTURE	02/13/42
EL CHOCLO	02/13/42

HARLAN LEONARD

& The Rockets, Instrumentals

ROCKIN' WITH THE ROCKETS	01/11/40
HAIRY JOE JUMP	01/11/40
MY GAL SAL	01/11/40
SKEE	01/11/40
PARADE OF THE STOMPERS	03/11/40
ROCK AND RIDE	07/15/40
400 SWING	07/15/40
A LA BRIDGES	07/15/40
DAMERON STOMP	11/13/40
KEEP ROCKIN'	11/13/40
TAKE 'EM	11/13/40

& The Rockets, Vocals

I DON'T WANT TO SET THE WORLD ON FIRE, *vo Myra Taylor*	03/11/40
RIDE MY BLUES AWAY, *vo Ernie Williams*	03/11/40
MISTREATED, *vo EW*	11/13/40

WILLIE LEWIS

& His Negro Band

HAPPY FEET	06/19/41
LOVER COME BACK TO ME	06/19/41
BACON'S BLUES	06/19/41
CHRISTMAS NIGHT IN HARLEM	06/27/41
OL' MAN RIVER	06/27/41
CHRISTOPHER COLUMBUS	06/27/41
I'VE FOUND A NEW BABY	06/27/41
AFTER YOU'VE GONE, *vo June Cole*	06/27/41
BODY AND SOUL	06/27/41

JOE MARSALA

& His Delta Four

WANDERING MAN BLUES, *vo Dell St. John*	04/04/40
SALTY MAMA BLUES, *vo Bill Coleman*	04/04/40
THREE O'CLOCK JUMP, *vo DSJ*	04/04/40
REUNION IN HARLEM	04/04/40

& His Orchestra

BULL'S EYE	03/21/41
LOWER REGISTER	03/21/41
I KNOW THAT YOU KNOW	03/21/41
SLOW DOWN	03/21/41

& His Chosen Seven

LAZY DADDY	07/06/42

GLENN MILLER

& His Orchestra, Instrumentals

IN THE MOOD	08/01/39
JOHNSON RAG	11/05/39
STARDUST	01/29/40
RUG CUTTERS SWING	01/29/40
TUXEDO JUNCTION	02/05/40
DANNY BOY	02/05/40
TAKE THE "A" TRAIN	05/28/41
ADIOS	06/25/41
STRING OF PEARLS	11/03/41
LONG TALL MAMA	11/03/41
I GOT RHYTHM	01/01/42
AMERICAN PATROL	04/02/42
RHAPSODY IN BLUE	07/16/42

& His Orchestra, Vocals

CHATTANOOGA CHOO CHOO, *vo Tex Beneke & The Modernaires*	05/07/41
SERENADE IN BLUE, *vo Ray Eberle & TM*	05/20/42
THAT OLD BLACK MAGIC, *vo Skip Nelson & TM*	07/14/42

LUCKY MILLINDER

& His Orchestra

SHOUT, SISTER, SHOUT, *vo Sister Rosetta Tharpe*	09/05/41
APOLLO JUMP	09/05/41
ROCK ME, *vo SRT*	09/05/41
THAT'S ALL, *vo SRT*	11/06/41
MASON FLYER	07/29/42
LITTLE JOHN SPECIAL	07/29/42

JIMMIE NOONE

& His Orchestra

NEW ORLEANS HOP SCOP BLUES	06/05/40
KEYSTONE BLUES	06/05/40

Quartet

SWEET LORRAINE	07/17/41

ORAN "HOT LIPS" PAGE

& His Band

LAYAYETTE	11/11/40
SOUTH	11/11/40

Trio

THIRSTY MAMA BLUES, *vo Hot Lips Page*	12/10/40
JUST ANOTHER WOMAN, *vo HLP*	12/10/40
MY FIGHTIN' GAL, *vo HLP*	12/10/40
EVIL MAN'S BLUES, *vo Teddy Bunn*	12/10/40
DO IT IF YOU WANNA	12/10/40

SAM PRICE
& His Texas Blusicians

THE DIRTY DOZENS	09/26/40
JUST JIVIN' AROUND	04/03/41
DO YOU DIG MY JIVE? *vo Chorus*	06/13/41
HARLEM GIN BLUES, *vo Ruby Smith*	12/10/41
MATCH BOX BLUES, *vo Jack Meredith*	12/10/41
BLOW, KATY, BLOW	01/20/42

DON REDMAN
& His Orchestra

YOU AIN'T NOWHERE, *vo DR*	01/17/40
ABOUT RIP VAN WINKLE	01/17/40
SHIM-ME-SHA-WABBLE	01/17/40
CHANT OF THE WEED	01/17/40

GEORGE SHEARING
Piano Solos

MISSOURI SCRAMBLER	03/03/41
OVERNIGHT HOP	03/03/41
BEAT ME DADDY, EIGHT TO THE BAR	04/23/41
MORE THAN YOU KNOW	08/01/41
SOFTLY AS IN A MORNING SUNRISE	12/09/41
SPOOKIE WOOGIE	01/28/42
ROSETTA	04/28/42
TIME ON MY HANDS	12/12/42

EDDIE SOUTH
& His Orchestra

ZIGEUNER	06/10/40
PRAELUDIUM AND ALLEGRO	06/10/40
OH, LADY BE GOOD	03/12/41

JESS STACY
& His Orchestra

NONI	09/26/39
JESS STAY BLUES	09/26/39

BREEZE, 1 & 2	11/30/39
I CAN'T BELIEVE THAT YOU'RE IN LOVE WITH ME	11/30/39
CLARINET BLUES	11/30/39

MAXINE SULLIVAN

Vocals, accompanied by various groups

JACKIE BOY	08/22/39
ILL WIND	08/22/39
ST. LOUIS BLUES	05/01/40
THE HOUR OF PARTING	05/01/40
IF I HAD A RIBBON BOW	08/01/40
MOLLY MALONE	08/01/40
BARBARA ALLEN	08/01/40

LU WATTERS

& His Yerba Buena Jazz Band

MAPLE LEAF RAG	12/19/41
IRISH BLACK BOTTOM	12/19/41
LONDON BLUES	03/29/42
TIGER RAG	03/29/42

MARY LOU WILLIAMS

Piano Solo

LITTLE JOE FROM CHICAGO	10/12/39

Six Men & A Girl

TEA FOR TWO	01/26/40
MARY LOU WILLIAMS BLUES	01/26/40
SCRATCHIN' THE GRAVEL	01/26/40
ZONKY	01/26/40

& Her Kansas City Seven

BABY DEAR	11/18/40
HARMONY BLUES	11/18/40

4. Fourth Tier – *WORTH A LISTEN*

GEORGE AULD
& His Orchestra

JUKE BOX JUMP 01/40
SWEET SUE 02/40

WILL BRADLEY
& His Orchestra

CELERY STALKS AT MIDNIGHT 01/17/40
JIMTOWN BLUES 01/17/40
BEAT ME DADDY, EIGHT TO THE BAR, *vo Ray McKinley* 05/21/40
IN THE HALL OF THE MOUNTAIN KING 05/12/41

Trio

DOWN THE ROAD A-PIECE, *vo RMcK* 08/12/40

Ray McKinley Quartet

TEA FOR TWO 01/21/41

Six Texas Hot Dogs

BASIN STREET BOOGIE 07/23/41

LES BROWN
& His Orchestra, Instrumentals

A MELLOW BIT OF RHYTHM 04/09/40
WALKIN' AND SWINGIN' 04/09/40
MARCHE SLAV 04/08/41
JOLTIN' JOE DI MAGGIO 08/08/41
BIZET HAS HIS DAY 09/17/41
MEXICAN HAT DANCE 09/17/41
OUT OF NOWHERE 07/20/42

& His Orchestra, Vocals

NOTHIN', *vo Betty Bonney* 08/08/41
SUNDAY, *vo Butch Stone* 07/20/42

SONNY BURKE
& His Orchestra

JIMMIE MEETS THE COUNT 09/03/40
THE COUNT BASICALLY 10/03/40

BOBBY BYRNE
& His Orchestra

DANNY BOY 09/04/40

UNA MAE CARLISLE
Vocals, accompanied by various groups

WALKIN' BY THE RIVER, *vo UMC*	11/13/40
BLITZKRIEG BABY, *vo UMC*	03/10/41
BEAUTIFUL EYES, *vo UMC*	03/10/41

HOAGY CARMICHAEL
Vocals & Piano Solos

OLD MAN HARLEM	03/27/42
JUDY	05/11/42
STARDUST	05/11/42
HONG KONG BLUES	05/11/42

CHAMBER MUSIC SOCIETY OF LOWER BASIN STREET

WININ' BOY BLUES *(with Jelly Roll Morton)*	07/14/40
KING PORTER STOMP *(with JRM)*	07/14/40
MUSKRAT RAMBLE *(with Sidney Bechet)*	11/11/40
DINAH'S BLUES, *vo Dinah Shore*	11/11/40
AUNT HAGAR'S BLUES, *vo Lena Horne*	06/25/41
MOOD INDIGO, *vo DS*	09/41
BODY AND SOUL, *vo DS*	09/41
STARDUST, *vo DS*	09/41
BEALE STREET BLUES, *vo LH*	09/41
MOUND BAYOU, *vo Linda Keene*	02/02/42

BOB CHESTER
& His Orchestra

57TH STREET DRAG	10/12/39
EASY DOES IT	01/02/40
FROM MAINE TO CALIFORNIA	09/25/41
HARLEM CONFUSION	10/28/41
TANNING DR. JEKYLL'S HIDE	03/04/42
STRICTLY INSTRUMENTAL	05/27/42

LARRY CLINTON
& His Orchestra

STUDY IN SCARLET	07/14/39
STUDY IN SURREALISM	01/02/40
STUDY IN MODERNISM	03/27/40
BOLERO IN BLUE	08/09/40

AL COOPER
& The Savoy Sultans

JUMPIN' THE BLUES	10/16/39
FRENZY	03/29/40
SOPHISTICATED JUMP	03/29/40
SECOND BALCONY JUMP	02/28/41
SEE WHAT I MEAN	02/28/41

JOHNNY DODDS
& His Orchestra

RED ONION BLUES	06/05/40
GRAVIER STREET BLUES	06/05/40

SAM DONAHUE
& His Orchestra

SIX MILE STRETCH	05/20/41
FLO-FLO	11/12/41

JIMMY DORSEY
& His Orchestra, Instrumentals

MAJOR AND MINOR STOMP	11/03/39
CONTRASTS	04/30/40
DOLIMITE	07/17/40
ON THE TRAIL	09/03/40
TURN LEFT	12/09/40
TURN RIGHT	02/03/41
BAR BABBLE	03/19/41
CHARLESTON ALLEY	08/01/41
MURDERISTIC	12/22/41
HOBOKEN ROCK	12/22/41

& His Orchestra, Vocals

HEP-TEE-HOOTIE, *vo Helen O'Connell*	07/17/40
APAPOLA, *vo Bob Eberly & HO'C*	02/03/41
MARIA ELENA, *vo BE*	03/19/41
GREEN EYES, *vo BE & HO'C*	03/19/41
TANGERINE, *vo BE & HO'C*	12/10/41
I'M GLAD THERE IS YOU, *vo BE*	12/22/41

SONNY DUNHAM
& His Orchestra

MEMORIES OF YOU	07/23/41

EDDIE DURHAM
& His Orchestra

I WANT A LITTLE GIRL	11/11/40
MOTEN'S SWING	11/11/40

ZIGGY ELMAN
& His Orchestra

AM I BLUE?	08/29/39
DEEP NIGHT	11/27/39
I'M THROUGH WITH LOVE	12/26/39

SHEP FIELDS
& His New Music

AMERICAN PATROL	1942

GLEN GRAY
& His Casa Loma Orchestra

PRELUDE IN C SHARP MINOR	08/13/39
SHADOWS	08/13/39
COME AND GET IT	09/28/39
NO NAME JIVE, *Parts 1 & 2*	03/18/40

HAITIAN ORCHESTRA

TROPICAL MOOD RHUMBA	11/22/39
SOUS LES PALMIERS	11/22/39
ROSA RHUMBA	11/22/39
TI RALPH	11/22/39
BABA RHUMBA	11/22/39
ORIGINAL MUSIC – PART ONE	11/22/39
MAGIC ISLAND MERINGUE	11/22/39
MEYETTE MERINGUE	11/22/39

LES HITE
& His Orchestra

T-BONE BLUES, *vo T-Bone Walker*	06/40
JERSEY BOUNCE, *vo Jimmy Anderson*	01/42

CLAUDE HOPKINS
& His Orchestra

YACHT CLUB SWING	02/40

BUD JACOBSON
Jungle Kings

CLARINET MARMALADE	03/09/41

JACK JENNEY
& His Orchestra

STAR DUST	10/19/39
THE WORLD IS WAITING FOR THE SUNRISE	12/06/39

BUNK JOHNSON
Jazz Band

BUNK'S BLUES	06/11/42
PANAMA	06/11/42
SOBBIN' BLUES	10/02/42
WEARY BLUES	10/02/42

LONNIE JOHNSON
Guitar Solos

JERSEY BELLE BLUES	11/02/39
RAMBLER'S BLUES	02/13/42

CRIPPLE CLARENCE LOFTON
Piano Solos

I HAD A DREAM	11/39
STREAMLINE TRAIN	11/39
I DON'T KNOW	11/39
PINETOP'S BOOGIE WOOGIE	11/39
BLUE BOOGIE	11/39

WINGY MANONE
& His Orchestra

BLUE LOU	09/06/39
MY HONEY'S LOVIN' ARMS, *vo W. Manone*	09/06/39
WHEN MY SUGAR WALKS DOWN THE STREET, *vo WM*	09/06/39
RHYTHM ON THE RIVER, *vo WM*	08/06/40
OCHI CHORNYA, *vo WM*	03/19/41
MAMA'S GONE, GOODBYE, *vo WM & Chorus*	03/19/41
STOP THE WAR, *vo WM*	03/19/41

JIMMY McPARTLAND
& His Orchestra

JAZZ ME BLUES	10/11/39
CHINA BOY	10/11/39
THE WORLD IS WAITING FOR THE SUNRISE	10/11/39
SUGAR	10/11/39

JOHNNNY MERCER
Vocals

STRIP POLKA	06/12/42
GI JIVE	06/12/42

TOOTS MONDELLO
& His Orchestra

ST. LOUIS GAL	11/39
LOUISIANA	11/39
SWEET LORRAINE	11/39
BEYOND THE MOON	11/39

RED NICHOLS

WAIL OF THE WINDS	08/04/39
MOONLIGHT SERENADE	09/02/39

RAY NOBLE
& His Orchestra

COMANCHE WAR DANCE	09/29/39
IROQUOIS	09/29/39
SEMINOLE	01/19/40
SIOUX	01/19/40
HARLEM NOCTURNE	08/08/40

TEDDY POWELL
& His Orchestra

FLEA ON A SPREE	11/13/39
RIDIN' THE SUBWAY	02/01/40
FEATHER MERCHANTS' BALL	05/20/40
BLUE DANUBE	03/24/41
TAPESTRY IN BLUE, *vo Peggy Mann*	06/12/42

LOUIS PRIMA
& His New Orleans Gang

OF THEE I SING, *vo LP*	07/12/39

CLARENCE PROFIT
Trio

AZURE	09/11/40

HENRY "KID" RENA
Jazz Band

PANAMA	08/21/40
GETTYSBURG MARCH	08/21/40
MILENBERG JOYS	08/21/40
LOWDOWN BLUES	08/21/40
HIGH SOCIETY	08/21/40
CLARINET MARMALADE	08/21/40
WEARY BLUES	08/21/40
GET IT RIGHT	08/21/40

FREDDIE RICH

& His Orchestra, Instrumentals

'TIL WE MEET AGAIN	02/14/40
I'M FOREVER BLOWING BUBBLES	02/14/40

& His Orchestra, Vocals

A HOUSE WITH A LITTLE RED BARN, *vo Rosemary Calvin*	02/14/40
HOW HIGH THE MOON, *vo RC*	02/14/40

ALVINO REY

& His Orchestra

SANTA CLAUS IS COMING TO TOWN, *vo King Sisters*	10/24/41
THE MAJOR AND THE MINOR	07/24/42

ADRIAN ROLLINI

Trio

I CAN'T BELIEVE THAT YOU'RE IN LOVE WITH ME & I CAN'T GIVE YOU ANYTHING BUT LOVE	09/28/39
STARDUST & SOLITUDE	09/28/39
DIGA DIGA DOO	09/28/39
DARDANELLA	10/05/39
HONKY TONK TRAIN BLUES	05/07/40
ISLE OF CAPRI	05/07/40
MARTHA	05/07/40
THE GIRL WITH THE LIGHT BLUE HAIR	05/07/40

JAN SAVITT

& His Top Hatters, Instrumentals

720 IN THE BOOKS	09/23/39
KANSAS CITY MOODS	01/24/40
BLUES IN THE GROVE	02/04/40
IT'S TIME TO JUMP AND SHOUT	02/04/40
GREEN GOON JIVE	01/03/41
MY HEART AT THY SWEET VOICE	01/03/41
BIG BEAVER	02/27/41
HORIZON	04/03/41
THE SORCERER'S APPRENTICE	05/05/41

& His Top Hatters, Vocals

VOL VISTU GAILY STAR, *vo Bon Bon*	08/29/39
THE PAPER PICKER, *vo BB*	08/29/39
ALLA EN EL RANCHO GRANDE, *vo BB*	09/23/39
ROSE OF THE RIO GRANDE, *vo BB*	02/04/40

RAYMOND SCOTT
& His New Orchestra

FOUR BEAT SHUFFLE	06/17/40
AT AN ARABIAN HOUSE PARTY	06/17/40
COPYRIGHT 1950	11/29/40
WHEN COOTIE LEFT THE DUKE	01/06/41
ON THE JERSEY SIDE	04/07/41

STUFF SMITH
& His Orchestra, Instrumentals

MY THOUGHTS	12/39
CRESCENDO IN DRUMS	c.4/40

& His Orchestra, Vocals

SAM THE VEGETABLE MAN, *vo SS*	12/39
MY BLUE HEAVEN, *vo SS*	12/39
WHEN PA WAS COURTIN' MA, *vo SS*	12/39
IT'S UP TO YOU, *vo Stella Brooks*	c.4/40
I'VE GOT YOU UNDER MY SKIN, *vo SS*	c.4/40
JOSHUA, *vo SS & Jonah Jones*	c.4/40

WILLIE "THE LION" SMITH
& His Orchestra

RUSHIN'	02/17/40
NOODLIN'	02/17/40

SKEETS TOLBERT
& His Gentlemen of Swing, Instrumentals

THE STUFF'S OUT	07/05/39
RAILROAD BLUES	07/05/39
SWING OUT	07/05/39
BUGLE BLUES	12/17/40
UNCLE EPH'S DREAM	05/22/41
FILL UP	01/29/42

& His Gentlemen of Swing, Vocals

W.P.A., *vo Chorus*	03/12/40
JUMPIN' LIKE MAD, *vo C*	10/02/40
FOUR O'CLOCK BLUES, *vo Babe Wallace*	12/17/40
BIG FAT BUTTERFLY, *vo C*	05/22/41
C.O.D., *vo C*	07/25/42

GEORGE WETTLING
Chicago Rhythm Kings

I FOUND A NEW BABY	01/16/40
BUGLE CALL RAG	01/16/40
I WISH I COULD SHIMMY LIKE MY SISTER KATE	01/16/40
DARKTOWN STRUTTERS' BALL	01/16/40

BOB ZURKE
& His Delta Rhythm Band, Instrumentals

SOUTHERN EXPOSURE	07/18/39
HOBSON STREET BLUES	07/18/39
HONKY TONK TRAIN BLUES	08/10/39
I'VE FOUND A NEW BABY	08/10/39
TOM CAT ON THE KEYS	09/26/39
EVERYBODY STEP	09/26/39
CUBAN BOOGIE WOOGIE	10/30/39
NICKEL NABBER BLUES	12/15/39
TEA FOR TWO	01/08/40
COW COW BLUES	05/08/40

& His Delta Rhythm Band, Vocals

IT'S A HAP-HAP-HAPPY DAY, *vo Claire Martin*	09/26/39
RHUMBOOGIE, *vo Evelyn Poe*	05/08/40

Selected list of blues records from the period:

BIG BILL BROONZY
Vocals & Guitar

WHEN I BEEN DRINKING	05/02/41
I FEEL SO GOOD	12/02/41

EDDIE "SON" HOUSE
Vocals & Guitar + Comments by Alan Lomax

CAMP HOLLERS	08/41
LOW DOWN DIRTY DOG BLUES	1942
AM I RIGHT OR WRONG	1942
WALKING BLUES	1942
THE PONY BLUES	1942

ROBERT LOCKWOOD, JR.
Vocals & Guitar

LITTLE BOY BLUE	07/30/41
TAKE A LITTLE WALK WITH ME	07/30/41

BIG MACEO (MERRIWEATHER)

WORRIED LIFE BLUES	06/24/41

MEMPHIS MINNIE
Vocals & Guitar

ME AND MY CHAUFFEUR BLUES	05/21/41
I'M NOT A BAD GAL	12/12/41

TAMPA RED
Vocals, Guitar & Kazoo

DON'T YOU LIE TO ME	05/10/40
IT HURTS ME TOO	05/10/40

JOHNNIE TEMPLE
Vocals

CHERRY BALL	09/19/39

T-BONE WATERS
Vocals & Guitar, accompanied by piano

MEAN OLD WORLD	07/20/42

MUDDY WATERS
Vocals & Guitar

COUNTRY BLUES	1942
I BE'S TROUBLED	1942

BUKKA WHITE
Vocals & Guitar

A STRANGE PLACE BLUES	03/08/40
WHEN CAN I CHANGE MY CLOTHES	03/08/40
A PARCHMAN FARM BLUES	03/08/40
A GOOD GIN BLUES	03/08/40
A BUKKA'S JITTERBUG SWING	03/08/40

BIG JOE WILLIAMS

CRAWLIN' KING SNAKE	03/27/41
MEET ME AROUND THE CORNER	03/27/41

JOHN LEE "SONNY BOY" WILLIAMSON
Vocals

WELFARE STORE BLUES	05/17/40
MY LITTLE MACHINE	05/17/40
MILLION YEARS BLUES	07/02/41
GROUND HOG BLUES	12/11/41

Selected list of recordings by British groups:

JOE DANIELS
& His Hot Shots

WAR DANCE FOR WOODEN INDIANS	02/01/40

NAT GONELLA
& His New Georgians

DINAH, *vo Nat Gonella*	10/04/40
AT THE WOODCHOPPERS BALL	10/30/40

SID PHILLIPS
Trio

I GOT RHYTHM	05/06/40

ROYAL AIR FORCE DANCE ORCHESTRA

I FOUND A NEW BABY	03/13/42
OH, YOU BEAUTIFUL DOLL	05/21/42

Appendix C

CUMULATIVE PERSONNEL LIST OF LIONEL HAMPTON'S VICTOR RECORDING SESSIONS

February 8, 1937 through April 8, 1941

Trumpet: Red Allen, Ziggy Elman, Walter Fuller, Karl George, Dizzy Gillespie, Harry James, Jonah Jones, Irving Randolph, Rex Stewart, Cootie Williams

Trombone: Lawrence Brown, J. C.Higginbotham

Clarinet: Buster Bailey, Eddie Barefield, Ed Hall, Mezz Mezzrow, Vido Musso, Marshall Royal, Omer Simeon

Alto Sax: Earl Bostic, Benny Carter, Buff Estes, Johnny Hodges, George Koenig, Dave Matthews, Toots Mondello, George Oldham, Russell Procope, Hymie Schertzer

Tenor Sax: Chu Berry, Robert Crowder, Herschel Evans, Coleman Hawkins, Jerry Jerome, Budd Johnson, Vido Musso, Art Rollini, Babe Russin, Ben Webster

Baritone Sax: Harry Carney, Edgar Sampson

Piano: Nat Cole, Clyde Hart, Billy Kyle, Marlowe Morris, Spencer Odon, Jess Stacy, Joe Sullivan, Sir Charles Thompson

Guitar: Irving Ashby, Ernest Ashley, Danny Barker, Bobby Bennett, Teddy Bunn, Al Casey, Charlie Christian, Freddy Green, Oscar Moore, Allan Reuss

Bass: Hayes Alvis, Vernon Alley, Artie Bernstein, Harry Goodman, Milt Hinton, John Kirby, Johnny Miller, Wesley Prince, Jess Simpkins, Billy Taylor, Mack Walker

Drums: Alvin Burroughs, Sid Catlett, Cozy Cole, Nick Fatool, Sonny Greer, Lionel Hampton, Jo Jones, Slick Jones, Gene Krupa, Kaiser Marshall, Al Spieldock, Zutty Singleton, Shadow Wilson, Lee Young

Vibraphone: Lionel Hampton

Violin: Ray Perry

CUMULATIVE PERSONNEL LIST OF TEDDY WILSON with BILLIE HOLIDAY & BILLIE HOLIDAY & HER ORCH. RECORDING SESSIONS

July 2, 1935 through February 10, 1942

Trumpet: Red Allen, Bunny Berigan, Emmett Berry, Richard Clarke, Buck Clayton, Bill Coleman, Shad Collins, Harry Edison, Roy Eldridge, Chris Griffin, Bobby Hackett, Harry James, Jonah Jones, Frankie Newton, Hot Lips Page, Irving Randolph, Charlie Shavers, Eddie Tompkins, Cootie Williams

Trombone: Tyree Glenn, Benny Morton, Dicky Wells, Trummy Young

Clarinet: Buster Bailey, Irving Fazola, Benny Goodman, Ed Hall, Jimmy Hamilton, Tom Mace, Ernie Powell, Cecil Scott, Artie Shaw

Alto Sax: Eddie Barefield, Lester Boone, Bill Bowen, Ted Buckner, Benny Carter, Joe Eldridge, Carl Frye, Johnny Hodges, Hilton Jefferson, Leslie Johnakins, Toots Mondello, Jimmy Powell, Don Redman, Hymie Schertzer, Tab Smith, Earle Warren

Tenor Sax: George Auld, Charlie Barnet, Chu Berry, Don Byas, Herschel Evans, Bud Freeman, Coleman Hawkins, Kenneth Hollon, Ted McRae, Vido Musso, Stanley Payne, Prince Robinson, Babe Russin, Kermit Scott, Joe Thomas, Ben Webster, Lester Young

Baritone Sax: Harry Carney, Jack Washington

Piano: Joe Bushkin, Clyde Hart, Eddie Heywood, Queenie Johnson, Kenny Kersey, James Sherman, Joe Sullivan, Claude Thornhill, Sonny White, Teddy Wilson

Guitar: Bernard Addison, Dave Barbour, Danny Barker, Al Casey, Paul Chapman, John Collins, Gene Fields, Freddy Green, Ulysses Livingston, Lawrence Lucie, Jimmy McLin, Allan Reuss, Carmen Mastren, Dick McDonough, John Trueheart

Bass: Artie Bernstein, Al Hall, Milt Hinton, John Kirby, Grachan Moncur, Wilson Myers, Walter Page, Pete Peterson, Ted Sturgis, John Williams

Drums: Kenny Clarke, Cozy Cole, Herbert Cowens, Eddie Dougherty, J. C. Heard, Jo Jones, Gene Krupa, Yank Porter, Alphonse Steele, Hal West

Appendix D: Recordings Based on Classical Compositions

mid-1939 to mid-1942

Ambrose & His Orch. (English)

Chopin, NOCTURNE	06/40

Will Bradley & His Orch.

Grieg, IN THE HALL OF THE MOUNTAIN KING	05/41

Les Brown & His Orch.

Ippolitov-Ivanov, PROCESSION OF THE SARDA	02/41
Tchaikovsky, MARCHE SLAV	02/41
Verdi, ANVIL CHORUS	02/41
Bizet, BIZET HAS HIS DAY	09/41

Una Mae Carlisle, vocals

Albeniz, MOONLIGHT MASQUERADE	10/41

Casa Loma Orch.

Rachmaninoff, PRELUDE IN C SHARP MINOR	08/39

Larry Clinton & His Orch.

Tchaikovsky, DANCE OF THE SUGAR PLUM FAIRY	08/40
DANCE OF THE FLOWERS	09/40
DANCE OF THE REED FLUTES	10/40

Xavier Cugat & His Waldorf-Astoria Orch.

Offenbach, LET'S STEAL A TUNE	01/41
Albeniz, MOONLIGHT MASQUERADE	09/41
Chopin, NOCTURNE	10/41
Tchaikovsky, PIANO CONCERTO IN B FLAT MINOR	10/41

Al Donahue & His Orch.

Beethoven, BEETHOVEN BOUNCE	01/40

Jimmy Dorsey & His Orch.

Tchaikovsky, IN THE HUSH OF NIGHT	03/41
Albeniz, MOONLIGHT MASQUERADE	08/41
Rubinstein, IF YOU ARE BUT A DREAM	02/42

Tommy Dorsey & His Orch.

Rimsky-Korsakov, SONG OF INDIA	10/40
Tchaikovsky, NONE BUT THE LONELY HEART	09/41
Grofe, DAYBREAK	07/42

Shep Fields & His New Music	
Tchaikovsky, MARCHE SLAV	04/41
Brahms, HUNGARIAN DANCE NO. 5	04/41
Bizet, HABANERA	05/41
deFalla, FIRE DANCE	12/41
Tchaikovsky, PETER & THE WOLF	03/42
Benny Goodman & His Orch.	
Ravel, BOLERO	08/39
Mendelssohn, SPRING SONG	08/39
Paganini, CAPRICE XXIV	10/41
Rachmaninoff, BEFORE	03/42
Tchaikovsky, PETER & THE WOLF	03/42
Horace Heidt & His Orch.	
Rossini, WILLIAM TELL OVERTURE	08/39
Rachmaninoff, PRELUDE IN C SHARP MINOR	01/40
Offenbach, BARCAROLLE	02/40
Woody Herman & His Orch.	
Tchaikovsky, ON THE ISLE OF MAY	01/40
PIANO CONCERTO NO. 1 IN B FLAT	08/41
Rachmaninoff, I THINK OF YOU	12/41
Tchaikovsky, THE STORY OF A STARRY NIGHT	04/42
Richard Himber & His Orch.	
Chopin, NOCTURNE IN E FLAT	12/40
Harry James & His Orch.	
Rimsky-Korsakov, FLIGHT OF THE BUMBLEBEE	02/41
Tchaikovsky, DODGERS FAN DANCE	06/42
Grofe, DAYBREAK	07/42
Swing and Sway with Sammy Kaye	
Tchaikovsky, ON THE ISLE OF MAY	01/40
John Kirby & His Orch.	
Dvorak, HUMORESQUE	10/39
Schubert, SERENADE	10/39
Chopin, POLONAISE	05/40
Lehar, FRASQUITA SERENADE	07/40
Donizetti, SEXTET FROM LUCIA	07/40
Tchaikovsky, BOUNCE OF THE SUGAR PLUM FAIRY	01/41
Beethoven, BEETHOVEN RIFFS ON	01/41
Chopin, REVOLUTIONARY ETUDE	Summer 41
Sinding, RUSTLE OF SPRING	Summer 41

Gene Krupa & His Orch.
Rachmaninoff, I THINK OF YOU 10/41

Donald Lambert, piano solos
Donizetti, SEXTET FROM LUCIA 01/41
Grieg, ANITRA'S DANCE 01/41
Massenet, ELEGIE 01/41
Wagner, PILGRIMS CHORUS 01/41

Guy Lombardo & His Royal Canadians
Grieg, ANITRA'S DANCE 11/40
Tchaikovsky, PIANO CONCERTO 09/41

Johnny Long & His Orch.
Bach, SWING ME BACH 09/40

Jimmie Lunceford & His Orch.
Beethoven, SONATA (PATHETIQUE) 02/40
Chopin, PRELUDE NO. 7 05/40

Enric Madriguera & His Orch.
Rimsky-Korsakov, SONG OF INDIA 03/41
Tchaikovsky, PIANO CONCERTO 09/41
Rubinstein, IF YOU ARE BUT A DREAM 03/42

Matty Malneck & His Orch.
Beethoven, THEN I WROTE THE MINUET IN G 08/39
Rossini, WILLIAM TELL OVERTURE 08/39
Massenet, MEDITATION (THAIS) 05/41

Freddie Martin & His Orch.
Tchaikovsky, PIANO CONCERTO IN B FLAT 06/41
Grieg, PIANO CONCERTO 12/41
Tchaikovsky, SERENADE FOR STRINGS 12/41
ARAB DANCE 04/42
CHINESE DANCE 04/42
DANCE FOR THE SUGAR PLUM FAIRY 05/42
OVERTURE MINIATURE 05/42
DANCE OF THE REED FLUTES 05/42
WALTZ OF THE FLOWERS 05/42
RUSSIAN DANCE 05/42
MARCH 05/42
Addinfell, WARSAW CONCERTO 07/42

Frankie Masters & His Orch.
Tchaikovsky, NOW AND FOREVER 02/42

Hal McIntyre & His Orch.	
Tchaikovsky, STORY OF A STARRY NIGHT	03/42
Glenn Miller & His Orch.	
Verdi, ANVIL CHORUS	12/40
Beethoven, MOONLIGHT SONATA	12/41
Tchaikovsky, STORY OF A STARRY NIGHT	01/42
Vaughan Monroe & His Orch.	
Leoncavallo, VESTI LA GIUBBA	03/41
Teddy Powell & His Orch.	
Strauss, BLUE DANUBE	03/41
Joe Reichman & His Orch.	
Tchaikovsky, ADANTE CANTABILE	01/42
Alvino Rey & His Orch.	
Rossini, WILLIAM TELL OVERTURE	02/41
vonSuppe, LIGHT CAVALRY OVERTURE	03/41
Greig, IN THE HALL OF THE MOUNTAIN KING	06/41
Liszt, LIBESTRAUM	11/41
Jan Savitt & His Orch.	
Herbert, PARADE OF THE WOODEN SOLDIERS	02/40
Liszt, LIBESTRAUM	01/41
Chopin, NOCTURNE IN E FLAT MAJOR	01/41
Rimsky-Korsakov, YOUNG PRINCE & YOUNG PRINCESS	01/41
Massenet, MEDITATION (THAIS)	01/41
Liszt, LES PRELUDES	01/41
Saint-Saens, MY HEART AT THY SWEET VOICE	01/41
Bizet, PRELUDE TO CARMEN	05/41
Dukas, SORCERER'S APPRENTICE	05/41
Grieg, IN THE HALL OF THE MOUNTAIN KING	05/41
Debussy, AFTERNOON OF A FAUN	08/41
Bach, LITTLE FUGUE (G MINOR)	08/41
Albeniz, MOONLIGHT MASQUERADE	10/41
Hazel Scott, piano solos	
Bach, TWO PART INVENTION	12/40
Chopin, VALSE IN D FLAT MAJOR	12/40
deFalla, RITUAL FIRE DANCE	12/40
Grainger, COUNTRY GARDENS	12/40
Liszt, HUNGARIAN RHAPSODY	12/40
Rachmaninoff, PRELUDE IN C SHARP MINOR	12/40

Artie Shaw & His Orch.	
Borodin, MY FANTASY	03/40
Eddie South & His Orch.	
Kreisler, PRAELUDIUM & ALLEGRO	06/40
Charlie Spivak & His Orch.	
Tchaikovsky, STORY OF A STARRY NGIHT	02/42
Art Tatum, piano solos	
Dvorak, HUMORESQUE	02/40
Massenet, ELEGIE	02/40
Jack Teagarden & His Orch.	
Rachmaninoff, PRELUDE IN C SHARP MINOR	01/41
Claude Thornhill & His Orch.	
Brahms, HUNGARIAN DANCE NO. 5	03/41
Schumann, TRAUMEREI	03/41
Albeniz, MOONLIGHT MASQUERADE	08/41
Grieg, PIANO CONCERTO	02/42

Appendix E: Recording Sessions of Future Stars

SINGERS

1939

August 29 George "Bon Bon" Tunnel, "Vol Vistu Gaily Star" with Jan Savitt and His Top Hatters. "Bon Bon," a good singer, was a rarity – a black male singer with a white band.

September 27 Dinah Shore, "La Cumparsita" with Xavier Cugat & His Waldorf-Astoria Orchestra. Dinah Shore would go on to TV super-stardom in the 1950s. She became popular during this triennium, appearing on the Chamber Music Society of Lower Basin Street radio program where she was called "Mademoiselle" Dinah Shore. (See 1942 Million Sellers.)

October 5 Art Carney, "Piggy Wiggy Woo" with Horace Heidt and His Musical Knights. Carney was part of Heidt's Donna & Her Don Juans. He was first noticed on early TV with comedian Morey Amsterdam, and then went on to stardom as Jackie Gleason's buddy on "The Honeymooners."

November 17 Gertrude Niesen, "Katie From Haiti" with Leo Reisman & His Orchestra. Niesen later starred on Broadway and had a hit record, "I Wanna Get Married."

December 2 Arthur Godfrey, "I'd Give A Million Tomorrows." A Washington disc jockey at this time, Godfrey later became a super-star on radio, TV, and recordings.

1940

January 5 Janet Blair, "I've Got No Strings" with Hal Kemp & His Orchestra. Later Blair became a Hollywood leading lady.

November 18 King Sisters, "St. Louis Blues" with Alvino Rey & His Orchestra. From this first recording session of this band to the last, the Sisters sang with Rey, who later married Louise King. In the '60s the Sisters hosted a popular TV show called "The King Family" which featured their children and spouses. Playing guitar in the background was their former boss, Alvino Rey.

November 29 Doris Day, "I Ain't Hep To That Step But I Dig It" with Les Brown & His Orchestra. Doris Day (nee Kappelhoff), one of the very best big band female vocalists, became one of the top Hollywood stars. (As one wag noted, her big band career was "before she was a virgin" – her stereotypical role in her major Hollywood movies.)

1941

January 7 Lena Horne, "Good-For-Nothin' Joe" with Charlie Barnet & His Orchestra. In June, she recorded "Love Me A Little Little" with Artie Shaw. As a black singer with popular white bands Lena Horne reached wide audiences. She was a major figure in music and a highly respected individual all through her life.

January 20 Jo Stafford, "For You" with Tommy Dorsey & His Orchestra. She was a member of the Pied Pipers singing group but did occasional solo vocals with Dorsey. Later, she became a well-known singer, including the hilarious Jonathan and Darlene just-out-of-tune recordings with husband Paul Weston.

April 21 Gordon Macrae, "Goodbye Dear, I'll Be Back In A Year" as one of Donna's Don Juans with Horace Heidt. Macrae was later a singing star both on Broadway and in Hollywood.

December 9 Perry Como, "Deep In The Heart of Texas" with Ted Weems & His Orchestra. This was Como's last side with Weems, his boss since 1936. Later, on his own, Como was a highly successful, relaxed singing star on records, radio, and TV.

1942

January 20 Fredda Gibson, "Somebody Nobody Loves" with Artie Shaw & His Orchestra. Fredda later changed her name to Georgia Gibbs and became well known on network radio with Jimmy Durante and Garry Moore as "Her Nibs, Miss Gibbs."

July 28 Gloria DeHaven, "Romance a la Mode" with Jan Savitt & His Top Hatters. Later DeHaven starred in a series of MGM musicals.

INSTRUMENTALISTS

1940

February 12 Trumpeter, "Wild Bill" Davison recorded with the Collector's Item Cats, his first session since 1928. In late 1943, he exploded on the jazz scene with Commodore records and remained a major traditional jazz star until his death in 1988.

February 16 Pianist George Shearing recorded his first two solo records for His Master's Voice label in London. Later in 1940 he recorded with Sid Phillips and Stephane Grappelly. He made his first U.S. recordings in 1947, became a major jazz figure in the '50s, and remained so into the '90s.

June 24 Drummer Shelly Manne with Bobby Byrne and His Orchestra. Manne became well-known with Stan Kenton in the '40s and remained a major figure in jazz.

1941

March 19 Pianist Mel Powell with Wingy Manone and His Orchestra. Powell joined Benny Goodman later that year and, still later, taught classical music at Yale and in California.

September 1 Trumpeter Willie "Cat" Anderson with Doc Wheeler and His Sunset Orchestra. Anderson became a featured "high note" trumpeter with Lionel Hampton and then Duke Ellington.

November 3 Cornetist Bobby Hackett recorded his short but eloquent solo on "String of Pearls" with Glenn Miller and His Orchestra. Benny Goodman had chosen Hackett to perform a Bix Beiderbecke imitation at his 1938 Carnegie Hall concert; Miller admired his work. But he didn't come to public attention until the '50s when Jackie Gleason chose him to solo on the "For Lovers Only" albums.

1942

January 19 Bassist Ed Safranski with Hal McIntyre & His Orchestra. Safranski went on to his reputation with Stan Kenton in the mid '40s.

February 17 Reed player Michael "Peanuts" Hucko with Bob Chester & His Orchestra. Hucko had been with the Will Bradley band which broke up at this time; he later starred with the Glenn Miller Army Air Force Orchestra and with Louis Armstrong's All Stars.

March 10 Saxophonist Sid Caesar with Shep Fields and His New Music, an experimental all-reed orchestra. Later Caesar confined himself to comedy and became a Broadway and TV star.

ARRANGERS AND LEADERS

1939

July 21 Trumpeter Russ Case with Raymond Scott Quintette. In the '40s and '50s Case was an important arranger-conductor.

August 24 Trumpeter Randy Brooks with Hal Kemp & His Orchestra. Brooks led a popular band in the mid-'40s.

October 2 Pianist Billy Maxted with Red Nichols and His Orchestra. Maxted became a popular leader in the '60s.

October 19 Alto saxophonist Hugo Winterhalter with Jack Jenney & His Orchestra. Winterhalter was a well-known arranger-conductor of the '50s.

November 3 Arranger Jerry Gray, saxophonists Tony Pastor and George Auld, guitarist Dave Barbour, and drummer Buddy Rich with Artie Shaw & His Orchestra. Eventually all five led their own bands.

1940

January 18 Trombonist Moe Zudecoff with Tony Pastor & His Orchestra. Zudecoff changed his name to Buddy Morrow and led a successful band in the '50s. The theme was "Night Train," a tune based on, but never credited to, Duke Ellington's 1945 "Happy-Go-Lucky Local."

1941

February 24 Trombonist-arranger Nelson Riddle with Charlie Spivak & His Orchestra. Riddle became a famous arranger-conductor, working with major singers such as Frank Sinatra and Linda Ronstadt.

March 8 Violinist Frank DeVol with Horace Heidt & His Musical Knights. DeVol later became chief arranger for Alvino Rey, but his most visibility was as bandleader "Slappy" on TV's "Fernwood Tonight."

May 22 Trombonist Si Zentner with Les Brown & His Orchestra. Zentner was a popular leader of the '50s and '60s.

July 15 Arranger Tadd Dameron with Harlan Leonard & His Rockets. The band's name misrepresented a smooth, modern step in the career of one of the most influential composers and arrangers in jazz.

November 17 Arranger Gil Evans with Claude Thornhill & His Orchestra. Evans produced many striking arrangements for Thornhill, and in 1949 led the "Birth of The Cool" session featuring Miles Davis and Gerry Mulligan. He was associated with Davis on many other musical projects.

1942

February 6 Drummer Spike Jones with Rudy Vallee & His Orchestra and one month later with Hoagy Carmichael. In July, Jones recorded "Der Fuhrer's Face" with his City Slickers. It became a million-seller and Jones was on his way to a career of musical parody, satire, mayhem, and fun.

March 11 Trombonist Ray Conniff with Vaughn Monroe & His Orchestra. Conniff became a well-known arranger-conductor in the '50s and '60s specializing in blending voices and orchestra.

Appendix F: List of Noteworthy Records

1939

1. Charlie Barnet & His Orchestra, CHEROKEE, 17 July 1939
2. Erskine Hawkins & His Orchestra, TUXEDO JUNCTION, 18 July 1939
3. Fats Waller & His Rhythm, SQUEEZE ME, 10 Aug. 1939
4. Eddie Condon & His Chicagoans, NOBODY'S SWEETHEART, 11 Aug. 1939
5. Quintette of The Hot Club of France, H. C. Q. STRUT, 25 Aug. 1939, London
6. Count Basie's Kansas City Seven, LESTER LEAPS IN, 5 Sept. 1939
7. Lionel Hampton & His Orchestra, WHEN LIGHTS ARE LOW, 11 Sept. 1939
8. Bob Crosby & His Orchestra, HIGH SOCIETY, 2 Oct. 1939
9. Coleman Hawkins & His Orchestra, BODY AND SOUL, 11 Oct. 1939
10. John Kirby & His Orchestra, SHUBERT'S SERENADE, 12 Oct. 1939
11. Earl Hines, piano solo, ROSETTA, 21 Oct. 1939
12. Muggsy Spanier & His Ragtime Band, DIPPER MOUTH BLUES, 10 Nov. 1939
13. Billie Holiday and Her Orchestra, THE MAN I LOVE, 13 Dec. 1939
14. Jimmie Lunceford & His Orchestra, LUNCEFORD SPECIAL, 14 Dec. 1939
15. Jelly Roll Morton, piano & vocal, MAMIE'S BLUES, 18 Dec. 1939

1940

16. Duke Ellington & His Famous Orchestra, KO-KO, 6 March 1940
17. Cab Calloway & His Orchestra, PICKIN' THE CABBAGE, 8 March 1940
18. Jam Session at Commodore, A GOOD MAN IS HARD TO FIND, 24 March 1940
19. Bechet-Spanier Big Four, FOUR OR FIVE TIMES, 28 March 1940
20. Mildred Bailey, I'M NOBODY'S BABY, 2 April 1940
21. Tommy Dorsey & His Sentimentalists, EAST OF THE SUN, vocals Frank Sinatra & Chorus, 23 April 1940
22. Chocolate Dandies, I CAN'T BELIEVE THAT YOU'RE IN LOVE WITH ME, 25 May 1940
23. Louis Armstrong & His Orchestra with Sidney Bechet, COAL CART BLUES, vocals: Louis Armstrong, 27 May 1940
24. Lee Wiley, SUGAR, 10 July 1940
25. Bud Freeman & His Famous Chicagoans, JACK HITS THE ROAD, vocals: Jack Teagarden, 23 July 1940
26. Art Tatum, piano solo, BEGIN THE BEGUINE, 26 July 1940

27. Will Bradley Trio, DOWN THE ROAD A PIECE, vocals: Ray McKinley & Don Raye, 12 Aug. 1940
28. Artie Shaw & His Gramercy Five, SUMMIT RIDGE DRIVE, 3 Sept. 1940
29. Meade Lux Lewis, HONKY TONK TRAIN BLUES, 4 Oct. 1940
30. Artie Shaw & His Orchestra, STAR DUST, 7 Oct. 1940
31. Johnny Hodges & His Orchestra, DAY DREAM, 2 Nov. 1940
32. Benny Carter & His Orchestra, ALL OF ME, 19 Nov. 1940
33. Big Joe Turner, CARELESS LOVE, 26 Nov. 1940
34. King Cole Trio, SWEET LORRAINE, vocals: Nat "King" Cole, 6 Dec. 1940

1941

35. Benny Goodman & His Sextet Featuring Count Basie, I FOUND A NEW BABY, 15 Jan. 1941
36. Metronome All Star Band, ONE O'CLOCK JUMP, 16 Jan. 1941
37. Woody Herman & His Orchestra, BLUE FLAME, 13 Feb. 1941
38. Count Basie & His Orchestra, 9:20 SPECIAL, 4 April 1941
39. Teddy Wilson, piano solo, CHINA BOY, 11 April 1941
40. Jay McShann & His Orchestra, HOOTIE BLUES, vocals: Walter Brown, 30 April 1941
41. Pete Johnson & Al Ammons, piano duet, CUTTIN' THE BOOGIE, 7 May 1941
42. Gene Krupa & His Orchestra, LET ME OFF UPTOWN, vocals: Anita O'Day & Roy Eldridge 8 May 1941
43. Claude Thornhill & His Orchestra, SNOWFALL, 21 May 1941
44. Ella Fitzgerald & Her Famous Orchestra, I GOT IT BAD, 31 July 1941
45. Stan Kenton's Orchestra, ADIOS, 11 Sept. 1941
46. Glenn Miller & His Orchestra, A STRING OF PEARLS, 3 Nov. 1941
47. Jimmy Dorsey & His Orchestra, TANGERINE, vocals: Bob Eberly & Helen O'Connell, 10 Dec. 1941
48. Lu Watters' Yerba Buena Jazz Band, MUSKRAT RAMBLE, 19 Dec. 1941
49. Harry James & His Orchestra, THE MOLE, 30 Dec. 1941

1942

50. Mel Powell & His Orchestra, THE WORLD IS WAITING FOR THE SUNRISE, 4 Feb. 1942
51. Red Norvo & His Orchestra, JERSEY BOUNCE, 5 March 1942
52. Tommy Dorsey & His Orchestra, WELL GIT IT!, 9 March 1942
53. Earl Hines & His Orchestra, STORMY MONDAY BLUES, vocals: Billy Eckstine, 1942
54. James P. Johnson, piano solo, SNOWY MORNING BLUES, 2 July 1942
55. Benny Goodman & His Orchestra, WHY DON'T YOU DO RIGHT?, vocals: Peggy Lee, 27 July 1942

Picture Credits

All non-record label pictures obtained by Getty Images, Chicago.
122 South Michigan Avenue, Suite 900
Chicago, IL 60603
USA

Prelude

1. *Helicline, Perisphere, & Trylon At 1939 World's Fair*
   Collection: Time & Life Pictures
   Photographer: Alfred Eisenstaedt

2. *Benny Goodman And Charlie Christian*
   Collection: Michael Ochs Archives
   Photographer: Frank Driggs

Chapter Two

1. *Duke Ellington*
   Collection: Time & Life Pictures
   Photographer: Gjon Mili

2. *Charlie D. Barnet*
   Collection: Time & Life Pictures
   Photographer: Charles Peterson

3. *Fats Waller; Charles Peterson; Eddie Condon; Bobby Hackett*
   Collection: Time & Life Pictures
   Photographer: Charles Peterson

4. *Lionel Hampton*
   Collection: Time & Life Pictures
   Photographer: Rex Hardy Jr.

5. *Bob Crosby; Bing Crosby*
   Collection: Time & Life Pictures
   Photographer: Bernard Hoffman

6. *Jam Session*
   Collection: Hulton Archive
   Photographer: Charles Peterson

7. *Portrait Of Billy Holiday*
   Collection: Hulton Archive
   Photographer: Frank Driggs Collection

8. *Lester Young At The Village Vanguard*
   Collection: Hulton Archive
   Photographer: Charles Peterson

Chapter Three

1. *Muggsy Spanier*
   Collection: Time & Life Pictures
   Photographer: Robert Parent

2. *Jazz Giants*
   Collection: Hulton Archive
   Photographer: Hulton Archive

3. *Artie Shaw; Robert Benchley*
   Collection: Time & Life Pictures
   Photographer: Ralph Morse

Chapter Four

1. *Late 1940s, New York City, Woody Herman*
   Collection: Michael Ochs Archives
   Photographer: Michael Ochs Archives

2. *Duke Ellington*
   Collection: Hulton Archive
   Photographer: Metronome

3. *Count Basie*
   Collection: Hulton Archive
   Photographer: American Stock

4. *Dorsey Duet*
   Collection: Hulton Archive
   Photographer: American Stock

5. *Swinging Miller*
   Collection: Hulton Archive
   Photographer: Charles Peterson

Chapter Five

1. *Too Loud*
   Collection: Hulton Archive
   Photographer: Metronome

2. *Frank Sinatra*
   Collection: Hulton Archive
   Photographer: Gene Lester

3. *Harry James Band*
   Collection: Hulton Archive
   Photographer: Frank Driggs Collection

4. *Barnet And Carter*
   Collection: Hulton Archive
   Photographer: Metronome

www.ingramcontent.com/pod-product-compliance
Lightning Source LLC
LaVergne TN
LVHW061221100826
845148LV00004B/821
9780916182151